Complete Guide to Competency-Based Education

Practical Techniques for
Planning, Developing, Implementing,
and Evaluating Your Program

Leo H. Bradley, Ed.D.

PRENTICE HALL
Englewood Cliffs, New Jersey 07632

Prentice-Hall International (UK) Limited, *London*
Prentice-Hall of Australia Pty. Limited, *Sydney*
Prentice-Hall Canada Inc., *Toronto*
Prentice-Hall Hispanoamericana, S.A., *Mexico*
Prentice-Hall of India Private Limited, *New Delhi*
Prentice-Hall of Japan, Inc., *Tokyo*
Simon & Schuster Asia Pte. Ltd., *Singapore*
Editora Prentice-Hall do Brasil, Ltda., *Rio de Janeiro*

10 9 8 7 6 5 4 3 2 1

Library of Congress Cataloging-in-Publication Data

Bradley, Leo H.
  Complete guide to competency-based education: practical
techniques for planning, developing, implementing, and evaluating
your program / Leo H. Bradley.
      p.   cm.
  Bibliography: p.
  Includes index.
  ISBN 0-13-160078-8
  1. Competency based education—United States.   I. Title.
LC1032.B72 1987   87-17628
370'.7'32—dc19   CIP

ISBN 0-13-160078-8

PRENTICE HALL
BUSINESS & PROFESSIONAL DIVISION
A division of Simon & Schuster
Englewood Cliffs, New Jersey 07632

Printed in the United States of America

Dedication

To the teachers and administrators of the Clermont County, Ohio, local schools, who have lived this book, thus making it possible.

And to my colleagues at the Clermont County, Ohio, Office of Education, who have proven the viability and usefulness of the intermediate agency in public education.

Acknowledgments

For me, writing is a combination of study and research, experience and imagination. I can't imagine being able to write without all of these. I've often tried to determine for myself which element makes the most important contribution to the writing process. I can't decide.

One thing I have decided, though, is that within the experience realm it is the people with whom an author interacts that make the difference. Two such people for me are Carolyn Martin and Diane Lowman. Their influence on the intervention sections of this book is too significant to be acknowledged by only a footnote. Both being excellent instructional analysts, they helped me conceptualize what this part of the book should say and how best to present the topics. Carolyn and Diane also contributed significantly to the language arts and mathematics competency material that appears in this book.

I once asked my father what to say to someone who has been so kind or good or helpful that words are just not sufficient to express one's gratitude. He told me a long time ago, one day in the meadow, "Son, thanks is a big word. Just say thanks."

So, Carolyn and Diane, "Thanks."

About the Author

Leo H. Bradley holds an A.B. from Morehead State University, an M.Ed. from Xavier University, and an Ed.D. from the University of Cincinnati. He has spent over twenty-four years in public education as a teacher and as an administrator. At the local level, Dr. Bradley has held the position of principal, curriculum director, assistant superintendent, and local superintendent. He is currently the Assistant Superintendent for Curriculum and Instruction for the Clermont County, Ohio, Schools.

Dr. Bradley is also an assistant adjunct professor in educational administration at the University of Cincinnati, a post he has held for over eleven years. He has had numerous articles published, mostly on curriculum and rural education, and is the author of *Curriculum Leadership and Development Handbook* (Prentice-Hall, 1985).

Dr. Bradley is a frequent presenter on curriculum and educational leadership topics at state, regional, and national meetings. Over the past seven years he has led the planning, development, implementation, and evaluation of a competency-based education program in the Clermont County, Ohio, local schools. This program is considered exemplary by the schools of Ohio.

Dr. Bradley does not confine himself to educational writing. He also writes baseball history and fiction, and has composed hundreds of songs, twelve of which have been recorded on the Fraternity record label.

About This Guide

American schools are being asked to answer the public's demand for educational excellence, and at the forefront of education's response to this demand for excellence is the competency movement.

Unfortunately, the early competency programs of the late 1970s and early 1980s were little more than standardized testing programs. Needless to say, they failed to take into account individual differences in ability and aptitude. Neither did they address the differences in local curriculum scope and sequence.

These failures have not negated the call for nor the need for competency-based education. However, they have pointed out the need for the competency movement to include additional components to testing and the desirability of correlating competency with the local curriculum.

For competency-based education to be effective, it must be locally developed so that curriculum, instruction, and assessment can be correlated. Competency-based education should also have an instructional emphasis so that the program is not another form of standardized testing. If standardized testing was going to cure the ills of education, it would already have done so.

A vast number of states have passed legislation that mandates competency-based education in some form. School districts throughout the nation are attempting to meet these mandates in a manner that will enhance their educational programs, and not just add more testing to an already crowded agenda.

Complete Guide to Competency-Based Education speaks to a process that will accomplish locally developed competency-based education with instructional emphasis. The processes of planning, developing, implementing, and evaluating are explained in step-by-step activities.

This is not a book on minimum competency testing alone. The *Guide* explains all the competency-based education components—assessment, instruction, intervention, and testing. Most important, the entire process is explained from the instructional point of view and accepts as a prerequisite that competency-based education is feasible only when approached at the local and not the state or national level.

Here is a sample of what you will find in *Complete Guide to Competency-Based Education:*

• Chapter 1 presents the rationale for using competency-based education as a vehicle for improving curriculum and instruction. It details why competency should be developed and implemented locally. This chapter tells you what resources are necessary to utilize competency-based education. It also speaks to the role that administrators and teachers play in the planning and development of competency-based education. In summary, this chapter addresses the "why" and "how" of competency-based education.

• Chapter 2 describes the planning process, from the formulation of the leadership group through the implementation models. A complete flowchart and time line are presented and explained.

• Chapter 3 takes you through the developmental process. Included are strategies on how to identify competencies from the course of study, develop and sequence test items, field test, set up management systems, keep records, develop policies, and staff inservice activities.

• Chapter 4 explores implementation. The emphasis is on intervention, the heart of the instructional program. This chapter tells you what happens in the classroom when competency-based education is in full swing.

• Chapter 5 covers both process and product evaluation. Both must be done properly to make competency-based education effective.

• Chapter 6 concludes with strategies to combat the obstacles, constraints, and facades (which invariably occur) that stand in the way of effectively implementing competency-based education. If these oppositions are not successfully countered, competency-based education will not reach its potential. This chapter gives you tips on how to "run those roadblocks."

• A special feature of *Complete Guide to Competency-Based Education* is the Appendix, which presents 96 competency test items for language arts assessment in grades kindergarten through seven. These are included so that you have an overview of exactly what, and how, test items are given at each particular grade.

Found throughout this book are forms, guides, samples, and policies that are needed to implement competency-based education. All these samples can easily be adapted to any local school setting. Many can be used as they appear. The methodology presented is not an untried theory—it has been done . . . recently . . . and it has worked! The methodology is designed for the practitioner who has responsibility for competency-based education. The superintendent, curriculum director, principal, or department head will find answers and suggestions applicable to his or her situation.

So, if you want to pursue competency-based education as a viable option to improve education or if competency-based education is a standard/mandate in your school, then *Complete Guide to Competency-Based Education* was written for you.

Leo H. Bradley

Contents

CHAPTER 1

The Rationale for Competency-Based Education

There are two major reasons to have competency-based education. The first is that competency-based education is a good method for ensuring the total correlation of curriculum, assessment, instruction, and testing. The second is that competency-based education is a good method for validating the achievement of basic skills.

CORRELATION OF CURRICULUM, ASSESSMENT, INSTRUCTION, AND TESTING

Let's first explore the correlation of curriculum, assessment, instruction, and testing. It is often assumed that these processes are correlated in all schools. Sometimes they are not, and when this is the case, each is often a separate entity. Curriculum is often nothing more than a document—sometimes referred to, sometimes not, by some teachers, but not by all teachers. In some cases, it is used as a reference document. Sometimes it is tolerated because it meets a standard and is treated as such. Sometimes it gathers dust on some distant shelf or in some storage box in a far-off closet.

Too often the curriculum being implemented in the classroom is determined by each classroom teacher in isolation. Therefore, it may or may not be tied to the formal or planned curriculum, or to what other teachers of the same grade level or subject are teaching. Most of the time it is tied together, in a loose sort of way, through the use of common textbooks.

The testing program is often a commercially developed, nationally normed test that only partially correlates with the planned or "real" curriculum. The method of testing may or may not be in agreement with the school's philosophy, method of instruction, or curriculum.

Too many times, in educational practice, the planned or formal curriculum is present only to meet a standard. The actual curriculum depends on teacher expertise and opinion and the textbook being used. Testing consists of comparative data normed on a "national curriculum" and is accepted as valid without regard to its correlation with local expectations.

Competency-based education, if properly planned, developed, and implemented, can successfully correlate the four processes of curriculum, assessment, instruction, and testing. (See Figure 1-1.) The competencies are derived from the course of study (curriculum). Instruction begins with the competencies, and assessment and testing are criterion-referenced to the competencies. Curriculum development becomes more meaningful because the principals and teachers know that student evaluation will be based on the planned curriculum. Instruction is, therefore, more closely correlated with the planned curriculum because of the eventual evaluation process. Accountability is inevitable. Currently, that accountability does not exist for the following reason: it can always be claimed that the testing program does not measure what is being taught, that is, the curriculum or the instructional program.

Figure 1-1

CORRELATING CURRICULUM, ASSESSMENT, INSTRUCTION, AND TESTING
THROUGH COMPETENCY-BASED EDUCATION

Curriculum	→	Assessment	→	Instruction	→	Testing

Determining what is to be taught

—Course of Study

—Pupil Performance Objective

—Competency Items

Sources

Course of Study

1. Philosophy of Education
2. Research
3. Community Concerns
4. Evaluative Data

Determining in which parts of the course of study each student does or does not need instruction

—Ongoing

—Diagnostic

Sources

Course of Study

Teaching based on course of study and assessment information

Sources

Course of Study
Assessment

Measuring competency of each student on competency items derived from course of study

Sources

Course of Study
Instruction

With competency-based education, there is no way to claim that any of the processes—curriculum, assessment, instruction, or testing—are invalid because they are not correlated, and are, therefore, questionable.

Weaknesses and strengths in the educational program can be pinpointed and rectified or reinforced, whichever is called for. What is sorely needed by schools is a control of the educational process and the product. Schools need a feeling of control over the success of basic skills curriculum. Competency-based education focuses the school's attention on at least one controllable process, basic skill development. Knowledge and confidence that all four processes are correlated, and thus identifiable, is a tremendous first step toward meaningful self-evaluation. The fact that it is impossible to measure all the processes and products of a school is no excuse not to measure what we have the ability to measure.

ACHIEVEMENT OF BASIC SKILLS

A second major reason to implement competency-based education concerns the current status of knowledge. The current state is usually referred to as an explosion. Goodlad's time line of knowledge[1] claims that knowledge development has followed a rapidly advancing pattern. The knowledge of the world doubled between 1 A.D. and 1750, which means it took 1750 years. Knowledge next doubled in the year 1900. That was only 150 years. By the year 1950, knowledge had once again doubled in the world. That was only 50 years. Since 1950, knowledge has doubled every 10 years. Obviously, the knowledge explosion is not going to slow down. If anything, the rate of knowledge is going to speed up. For example, robotics and genetic engineering are being projected by demographers as the leading U. S. industries by 1990. Both are relatively new concepts and were only theories just a few short years ago. Goodlad's time line of knowledge points out the eduational dilemma for schools. How do the schools teach all the knowledge available? The answer is, of course, it can't be done.

Even more significant is that the future promises to magnify the problem. The amount of knowledge from which to select curriculum is going to become more and more voluminous. Education's answer to the knowledge explosion has been to expand and diversify, perhaps at the expense of attention to the basic skills. Current societal expectations are still very much centered around basic skills. Therefore, there is a conflict between the knowledge explosion and societal expectations.

Education needs to meet the expansion of knowledge. It also has no choice but to meet societal demands. But education must realize that it cannot be accountable for the total achievement of total knowledge by the total population. Education must realize that its role is to be involved in broad curriculum and instructional expectations but that it cannot be accountable in the traditional sense (testing) for all the learning that takes place in the schools. This, however, shouldn't keep education from expanding and diversifying to meet the needs of the modern and future world. What is needed is a narrowing down and a defining of that part of the educational program that all students of the schools will be held accountable for through testing/assessment. Competency-based education provides a means of achieving this specific need.

CURRICULUM DEVELOPMENT
VIA THREE LEARNING PROCESSES

Three learning processes are necessary for curriculum development now and in the foreseeable future. They are: (1) basic skills, (2) exploration, and (3) specialization. (See Figure 1-2.)

Figure 1-2

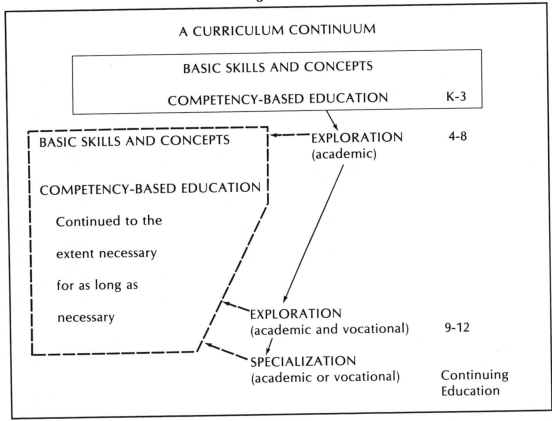

Basic Skills

Since schools can't teach all knowledge, or even a substantial portion of it, the basic skills take on even more vital importance. Only with the mastery of the basic skills can a student hope to master exploration and/or specialization. Basic skills should be the directive and the uniform part of the curriculum. It is here that competency-based education fits. Students must be continually exposed to this part of the curriculum until maximum potential achievement has been reached. Competency-based education should never be the total curriculum. It should be only a part. How much of a part is determined by the individual student. The fewer competencies the student has mastered, the more that competency-based education will be represented in the student's curriculum.

Exploration

Exploration is the process of broad exposure—providing the student with the necessary base of information from which to pursue specialization. Exploration is consistent with the demands of the knowledge explosion in today's world. It allows the student to pursue the many alternatives that are available to mankind today. Included in these alternatives is the pursuit of individual interests. Exploration is both academic and vocational, and should be occurring kindergarten through 12. Exploration would include both the general and college preparatory programs at the high school level.

Specialization

Specialization is, of course, vocational in nature. It is pursued in high school in most cases, but not in all. Some students will choose to spend their entire kindergarten through 12 curriculum on basic skills and exploration. Therefore, specialization could occur in college or through some other form of continuing education. The fact that people today change careers frequently throughout life is a strong case to not utilize this aspect of the curriculum at the expense of basic skills and exploration.

SUPPORTING REASONS FOR COMPETENCY-BASED EDUCATION

In discussing the rationale for competency-based education, one must be careful not to insinuate that it is the only method or process that can obtain the outcomes that competency-based education can produce. They could be achieved in other ways also. However, the fact that they (meaning the outcomes) can be verified through competency-based education implementation is a supporting reason for utilizing competency-based education.

The most significant supporting reasons for the competency-based education process are described below.

Student Achievement Is Verified

In the case of competency-based education, achievement is defined in terms of locally identified skills and concepts. There are many yardsticks you can use to define achievement. With competency-based education, locally developed skills and concepts are the yardstick.

Curriculum Continuity Is Created

Curriculum continuity, both horizontal and vertical, is created on basic skills and concepts. Vertical curriculum continuity means that there is a systematic introduction and reinforcement of significant learning objectives K–12, thus eliminating useless repetition and damaging voids. This is where curriculum is developed. Horizontal curriculum continuity means that all the teachers within a grade level or subject area are following the planned curriculum; this is how the curriculum is monitored. Again, curriculum voids and repetition in basic skills and concepts are eliminated.

Priorities Are Established

The establishment of curricular and instructional priorities is a necessity in today's education. It is impossible to teach all the knowledge and information available. Therefore, priorities must be established in the curriculum development process. The competency-based education program, by its nature and purpose, establishes these priorities.

Competency Coincides With the Public's Perception of the School's Functions and Goals

The public has always clamored for, and will continue to clamor for, no-nonsense basic education. They will clamor for other things also, but the most constant of the public's pleas is to produce quality education in the basic skill areas. To a vast part of the population, schools are best described as the place for the development of the three R's. Perhaps this expectation is an oversimplification of what education should be. It is a part, but not the whole. However, it is a legitimate part. Therefore, to promote competency-based education is educationally as well as politically sound. It gives the schools a chance to promote, rather than react to, the push for basic skill and concept emphasis. Best of all, from the educational as well as the political point of view, it presents attainable and measurable educational goals. So much of education is intangible that effectiveness is difficult to prove. Competency-based education provides an opportunity to attain and report goals without having to manufacture them to the detriment of the educational program.

A Staff Development Program Is Produced

The stabilization of teaching staffs has made staff development programs the best organizational vehicle for staff professional growth. No longer can schools depend on "new blood" to renew the school staff.

The main criterion for successful staff development programs is teacher acceptance. Staff developments that center around subject areas are very popular with teachers. There is, of course, a need for staff development in all areas of education; topics ranging from teacher stress to student motivation are important. But so is staff development, by subject area, in curriculum and instruction. Competency-based education is a vehicle through which subject area staff development can occur.

WHY HAVE LOCALLY DEVELOPED COMPETENCY-BASED EDUCATION?

The notion of locally developed competency-based education is a rejection of the theory of a national or uniform curriculum. Anyone supporting the theory of a national curriculum would recommend a national competency-based education program also.

Proponents of locally developed competency-based education base their position on various types of local concern. The following is a discussion of the concerns that form the rationale for locally developed competency-based education.

Local Uniqueness

Local uniqueness means not only that the demographic characteristics of a community may be unique, but that the community may have goals and objectives in curriculum that may not be widely accepted, but on which the local community has consensus.

Local Autonomy

This means that within the framework of national and state law and interest, and accepted educational research and practice, the local school is deciding policy and priority. There is no way any local school can have total autonomy today. There are too many federal and state laws, regulations, and standards that bind all schools. However, locally established curriculum priority is still possible.

Local Confidence

Local schools have lost confidence in their ability to lead in education. They still seem to have confidence in their ability to educate, but not to lead. Competency-based education could restore this lost confidence that could then be exerted in other areas also. A well developed and implemented competency-based education program will produce confidence in teaching, personnel, finances, testing, assessment, goal setting, self-evaluation. Those are characteristics that produce leadership.

Local Ownership

Local ownership of the schools' educational program is possible on an individual basis without any kind of organizational development. But staff ownership of the education program is possible only through staff development. Staff development designed to promote staff ownership of the total educational program is currently missing in many schools. That is why classroom teachers retreat and retrench to their own classrooms. There is no mechanism by which they can develop ownership of the total educational program, so they cling to that part of the program over which they can feel complete ownership, that is, the things that go on in their individual classrooms. Local ownership cannot occur until the system is identifiable by a singular nature. Teachers cling to their classroom because it is the only thing that is clearly identifiable to them in the school. They would take ownership of the total school curriculum if it had the same characteristics as their classroom, that is, self-development and control. Competency-based education provides this self-development and control, which is uniform within all classrooms.

The rationale of using competency-based education to create ownership of the total educational program by all the teachers would not be feasible if the competency-based education program included the total curriculum. That is asking too much. Teachers are not assembly line workers. They are professionals. Thus, they deserve autonomy in their teaching. But it is not unreasonable to expect them all to teach basic skills. Therefore, it is most feasible in the basic skill and concept approach.

Local Knowledge

The local knowledge that is needed is that the curriculum, assessment, instruction, and testing programs correlate. Only with locally developed competency-based education can the school be sure that these four elements do, in fact, correlate. Comparative and normed referenced data offer valuable information about the school and its students. It will not, however, verify the correlation of curriculum, assessment, instruction, and testing. Only competency-based education will provide and verify this correlation, which is being defined in the book as "local knowledge."

The application of the concept of "local knowledge" makes it possible to include concepts as a part of a competency-based education program. There is not universal consensus on what concepts should be assessed in the curriculum, on a regional, state, or national level. But on a local level, concepts can be established. This is especially pertinent in the nonskill subject areas that do not contain a lot of skills, but are mostly the study of concepts, such as history. Without the inclusion of concepts, competency is not feasible in the nonskill subject areas.

RESOURCES NECESSARY FOR LOCALLY DEVELOPED COMPETENCY-BASED EDUCATION

The resources necessary to develop competency-based education on a local level are of two kinds: monetary and human. The monetary resource need is not a particular dollar amount. A more important concern is, can the program be maintained on the "hard money" budget? If the answer is no, then the competency-based education program is not being developed at the proper level. Perhaps a bigger, more encompassing development is called for. If the program cannot be maintained within the normal budget, without dependence on grants or other "soft money," then the school should look for a cooperative venture, one that could be sustained on the regular budget.

On the other hand, competency-based education should be done at a level that is effective. Sometimes, cooperative ventures are sold on the basis of efficiency, often at the cost of effectiveness. Effectiveness is doing the right thing. Efficiency is doing things right. In education, doing things right is not sufficient if the right things are not being done. Monetarily, the correct level for competency-based education development has been achieved when there is efficiency without the loss of effectiveness.

COMMITMENT, ATTITUDES, AND VALUES NECESSARY FOR SUCCESSFUL LOCALLY DEVELOPED COMPETENCY-BASED EDUCATION

Any program that affects students, and therefore parents, as much as competency-based education does must have the support of the board of education. Perhaps this statement seems frivolous since the board is the policy-making body of a school district. However, the term support can have many meanings. Support could mean nothing more than the lack of opposition. It could mean apathetic tolerance. Or it could be support based on backing from the administration, but not necessarily of the program in question. Or it could be visible, vocal advocacy. Visible advocacy is the kind of support that competency-based education will require if it is to be successful. Since it requires considerable teacher and principal time, they must be aware of the board's support. If they are, they will be more likely to give competency-based education the commitment it will demand.

The board of education support must be of two kinds. First is the philosophical and political support. But just as important is their willingness to provide the financial support necessary to keep the program operating on an ongoing basis. This financial commitment should be based on "hard money." It should also be a long-term commitment, so that no one is guessing or speculating on how long the program is going to continue. The commitment of the community and staff is always stronger for programs that are considered permanent. That is the challenge for any facet of the educational program. No one doubts that the board will buy textbooks or provide a library. Competency-based education can begin to gain this status of permanence only if the board of education is obviously determined to make it work, and shows this commitment through the use of hard money and visible support.

The commitment of the principal needs to be discussed because too many principals do not give curriculum and instructional matters the priority they need. To add competency-based education in those situations will only compound the problems resulting from that neglect. Competency-based education will have little or no positive effect in any school if the principal does not give positive leadership through priority and constant involvement in all phases of the program. Of special significance is monitoring the implementation of the competency-based education program and assisting the teacher consultants in the staff input phase.

Regardless of how well trained the teacher consultants are, they cannot be effective with their fellow staff members unless the principal is supportive and cooperative.

It is assumed that a curriculum leader can lead any curriculum development, regardless of the subject. This assumption is made because it is process expertise that the curriculum leader is expected to provide. However, because testing and assessment are such a vital part of competency-based education, curriculum leaders may feel the need for outside consulting assistance in this area. Therefore, in relation to competency-based education, process expertise is defined as self-expertise or the ability to identify outside human resources who can provide any knowledge or skill needed by either the curriculum leader or anyone else involved in competency-based education.

It is not difficult to determine when teacher attitude toward competency-based education is positive. All a school administration ever wants from any teacher or employee is the willingness to defend their program when they feel it is justified. When teachers are willing to do this, then it can be assumed that the teachers have a positive attitude toward competency-based education.

WHAT CRITERIA MAKE COMPETENCY-BASED EDUCATION LOCALLY DEVELOPED?

To be truly locally developed, and to be truly a competency-based education program, two characteristics must be present. First, the competencies must be totally based on the local course of study. Second, competency-based education must be in the mainstream of classroom activities, that is, be an integral part of the instructional program.

The local course of study being the source of all competency makes it possible to include concepts as well as skills in the competency program. It has always been difficult in education to get universal agreement on what concepts are the most significant. As a matter of fact, universal agreement has not yet occurred, nor does it seem likely. However, it is not difficult to establish and defend concepts at the local level. The possibility of the inclusion of subject matter concepts in the competency program broadens the scope of the program significantly.

DIFFERENCES BETWEEN COMPETENCY-BASED EDUCATION ASSESSMENT/TESTING AND STANDARDIZED TESTING

Figure 1-3 illustrates the differences in competency-based education assessment/testing and norm-referenced standardized tests.

Figure 1-3

CBE Assessment/Testing	Standardized Testing
1. Origin: local course of study	1. Origin: national opinion
2. Does not have to depend totally on reading ability	2. Dependent on reading ability
3. Integral part of instructional program	3. Separate from instruction
4. Criterion-referenced (competencies)	4. Norm-referenced
5. Internally (locally) planned, developed, implemented, and evaluated	5. Externally planned, developed, implemented, and evaluated
6. Individual data analysis	6. Comparative data analysis
7. Immediate results	7. Delayed results
8. Various groupings for testing	8. Classroom grouping for testing
9. Can be given any time	9. Definite dates for testing
10. No time limits	10. Time limits
11. Teacher graded	11. Outside grading

This comparison naturally raises the question of whether both testing methods are necessary. The answer to that question depends on what information a school system wants. If a school system wants comparative data, the standardized tests are needed. If not, then they aren't. If a school wants data on how well students are doing on self- or school-identified competencies, then competency-based education is desirable. It seems to me that both are necessary for a good school evaluation program. Standardized tests will give the school a national and state comparison and a check on the validity of local competencies. Competency-based education will ensure the correlation between curriculum, assessment, instruction, and testing. Obviously, the two testing methods exist for separate purposes and cannot replace one another. Good education needs both.

Any competency-based program that is not in the mainstream of classroom activities (that is, an integral part of the instructional process) is doomed to failure. Why? Because if the competency program does not reflect the correlation of curriculum, assessment, instruction, and testing, then the testing done and the evaluation accomplished (that is, the results of the program) will be no different from all the standardized test results that we have had for years.

Educators should have learned by now that external testing programs will not cure the ills of education. If they could have, they would have. Standardized, norm-referenced tests leave too many questions unanswered, too many issues unchallenged. Just a few of these are:

a. Does the test reflect the curriculum?
b. How do the students rank in ability to the normed population?
c. How are the results used to improve instruction?
d. How can you involve the local educational community (teachers, citizens, businesses) in the development?
e. Although problems are revealed, why do the problems exist?
f. What about the assessment of the gifted and slower students?
g. Is there too much dependence on reading ability?

I am not saying that norm-referenced tests don't serve a purpose; they do, in that comparative data can be collected and inferences can be drawn. However, competency has no need for comparative data. The only pertinent question is, how did student "A" do on competency #1, and so on.

Making Assumptions

Some assumptions must be made if a local competency development is going to be utilized. First of all, you must accept that teachers are knowledgeable about what subject matter or basic skills should be classified as competencies. And second, you must accept that, if properly trained, teachers can be credible consultants to their fellow staff members.

These two assumptions are the same assumptions that are necessary for any local curriculum development process and are discussed in this chapter under "Resources Necessary for Locally Developed Competency-Based Education."

Also, it must be accepted that local school personnel are capable of assessment expertise. That is, that local school personnel can develop test items, establish their validity and reliability through field testing, and properly maintain testing conditions. In other words, can a school system maintain its own testing program and have confidence in its results? And, just as important, can the public have confidence in it also? If these questions can be answered yes, then an in-house developmental program is called for because it can be more closely correlated with the instructional program than can norm-referenced outside testing, which does not have the immediate feedback that good instruction demands.

One of the reasons many reject competency-based education is the testing validity and reliability issue. These concepts are almost mystical to most educators. However, validity and reliability can be established locally. This is accomplished through the field testing phase. In reality, it is the same process as testing companies use, only on a smaller scale. So be confident in assuming that validity and reliability can be established locally. And be ready to defend it because it will be an issue put forth by those who oppose a competency-based education program.

Using Competency-Based Education
As a Staff Development Tool

One of the most significant results of locally developed competency-based education is the staff development that it automatically creates. This results in teacher self-renewal through increasing his or her knowledge in the subject taught. This self-renewal is accomplished through two processes:

   a. The study and thought required to participate in a locally developed competency-based education program
   b. The dialogue that occurs among colleagues during the competency development process

Staff development designed to increase teachers' knowledge in their subject area is popular among teachers. One of their complaints about staff development programs is that the programs are too far removed from the teachers' immediate classroom needs. Staff development has involved too many one-day "dog and pony" shows which are more entertainment than education, too much theory and not enough practical application.

Locally developed competency-based education provides teachers the opportunity to improve their skills and understandings of their subject matter and the curriculum development process. We in education have too long assumed that teachers do not need additional subject matter knowledge beyond their college training. We have also assumed that pretraining acquaints teachers with curriculum development processes when, in fact, it often does not.

In summary, locally developed competency-based education provides the opportunity for extensive staff development. It provides the opportunity to make staff development an integral part of the school operation. Teachers will become more skilled and knowledgeable about the curriculum and the curriculum development process. The skills and understandings will have benefits far beyond the competency-based program. And, of course, that is what staff development is all about.

Staff Ownership Through Local Development

In deciding whether or not to develop competency-based education locally, quality is not the issue. Quality can be achieved through both local development or outside adaptation. The significant question is, which is more important, local ownership or efficiency in development? Local development takes longer and is less efficient. However, local ownership will be present. Outside adaptation can be achieved more quickly and efficiently. However, local ownership will be less present than in the local development.

Local competency development produces teacher ownership of both the process and product. Process ownership is very important in curriculum development. Most curriculum products (documents) look a lot alike. However, curriculum processes vary a great deal. It is in the process that local ownership is created. Extensive local involvement in the process of developing competency-based education will help alleviate the biggest obstacle to competency-based education. That obstacle is fear.

Teachers fear how the results will be used. How will it affect their teaching? How will it affect their evaluation? Will it be too hard? The way to alleviate these fears is to involve the teachers in the total process. Make them knowledgeable by allowing them to participate in the developmental process. It can be done only through local development.

COMPETENCY AND THE TEACHER EVALUATION ISSUE

Do not try to avoid this issue. It will always surface in any competency-based education program development. If the following decisions and processes are a part of the program development, the issue of competency and teacher evaluation can be addressed and settled in proper fashion.

First of all, teachers should be involved in the decision-making process concerning what critical skills should be competencies. Teachers are the group within the school structure who know the most about what should be taught. They should not be the sole decision makers, but they should be one of the decision-making groups.

Two other concepts must be present to keep this process from becoming a problem. First of all, the caliber of students that make up the teacher's classroom should always be taken into account.

Education has valid means of measuring ability and potential. Therefore, it is easy to know whether a teacher has students who should be expected to demonstrate competency with no intervention, with some intervention, or with much intervention. It should also be known if certain students will never demonstrate competency.

With this kind of information available, a teacher can be judged against student ability and achievement, not just against achievement.

Also, teacher performance in relation to the competency-based program should be one evaluation criterion. It should be considered along with all the other components of teacher evaluation, such as attendance, classroom management, disciplinary procedures, preparedness, etc.

As long as these components are present, the teacher evaluation issue can be addressed with confidence and forcefulness. The competency-based education program should be a part of the teacher evaluation process. If the above procedures are followed, it will enhance the process of evaluating teacher performance.

THE PRINCIPAL AND COMPETENCY-BASED EDUCATION—A CHALLENGE IN COMMUNICATION AND COMMITMENT

It has often been said that the principal is probably the key person in the implementation of any curriculum. That is a considerable understatement. The principal is definitely the key. In schools where the principal emphasizes curriculum, the course of study is extensively utilized. In schools where the principal does not emphasize curriculum, the course of study gathers dust. Therefore, it is imperative that principals be involved in the developmental process, both mentally and emotionally. The principal must understand what competency-based education is and be committed to its implementation.

Another thing that is constantly said about principals is that they are too busy for curriculum matters. That is probably more a matter of priority than of time. But whatever the cause, it does seem to be the perception of most principals. They want to be involved through decision making but they don't want to do the leg work or the "nitty-gritty" processes that must occur for curriculum development to take place.

The challenge is to involve them without making it appear that their input is of the after-the-fact rubber-stamp variety. The other challenge is to keep them from undoing or undermining the work of the teachers, who have made content decisions before them. This can best be accomplished by increasing their decision-making involvement during field testing and subsequent refining procedures. This is done by holding constant updating sessions with the principals and giving them the opportunity for input.

What should be constantly emphasized with principals is that competency-based education is a way to achieve curriculum accountability. That is a good reason for them to be involved. Also, give them the challenge of getting their highly competent teachers to accept the need for competency-based education. It is this group of teachers who offer the most significant opposition to the program. Being highly competent, and highly motivated, they cannot see the need for the program in their classroom. What needs to be emphasized to them is that not all classroom teachers are as successful as they. Also, emphasize that individual classroom excellence does not ensure excellent continuity of curriculum. Correlation is necessary. Competency-based education ensures that correlation through continuity of curriculum.

The key point in this discussion of the principal and competency-based education is that staff ownership is vital to its success. The principal is the only administrator close enough to the implementation process to facilitate the development of this ownership. During the initial implementation of competency-based education, problems and discontent are bound to occur. The principal must monitor these problems and respond to the discontent. As with all educational programs, ultimately the principal is the key.

NOTE FOR CHAPTER 1

1. John Goodlad, *School Curriculum and the Individual* (Waltham, MA: Blaisdell Publishing Company, 1966), page 162.

CHAPTER 2

Planning for Competency-Based Education

Figure 2-1 presents a chart of thirty-nine activities to help you with the local development of a competency-based education program. Each activity is placed in one of four program phases: planning, development, implementation, and evaluation. The involvement column lists who should be involved in the activity, and the leadership column tells who should be responsible for leading the activity. Each activity will be fully explained in this and the following chapters, discussing why it is an important part of local competency-based education development and how it can be accomplished.

Figure 2-1
Chart of Locally Developed Competency-Based Education

PROGRAM PHASE	ACTIVITY	INVOLVEMENT	LEADERSHIP
Planning	1. Forming a leadership group	Central Office Superintendent Curriculum Leader Principals Teacher Representation Board Representation Community Representation	Curriculum Leader
Planning	2. Establishing an implementation time line (by subject area, by year)	Leadership Group	Curriculum Leader
Planning	3. Selecting teachers who will act as teacher consultants for the program	Curriculum Leader Principals	Principals
Planning	4. Establishing a workshop schedule for selection of competencies and development or selection of test items	Curriculum Leader Principals	Curriculum Leader
Planning	5. Establishing a philosophical approach to be taken	Leadership Group	Curriculum Leader
Development	6. Planning workshops to tentatively identify competencies from course of study.	Curriculum Leader Principals (optional) Teacher Consultants	Curriculum Leader
Development	7. Training session for teacher consultants on how to gather staff input	Curriculum Leader Teacher Consultants	Curriculum Leader
Development	8. Staff input sessions	Teacher Consultants, Teachers, Principals	Teacher Consultants

Figure 2-1
(Continued)

PROGRAM PHASE	ACTIVITY	INVOLVEMENT	LEADERSHIP
Development	9. Feedback workshop to finalize competencies	Curriculum Leader Teacher Consultants Principals	Curriculum Leader
Development	10. Gathering resources for development and selection of test items	Curriculum Leader	Curriculum Leader
Development	11. Test item development and selection workshops	Curriculum Leader Teacher Consultants	Curriculum Leader
Development	12. First publication of test items	Curriculum Leader Clerical Personnel	Curriculum Leader
Development	13. Training session for teachers who will administer first field test	Curriculum Leader Field Test Classroom Teachers	Curriculum Leader
Development	14. First field test	Teachers	Teachers
Development	15. Factors to consider in analyzing field test results	Teachers	Teachers
Development	16. Compiling first field test results	Curriculum Leader Clerical Personnel	Curriculum Leader
Development	17. Analyzing first field test results	Curriculum Leader	Curriculum Leader
Development	18. Reporting first field test results	Curriculum Leader Principals Teacher Consultants Leadership Group	Curriculum Leader
Development	19. Workshop to revise test items based on first field test results	Curriculum Leader Teacher Consultants Principals	Curriculum Leader
Development	20. Second publication of test items	Curriculum Leader	Curriculum Leader
Development	21. Training session for teachers who will administer second field test	Curriculum Leader Teachers	Curriculum Leader
Development	22. Second field test	Teachers	Teachers
Development	23. Factors to consider in analyzing field test results	Teachers	Teachers
Development	24. Compiling second field test results	Curriculum Leader Clerical Personnel	Curriculum Leader
Development	26. Reporting second field test results NOTE: If further revision of test items is needed, go back to Activity 19 and repeat Activities 19 through 26 until test items are deemed valid.	Curriculum Leader Principals Teacher Consultants Leadership Group	Curriculum Leader
Development	27. Developing classroom management procedures and recordkeeping systems for competency-based education	Curriculum Leader Principals Teacher Consultants	Curriculum Leader

Figure 2-1
(Continued)

PROGRAM PHASE	ACTIVITY	INVOLVEMENT	LEADERSHIP
Development	28. Publication of final competency-based education documents	Curriculum Leader	Curriculum Leader
Development	29. Development of intervention program	Curriculum Leader Principals Teacher Consultants	Curriculum Leader
Development	30. Staff in-service on competency-based education	Curriculum Leader Principals, Teachers	Curriculum Leader
Development	31. Policy development	Superintendents Curriculum Leader Principals Teacher Representative	Superintendents
Development	32. Policy adoption (should come after first year of implementation)	Superintendents Board of Education Curriculum Leader	Board of Education
Development	33. Informing the public about competency-based education	Curriculum Leader Principals	Curriculum Leader
Implementation	34. Pretesting	Teachers	Teachers
Implementation	35. Intervention	Teachers	Teachers
Implementation	36. Posttesting	Teachers	Teachers
Implementation	37. Keeping records management simple	Teachers	Teachers
Evaluation	38. Evaluating the competency-based education program	Principal Curriculum Leader Teachers	Curriculum Leader
Planning Development Implementation Evaluation	39. For revision, repeat all steps		

ACTIVITY 1

Forming a Leadership Group

The competency leadership group should be made up of the curriculum leader, the superintendent, principals, teachers, board members, and community members. Each position will have a different function. These functions should be clearly spelled out from the beginning and should remain consistent.

The role/function of the leadership group is largely decision making in regards to the following aspects of competency-based education:

1. Philosophy
2. Rationale
3. Policy development
4. Scheduling

In addition, the leadership group is responsible for communication, both horizontal and vertical, to the rest of the school community. Despite the best-laid plans, all programs run into difficulties. The leadership group should provide the trouble-shooting when needed.

An informal role that the leadership group fills is the establishment of a base of legitimacy for competency-based education. Curriculum development is effective only when legitimacy is established. A leadership group composed of the people/positions described previously will establish that legitimacy.

Membership on the leadership group is easy to establish. The involvement of the different positions is a little more complex. The *board members* should be observers only. A board member is only an individual unless he or she is acting as part of a board in legal status. Therefore, the only role consistent with this legal position is that of observer. The board member's function is to act as the communicator to the board on the process. If the board member observes decisions or processes that are not acceptable to him as an individual, or if the board member does not think the total board would approve, the board member should take the issue to the board of education, and then the board can direct the superintendent accordingly.

The *superintendent* must be a participant. The position he or she holds leaves no other option. However, this participation should not undermine the curriculum leader's role. The superintendent must have thorough knowledge of the curriculum leader's strategies and techniques and take care not to destroy them. If the superintendent disagrees with the curriculum leader, this disagreement must be handled so as not to destroy the credibility of the curriculum leader. The presence of the superintendent adds great prestige to any curriculum development. If the relationship between the superintendent and curriculum leader is an open and trusting one, his or her presence at curriculum development meetings will enhance the process.

As with all curriculum development, the *principal's role* is significant and multiple in competency-based education. Since he or she is the administrator most involved in the implementation process, it is imperative that the principal be involved in the planning. The key is to keep the principal involved without piling on too much "nitty-gritty" work or taking up too much of his or her time. The principal's most significant role is to choose the teacher consultants for the project. The principal should also be asked to give input into the selection of competency items. The principal would also serve as a check on proposals that are not feasible in actual practice.

The *teachers* on the leadership group will serve as decision makers and communicators to the rest of the staff. Keep in mind that they will be the only teachers privy to the decision-making process of the leadership group, so their involvement and communication is vital. They should be teachers who are respected by their peers, knowledgeable in curriculum, and willing to take a stand. Sometimes, this stand may be contrary to the teachers' union stance.

The *community representatives* are in a consultative role. They should perform two functions: (1) ask questions to clarify points, and (2) give the public opinion on matters *prior to* the decision-making process. Of course, they also serve as communicators to the public in an informal manner. Don't ask them to communicate formally to the community. Competency-based education is too complex. Educators should perform this task.

The *curriculum leader's role* is vital throughout the planning stage. It is during the planning phase that control must be maintained because all participants will not yet be knowledgeable enough to function effectively without strong direct leadership. This direct leadership, which may lead to more control and less group ownership, is acceptable at this phase because ownership by the group is not yet established. That will come later, and when it does, the direct leadership should be reduced. At this early planning phase, establishment of the proper process is the vital concern.

This can best be assured through strong leadership by the person most knowledgeable and most responsible, the curriculum leader. During the formulation stages of the leadership group, the leadership styles most appropriate are the instructor and advocacy styles because at this jointure, "expertise" is the most significant characteristic the curriculum leader can exhibit.

ACTIVITY 2

Establishing an Implementation Time Line

The question of how much time a school system needs to implement competency-based education can be answered only through the assessment of available resources. The most important resources are the human resources. How much time does the leadership have to devote to the development of competency-based education? Is quality time available to the teaching staff? How extensive are the support services, such as clerical and secretarial?

Material resources are also vital. The significant question about material resources is, will they hold up the process at any point? If you have to wait for paper, or printing, or clerical tasks, then you are going to need more time to implement competency-based education.

Needless to say, the more extensive the human and material resources, the quicker you can implement competency-based education.

Regardless of the quantity and quality of resources available, there are a series of process steps that have to be accomplished. Because available resources vary from school to school, different implementation guidelines will be recommended.

Figure 2-2
Competency-Based Education Development
Two-Year Plan

FIRST

YEAR

1. Philosophical Emphasis
   - Basic *vs.* Optimal
   - Instructional *vs.* Evaluative
   - Availability *vs.* Security

2. Course of Study

3. Competency Item Selection

4. Test Item Development or Selection

5. Field Test

6. Revision Based on Field Test

7. Field Test

8. Revision Based on Field Test

9. Recordkeeping Management System

10. Staff In-Service

SECOND

YEAR

11. Implementation

12. Evaluation

Policy

Development

(Ongoing)

You can adapt the time line that best fits your resource level. Four time lines are presented. They are a two-year, three-year, four-year, and five-year plan. The two-year plan is not recommended. Two years is not sufficient time to adequately implement competency-based education. However, this author knows from experience that educational mandates and standards sometimes force educators to accomplish tasks quickly. So if you have only two years, this is the most intelligent way to accomplish the tasks. (See Figure 2-2.) If you wish to devote three years to the project, see Figure 2-3 for a time line. Figure 2-4 contains the four-year time line and Figure 2-5 contains the five-year program.

Figure 2-3
Competency-Based Education Development
Three-Year Plan

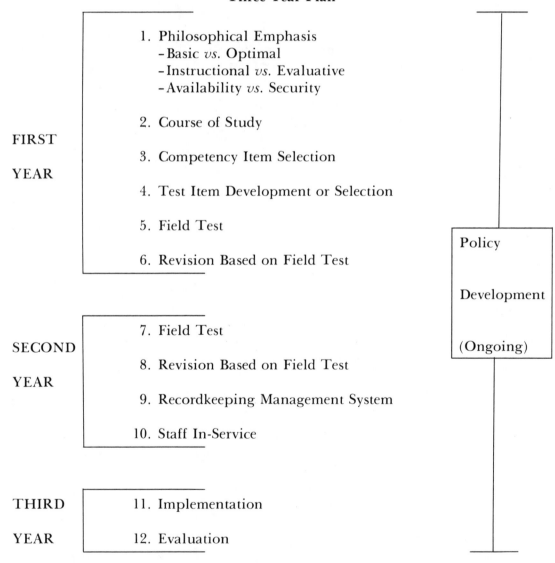

FIRST YEAR

1. Philosophical Emphasis
   - Basic *vs.* Optimal
   - Instructional *vs.* Evaluative
   - Availability *vs.* Security

2. Course of Study

3. Competency Item Selection

4. Test Item Development or Selection

5. Field Test

6. Revision Based on Field Test

SECOND YEAR

7. Field Test

8. Revision Based on Field Test

9. Recordkeeping Management System

10. Staff In-Service

THIRD YEAR

11. Implementation

12. Evaluation

Policy

Development

(Ongoing)

Figure 2-4
Competency-Based Education Development
Four-Year Plan

FIRST

YEAR

1. Philosophical Emphasis
   –Basic *vs.* Optimal
   –Instructional *vs.* Evaluative
   –Availability *vs.* Security

2. Course of Study

3. Competency Item Selection

4. Test Item Development or Selection

SECOND

YEAR

5. Field Test

6. Revision Based on Field Test

THIRD

YEAR

7. Field Test

8. Revision Based on Field Test

9. Recordkeeping Management System

10. Staff In-Service

FOURTH

YEAR

11. Implementation

12. Evaluation

Policy

Development

(Ongoing)

Figure 2-5
Competency-Based Education Development
Five-Year Plan

FIRST

YEAR

1. Philosophical Emphasis
   –Basic *vs.* Optimal
   –Instructional *vs.* Evaluative
   –Availability *vs.* Security

2. Course of Study

SECOND

YEAR

3. Competency Item Selection

4. Test Item Development or Selection

THIRD

YEAR

5. Field Test

6. Revision Based on Field Test

7. Field Test

8. Revision Based on Field Test

FOURTH

YEAR

9. Recordkeeping Management System

10. Staff In-Service (Intervention)

FIFTH

YEAR

11. Implementation

12. Evaluation

Policy

Development

(Ongoing)

ACTIVITY 3

Selecting Teacher Consultants

This is a very important outcome in the competency-based education development process. People are the most important resource in the process. The teacher consultants are the most important of the groups involved. "Just anybody" won't do. There should be a reason why certain teachers are picked, and why they were chosen.

There are five methods of choosing teacher representatives for curriculum development. These are by using: (1) volunteers, (2) rotation, (3) evolvement, (4) peer selection, or (5) administrative selection. Each method has its particular advantages and disadvantages. Following is a discussion of each method of selection, with recommendations as to when it should be used.

I. Volunteer
   A. Advantages
      1. People who volunteer are interested in the project. The motives for this interest may vary. For example, the motive may be purely political. The teacher may feel that volunteering for curriculum work may impress the administration. Or the motive could be purely educational. The teacher may see the need for the curriculum development and wish to participate in it. Regardless of the motive for the interest it can be assumed that a commitment is present.
      2. The use of volunteers is an open, democratic process.
   B. Disadvantages
      1. Incompetents may volunteer, in which case the product will probably be of poor quality.
      2. Calling for volunteers seems to indicate that the position is not too important since anyone is acceptable.
   C. Recommendation for Use
      Utilizing volunteers for curriculum development is feasible when the group from which the volunteers come is made up of people comparable in ability. In other words, everyone is acceptable because everyone is qualified. In this situation, the volunteer method may be the most desirable one because it produces an interested participant. Also, it is democratic in nature, and the use of democratic processes when possible is usually good for rapport and morale.
II. Rotation
   A. Advantages
      1. By rotating membership on curriculum committees, all possible participants can eventually be involved in curriculum development. The more that people

are involved in curriculum development, the more they tend to use the product. Therefore, rotating membership has the desirable effect of increasing involvement.

2. Rotating eliminates the need for selection. That is a strength in itself because selection is oftentimes a controversial process.

B. Disadvantages

1. The biggest problem with rotating membership on curriculum committees is that continuity is hampered. The degree of the problem will vary, but the problem will always be present. If rotation is used, the curriculum leader will have to keep in mind that two things will automatically occur: (1) there will have to be a lot of attention given to the communication process to ensure continuity, and (2) the curriculum development process will take longer because each time membership is rotated, there will have to be additional time set aside to bring new members up-to-date on the project.

2. Rotating membership seems to assure that all eligible participants have equal ability to serve. Such an assumption may be erroneous.

C. Recommendation for Use

Rotating membership for curriculum development should be used when involvement is more important than continuity or efficiency. Always expect rotating membership to increase the time necessary to achieve the goal. Rotation should be used when the eligible participants all have the ability to serve at a competency level that is acceptable or, put another way, the rotating membership will not prevent the development of an acceptable process or product.

III. Evolvement

A. Advantages

1. Evolvement will usually produce the "true curriculum leader" from the group. If a group works together long enough, the members of the group will recognize the qualities of its members. One of the qualities that will be recognized is that of "curriculum leader." The behavior of the group will display the confidence the group has in this person. The group will utilize him or her in an informal manner as their representative.

2. Cooperation from the group will probably be high because the group has chosen the "leader" or representative through their own processes. The selection has been an evolvement accomplished through their own informal structure without coercion or guidance. Therefore, this is probably the truest "leader" that could be identified.

B. Disadvantages

1. The evolvement process takes too long to occur to be feasible in any situation except one that is long-term. Most of the time, the long term is too long for curriculum development projects.

2. Leaders or representatives who have emerged are still without recognized authority. If you will recall, the gist of the discussion on the curriculum group was that it should have representatives who have authority. If curriculum representation is allowed to evolve, the problem of establishing recognized authority is left unsolved.

C. Recommendation for Use

Using evolvement as a method of choosing teacher representation for curriculum development is feasible only as a first and unfinished step. It would be useful as a means of determining which teachers are most competent in curriculum development. This information, gathered during the evolvement process, could then be used to choose teacher representatives utilizing one of the other methods of selection. If the evolvement process has been observed closely by the curriculum leader, the information gathered will improve the teacher selection process.

IV. Peer Selection

A. Advantages

1. By choosing their own representatives, the group will feel as though they have more control over their own destiny.

2. Since the group chose their own representatives, they are likely to cooperate with the project.

B. Disadvantages

1. The group may select representation for the wrong reasons, that is, friendship, apathy.

2. The peer selection method assumes that the group knows the kind of leadership and representation they need. In many instances, this may not be true.

C. Recommendation for Use

The peer selection process is highly recommended with the following conditions:

1. The group must have maturity and experience.

2. The group must be committed to the importance of curriculum development.

3. The group must be knowledgeable concerning the curriculum development. If they understand what kind of representation is needed, they can more intelligently choose a representative.

V. Administrative Selection

A. Advantages

1. Administrative selection tends to legitimize a position, and thus give it significance. Since one of the problems curriculum faces is its significance in the school power structure, administrative selection of teacher representation is helpful.

2. Administrators should know the best qualified person.

B. Disadvantages

1. The administration may not know who the best qualified person is for the job. Or, perhaps more likely, politics will dictate rather than reason or intellect.

2. As with all administrative decisions, this one may negatively affect group cooperation.

C. Recommendation for Use

Administrative selection should be used when peer selection is not feasible (see "C. Recommendation for Use" under "IV. Peer Selection" earlier in this outline). If administrative selection is utilized, be sure to treat the appointment as a significant one, and therefore, give it the time, energy, and thought that it deserves.

ACTIVITY 4

Establishing a Workshop Schedule

Refer to Figure 2-6 to see how a competency workshop schedule would be planned. Following are some helpful hints on the scheduling process that, if followed, will facilitate the item development. First of all, never schedule the workshop on Monday or Friday. Those are bad days for teachers to be out of the classroom. Monday is usually an organization day. The students have been away from school for the weekend. It is important that their regular teacher be there to start the week off on a positive note. Friday is often a test day, or at least a culmination of the week's activities. It is important that the regular teacher be there for this day also.

That leaves Tuesday, Wednesday, or Thursday for the competency workshops. Using these days will make it easier for substitute teachers to provide quality instruction.

It should be pointed out that anytime the regular teacher is out of the classroom, the quality of instruction will suffer for that day. However, by scheduling the workshop intelligently, the damage can be minimized for both student and teacher. The question that a school system must answer for itself is whether or not the quality time given for competency development is worth it in the long-term sense. Remember that both teaching and curriculum are important. Both need quality time from teachers. Quality time for curriculum development can come only from instructional time. Eventually, the time spent on curriculum development will improve the instruction. Therefore, it *is* worth it. If good substitute teaching is provided, the curriculum improvement resulting from the competency workshops will be worth the teacher time out of the classroom.

A real "nitty-gritty" consideration in scheduling competency selection workshops is to stay away from school days close to Christmas, Thanksgiving, and other holidays. These are always busy times in schools. Everything from student performances to feasts are occurring. This is a time of special events. The teachers won't want to be out of their classrooms during these times.

Workshops should also avoid exam weeks. As important as competency development is, it is no more important than other assessment procedures.

Figure 2-6

COMPETENCY WORKSHOP SCHEDULE

PHASE I   DEVELOPMENT OF COMPETENCY ITEMS

    Step 1   Planning Workshop
        Oct. 14 – Primary Language Arts
            20 – Primary Mathematics
            28 – Intermediate Language Arts
        Nov. 4 – Intermediate Mathematics
            12 – Middle/High School Language Arts
            18 – Middle/High School Mathematics

    Step 2   Staff Input
        Nov. 19 – January 12

    Step 3   Feedback Workshops
        Jan. 20 – Primary Language Arts
            27 – Primary Mathematics
        Feb. 3 – Intermediate Language Arts
            10 – Intermediate Mathematics
            17 – Middle/High School Language Arts
            24 – Middle/High School Mathematics

PHASE II   DEVELOPMENT OF COMPETENCY TEST ITEMS

    Step 1   Test Development Workshops
        April 14 – Primary Language Arts and Mathematics
              – Intermediate Language Arts and Mathematics
             28 – Middle/High School Language Arts and Mathematics

---

A vital part of the workshop schedule is the staff input phase. This part of the competency-based education development should last between four and six weeks. It should be no more, no less. If it is less than four weeks, the teacher consultants may not have the time to complete their tasks. If it is more than six weeks, the teacher consultants may have difficulty remembering the rationale for the selection of the competency items at the planning workshop. Both of these problems are of equal significance and can be avoided by keeping this input phase between four and six weeks in length.

ACTIVITY 5

Establishing a Philosophical Approach

Two very different philosophies of competency-based education are possible. The program can be instructionally oriented or have an evaluation emphasis. The fact that the program is instructionally oriented does not mean there are no evaluation components or vice versa. Any decent competency-based education program will have both instructional and evaluation components. But one will have to be emphasized more than the other. This emphasis will demonstrate the philosophical approach.

Since this book is recommending that competency-based education have an instructional emphasis, the characteristics of this orientation will be explained in detail. (See Figure 2-7.)

An advocate of any position should be knowledgeable about the alternatives. Therefore, Figure 2-7 also lists the counterpart characteristics of competency-based education with emphasis on evaluation. However, since they closely resemble the literature and practice long associated with educational evaluation, detailed discussion is not presented.

Let's take a closer look at the characteristics of competency-based education programs with instructional emphasis.

1. TESTS ARE HOUSED IN THE CLASSROOM

By housing the tests in the classroom, high availability of the test items is created. For the teacher in programs with instructional emphasis, this high availability is a necessity. The competency-based education tests must be a part of the regular classroom materials. They should be no different from the chalkboards, worksheets, textbooks, and all the other learning materials that are housed in the classroom. The competency test items should be kept in a filing cabinet in a looseleaf format. With this format the teacher can utilize any number of the test items that are needed.

Housing the tests in the classroom creates high availability and, thus, low security. Having the tests items means that the teacher has total access to the tests all the time. If you are concerned that teachers will cheat by practicing or giving out the answers and, thus, not utilizing the exams properly, you will have little confidence in the results. If trusting the teachers to properly implement competency-based education is in question, then housing the tests in the classroom is not an option you would choose, and you have a much bigger problem that should be solved before competency-based education is implemented.

It is reasonable to assume that teachers will be honest with competency-based

Figure 2-7

CHARACTERISTICS OF COMPETENCY TESTING WITH INSTRUCTIONAL EMPHASIS	CHARACTERISTICS OF COMPETENCY TESTING WITH EVALUATION EMPHASIS
1. Tests are housed in the classroom. a. High availability b. Low security c. Tests immediately available to teacher d. Tests given anytime (teacher-determined e. Results immediately available	1. Tests are housed outside the classroom. a. Low availability b. High security c. Tests unavailable to teacher except on testing days d. Tests given on scheduled days only (administratively determined) e. Results available at a later date
2. Tests are given to any number of students (from one student up).	2. Tests are given to a full classroom.
3. Teachers grade tests.	3. Outside grading of tests.
4. Teacher has previous knowledge of test content.	4. Teacher does not have previous knowledge of test content.
5. Results are used for instructional planning and student placement.	5. Results are used to evaluate student for purposes of advancement or retention.
6. Primary purpose is instructional improvement.	6. Primary purpose is student evaluation.
7. Secondary purpose is evaluation of students and instruction.	7. Secondary purpose is instructional improvement.
8. Multiple testing opportunities are provided.	8. One or few testing opportunities are provided.
9. Assumes local school personnel (teachers and administrators) can develop valid and reliable tests.	9. Seeks outside development of competency tests.
10. Assumes teachers can administer tests properly.	10. Seeks control of testing environment.
11. Assumes teachers will be honest in reporting results.	11. Prefers outside reporting of test results.
12. Puts testing in the mainstream of classroom instruction.	12. Keeps instruction and competency testing as separate entities.

Figure 2-7
(Continued)

CHARACTERISTICS OF COMPETENCY TESTING WITH INSTRUCTIONAL EMPHASIS	CHARACTERISTICS OF COMPETENCY TESTING WITH EVALUATION EMPHASIS
13. Provides constant assessment and intervention.	13. Provides periodic assessment and intervention.
14. Results are only one criterion for student promotion/detention.	14. Basis for promotion/retention.
15. No time limit on test items.	15. Time limit on test items.

education processes and results. If they aren't, no program, competency-based education or otherwise, is going to work effectively. Accessibility automatically reduces security. Therefore, the choice with any testing program is accessibility or security. If the emphasis is instruction, the choice of accessibility is easy to make. The purpose of competency-based education is to verify the success of each student on the competencies. Group data and norms are not significant. If test security is breached by the teacher, it really doesn't matter as long as the competency-based education results are achieved.

Further, no one will be wronged or hurt by the fact that the teacher "taught to the test." Test security is paramount only if group or comparative norms are going to be utilized. In that instance, teaching to the test could be harmful to students whose teacher did not teach to the test because they would suffer through the use of comparative norms.

The fact that the tests are immediately available to the teacher is an important key to the success of an instructionally oriented program. When the teacher plans for the next day, the next week, the next unit, and so on, competency testing is no more of an obstacle than getting the students to other learning materials. Competency-based education becomes a more integral part of the instruction. The teachers can plan to give tests to any number of students on any given day. The competency-based education testing can be in a small-group mode, or medium, or large-group mode. Or the teacher can utilize all the modes depending upon the instructional needs. Test items can serve as the pretest for an instructional unit or activity and as a posttest at the conclusion.

For competency-based education to be an integral part of instruction, the classroom teacher must have the option of giving a competency test at any time. This flexibility must also include the right to give as many test items as are needed to enhance the instructional plans.

Within the scope of the school year all the competencies will be prescribed in the course of study. After a competency has been taught as a part of the regular instructional program, the competency should be tested. If the student demonstrates achievement of the competency, then no further instruction on the competency is called for. If the student does not demonstrate achievement of the competency then intervention or reteaching should occur. The student should be retested and retaught until the competency is achieved.

Instructionally oriented competency-based education allows the teacher to spread the testing out so that student fatigue does not become a problem. It also allows the teacher to plan testing in such a way as to not significantly interrupt instruction.

Having competency-based education testing results immediately available is a necessary component for the instructionally oriented program. If competency-based education is to be utilized for the diagnosis of individual student's academic needs and to determine student grouping patterns, then test results must be immediately available.

Competency-based education can be implemented in different ways. There are two instructional models which lend themselves to competency-based education. These models will be referred to as *Verification Model* and *Course of Study Model*. (See Figures 2-8 and 2-9.) These two models will be discussed in more detail in Chapter 4.

2. TESTS ARE GIVEN TO ANY NUMBER OF STUDENTS

The learning modes that are characteristic of everyday instruction should be used for competency-based education assessment and testing. For example, an elementary classroom could look like the following diagram.

Group A	**Group B**	**Group C**	**Group D**
+		+ +	+ +
+ + +	+ +	+ +	
+	+ + +	+ +	+
		+ +	
		+ +	+ +

Activity	**Activity**	**Activity**	**Activity**
● Group Project	● Library Research	● Silent Reading	● Competency Testing

+ = Student

By studying this diagram, one can see that five out of twenty-eight students are engaged in competency testing. The rest of the students are involved in other instructional activities. Group D could have been involved in oral reading. The significant fact is that, in instructionally oriented programs, competency assessment and testing is just another grouping option. Therefore, instruction does not stop so that competency testing can begin. They occur simultaneously within the instructional program.

Figure 2-8

VERIFICATION MODEL

Preassessment

Given at beginning of school year.

Given to all students.

Given regardless of whether or not the competency has been taught.

Students passing competencies will not be tested again unless teacher wishes to check for retention.

Successful achievement is recorded.

Regular Instruction

Competencies taught when prescribed by the course of study.

Postassessment

Students not successful on the preassessment are postassessed.

Successful achievement is recorded.

Intervention

For those students not successful on either the pre- or postassessment.

Postassessment

The cycle of intervention.

Postassessment is continued until postassessment is successful.

Assumptions—Verification Model

Students may know competencies without being taught.

Implies that if a student is already competent in a skill, two strategies will be followed:

  A) Not taught

  B) Taught with less emphasis and time

Pretest results will be used for grouping.

Implies multiple posttests determined by where the competency falls within the course of study

Figure 2-9

COURSE OF STUDY MODEL

<u>Regular Instruction</u>

Competencies taught when prescribed by the course of study.

<u>Assessment</u>

Administered immediately after competency has been taught to all students.

<u>Intervention</u>

For those students who were not successful on assessment.

<u>Reassessment</u>

The cycle of intervention/reassessment is continued until postassessment is successful.

<u>Assumptions—Course of Study Model</u>

Does not wish to assess student achievement on competency until after it has been taught as a part of regular instruction.

Not used for grouping.

Eliminates an assessment phase.

Both models could have periodic testing.

    Every year

    Every three years, etc.

Differentiate between assessment and testing.

    Testing

        One setting

        All students

        Within time frame

        For evaluation purposes

            Program

            Student

3. TEACHERS GRADE TESTS

When teachers grade the tests, immediate feedback is possible. So is immediate diagnosis. And of course, based on this diagnosis, the teacher can immediately go to work on intervention.

The fact that the teacher grades the test and uses the results for instructional purposes only illustrates the emphasis on instruction. No norms are kept. Therefore, testing results are obviously not the emphasis. The fact that each student's performance on each competency item does not have to be reported to the principal illustrates the lack of administrative emphasis.

Of course, year-end results *would* become significant in both testing and administrative emphasis. But that is a product concern.

During the process of competency-based education it is the teacher who is the focus, who is in control, and who is accountable. Therefore, since the teacher is free of testing and administrative constraints, all the emphasis can be on instruction.

4. TEACHER HAS PREVIOUS KNOWLEDGE OF TEST CONTENT

Since normed group data is not one of the purposes of competency-based education, it doesn't matter if the teacher teaches to the test. This statement is not to suggest that the teacher teaches only to the test. However, knowledge of the testing content may, in fact, make them better teachers of the competencies. The only thing that matters is, did the student demonstrate achievement of the competency? Anything the teacher does to help the student achieve this goal is encouraged. The content of the competency tests should be thought of in the same way as other instructional materials in the classroom. The teacher knows what is in the textbook, the filmstrips, the computer software, and so on. This knowledge helps the teacher better utilize the materials. Since the competency-based education emphasis is on instruction, the more knowledge the teacher has of the test items, the better instructional use can be made of them.

5. RESULTS ARE USED FOR INSTRUCTIONAL PLANNING AND STUDENT PLACEMENT

Competency results are a basis for instructional planning. By scanning the class roster, the teacher can see what competencies are a problem for a large, or at least a significant, number of students. Instruction in those competencies can be emphasized. Students can also be placed and grouped based on the competency results.

So long as some of the competencies have not been achieved by some of the students, they remain a factor in the instructional plan. When all the students have demonstrated achievement of all the competencies, the competencies cease to be a part of the instructional plan unless the teacher feels that reinforcement to ensure retention is needed.

6. INSTRUCTIONAL IMPROVEMENT IS PRIMARY PURPOSE

It is assumed in the instructional emphasis program that all students can pass all the competency items. It is also assumed, and pursued, that all students will eventually pass all the competency items. Therefore, the primary purpose of competency-based education is to plan and carry out instruction that will accomplish this goal. The emphasis is not to evaluate either the instruction or the individual students for the purpose of hiring, firing, promoting, or retaining, but to get the information necessary to plan instruction.

7. EVALUATION OF STUDENTS AND INSTRUCTION IS SECONDARY PURPOSE

Any educational program that forms the basis for decision making must be evaluated. Although it may not be the primary purpose of competency-based education, teacher and student evaluation is inevitable. In relation to the student, the competency-based education results identify the incompetent. If all assessment, intervention, and testing efforts still do not result in the achievement of the competency, then the evaluation of this student for decision-making purposes is required.

In relation to teachers, the continual failure of students, regardless of their ability level, is an indication of an instructional problem. The teacher should be held accountable for this continual and universal failure.

8. MULTIPLE TESTING OPPORTUNITIES ARE PROVIDED

Since the primary use of the testing results is for instructional decision making, each testing session is an opportunity to get information. Therefore, it matters not how many times the item has been tested. Only one precaution should be taken. To ensure that the student is not memorizing the tests, a two-week interval between testing sessions should be observed, or a different form of the test utilized.

9. ASSUMES LOCAL SCHOOL PERSONNEL CAN DEVELOP OR SELECT VALID AND RELIABLE TESTS

From a technical viewpoint, the selection or development of competency-based education test items does not require an entire staff knowledgeable in test preparation. What is required is at least one person on the staff knowledgeable about testing and willing to share that knowledge with the rest of the staff. You also need a staff willing to make the commitment necessary to allow the learning to take place.

Of all the preparations that a person could go through to make up test items, teaching experience is among the best. If a school system has competent teachers it is a safe assumption that they also have competent test developers or selectors, whichever is needed.

10. ASSUMES TEACHERS CAN ADMINISTER TESTS PROPERLY

The rationale for this assumption is a lot like the rationale for the previous discussion on development or selection. Teaching experience is the best training ground. This fact coupled with adequate in-service will certainly create an environment where competency-based education tests are administered properly.

11. ASSUMES TEACHERS WILL BE HONEST IN REPORTING RESULTS

If a school system is going to implement competency-based education with instructional emphasis, this assumption must be made. Any school administrator who feels teachers would not be honest in reporting competency-based education test results should deal with this problem before ever initiating competency-based education. No educational assessment program will work effectively if the teachers aren't honest with the results. So, if this problem exists, it should be dealt with through the teacher evaluation process. If present, this indicates a problem that shouldn't be tolerated even if there is no competency-based education program.

Except with the incompetent teacher, the proper administration of a competency-based education program will eliminate any problem of teacher dishonesty. Proper administration of the program means that the goals and procedures of the competency-based education program are clearly stated and consistently followed. It also means that the administration demonstrates, through their actions, that they understand the individual ability differences in the students and take these differences into account when evaluating student achievement results.

In summary, any administration that doesn't trust its teachers had better correct that situation before embarking on any instructionally based assessment.

12. PUTS TESTING IN THE MAINSTREAM OF CLASSROOM INSTRUCTION

Locally developed competency-based education is the "purest" form of curriculum testing. If used properly, it is a diagnostic process that is totally curriculum-based. The question of whether or not the competency-based education test items measure what is being taught is not the question it is in norm-referenced testing. Because if all the competency-based education test items are taken from the course of study, it is certain that students are being tested on subjects or skills that they *have* been taught (that is, if the teacher is following the course of study). Competency-based testing takes all the guesswork out of testing. A school knows that if a student fails, it is because he or she has not mastered the skill or concept, and not because the skill hasn't been taught.

13. **PROVIDES CONSTANT ASSESSMENT AND INTERVENTION**

Immediate or short-term feedback is the key to providing effective assessment and intervention. If the school is not interested in quick feedback on test results, commercially prepared, norm-referenced tests with computerized scoring should be used. But these require testing of all students at once and there is a turnaround time before results are available. Neither of these characteristics is conducive to good instruction. Any component of good instruction must have the teacher as the controlling factor. With the competency-based education instructional emphasis model, the teachers control the competency-based education feedback process just as they do all the other classroom tests and activities. Constant assessment means constant intervention is possible. This constancy is consistent with good instructional practices.

14. **RESULTS ARE ONLY ONE CRITERION FOR STUDENT PROMOTION/RETENTION**

Since competency-based education is considered only one of the components of the instructional program, it is reasonable to assume that it would be only one criterion for the promotion/retention decision. There are many other factors that are usually considered when making the promotion/retention decision on a student. The most common are grades, attendance, age, social development, psychological development, teacher opinion, administration opinion, parent opinion, and psychologist opinion. If the competency-based education results were poor, then the other factors should be more positive if promotion is the decision. Conversely, if the competency-based education results are excellent, then the other factors could be less positive and promotion still occur.

The whole notion of instructionally oriented competency-based education is to integrate the program into the exemplary classroom activities and make it an integral part of the instructional program. To make it the sole criterion for promotion or retention would not be consistent with this notion.

15. **NO TIME LIMIT ON TEST ITEMS**

Instructionally oriented competency-based education is concerned with student demonstration of competency achievement, not with the speed in which he can answer. It accepts that some people learn faster than others, but insists that all can learn basic skills if given time. Common sense must be used, of course. However, accuracy—not time—is the main testing criterion.

CHAPTER 3

Development of Competency-Based Education

ACTIVITY 6

The Planning Workshop

The purposes of the planning workshop are to tentatively identify competencies from the course of study and train the teacher participants to properly gather staff input. (See Figure 3-1.)

Before presenting the agenda for the planning workshop, the role of the course of study in competency-based education should be discussed. Since the course of study is the foundation for competency-based education, it should be emphasized that without a good course of study competency-based education is not possible. Any school system wishing to embark upon the development of a competency-based educational program should not do so until the course of study, properly developed through teacher and community input, is in place. *Properly developed* is a phrase which means that the course of study truly represents the consensus of the school community as to what the schools should teach. This may sound trivial and obvious, but in actuality, some

Figure 3-1

COMPETENCY PLANNING WORKSHOP

1. Bring with you to the planning workshop the course of study for the subject areas being developed (language arts or math).

2. Your role as consultant involves five phases:

   Phase A—Development of a tentative list of competencies in the planning workshop.

   Phase B—Gathering input from your local staff on the tentative list of competencies developed in the planning workshop.

   Phase C—Developing a list of competencies to be recommended to the principals and curriculum leaders.

   Phase D—Finalizing a list of competencies based on all inputs, to be presented to the local superintendents.

   Phase E—Developing or selecting test items to measure the competency items.

---

courses of study are put together to meet the letter of the law, or standard, but not the intent of the law. They are the hasty assembling, probably by one or a few people, of educational jargon to pass an inspection of some kind. Such courses of study will not suffice as the foundation for competency-based education.

PROBLEMS FACED BY THE CURRICULUM LEADER

As decisions are being made about which student performance objectives in the course of study should be competency items, two problems often emerge for the curriculum leader. They are: (1) either teachers or other participants will want to consider possible competency items that are not present in the course of study, and (2) they will notice student performance objectives in the course of study that they would like to change, or at least discuss, and will thus divert the attention of the group away from the task at hand.

In dealing with both of these problems, the curriculum leader should emphasize that although the concerns may be legitimate, they cannot be considered because it is not compatible with the group objective, which is to select competency items from the course of study. Encourage the participants to pursue these problems when the course of study is revised.

A third concern that the curriculum leader must address intelligently before competency-based education can be developed is, how many competencies should there be? There is no magic number. The major criterion should be, how many competencies are manageable within the instructional system? Or, put another way, how many competencies can be utilized without interfering with the teaching and learning process? When the competency-based program ceases to be an aid to instruction and becomes an interference to instruction, then the program is too vast.

A good way to approach this problem is to be comprehensive in the developmental phase. The curriculum leader should emphasize to the participants involved in the developmental phase not to concern themselves about quantity, only quality. During the implementation phase, it may be revealed that there are too many competencies to make the program manageable. At that time, priorities will have to be established and the number of competencies reduced. The curriculum leader should see to it that the question of *how many* competencies not be addressed in the developmental phase, but rather during the implementation phase when accurate information is available concerning the manageable level of the program.

CRITERIA USED TO ESTABLISH COMPETENCIES

To accomplish the first goal of the planning workshop, which is the tentative identification of competencies, criteria for selecting a competency must be established. The first question the teacher consultants will ask is, "What makes an objective a competency?" If criteria are not established, there is no basis for the decision-making process except the participants' opinions based on their experiences. That is closer to "what is" rather than "what should be."

Many different criteria are proper and feasible. Four possible criteria will now be presented. If any of these is unacceptable to a school system, they should determine their own. The significant step is to establish criteria for competencies and base the decisions on those criteria.

Is It Significant?

The term *significant* is subjective in nature. To ask teachers to identify competencies that are significant without clarifying what significant means will not produce meaningful results. The word significant needs meaningful descriptors. Following are descriptors that will help teachers and administrators determine if a learning objective from the course of study is significant enough to be a competency.

1. *Is it needed for further learning?* In all disciplines there are skills and/or concepts that are prerequisites to learning other skills and/or concepts. For example, a student cannot do division problems if he or she cannot multiply. A student cannot read if he or she does not know the letters of the alphabet. A student must know symbols to work chemistry problems. If a learning objective is needed for further learning, it is a good candidate for competency selection.

2. *Is it something an adult needs to know?* Theoretically, all schooling comes under this criterion of significance; certainly, all competency items should meet this criterion. If a learning objective is not needed for adulthood, it is difficult to imagine it being a competency.

3. *Is it something that our students will need to know when they are adults?* These are prerequisites for the future. We must have the foresight to identify them now so we can help ready the students of today for the world of tomorrow. Some examples are computer literacy, viewing the world from the global perspective rather than from a national or regional perspective, leisure time competency to cope with the rapidly increasing leisure time of the future. These are three examples of future trends that will require competence according to our most knowledgeable futurists.

4. *Should a child of this age with "good schooling" know this?* In order to answer this question, some standard is implied. To arrive at this standard, some comparative data, based on experience and current norms for education, should be used. In setting the standards, ask the question, "What should be" not "what is." Using comparative data and norms will help the curriculum leader arrive at what "should be" good schooling.

5. *By the end of a school level (that is, primary, intermediate, middle, high school), about 80 percent of the students would know this.* This criterion implies that 80 percent of the students should be able to demonstrate achievement of a competency through normal instruction with little or no intervention. It also implies that with intervention, 100 percent achievement of the competency is possible, perhaps even feasible. If an 80 percent achievement level, without intervention, is not maintained, then intervention will become too expensive in both time and money. It would also appear to be politi-

cally unwise to have competencies that regularly fall below the 80 percent achievement level.

6. *It applies to important things outside of school.* This criterion helps avoid the tendency to make all the competencies too "school skill" oriented. Applying this criterion leads to the inclusion of life skills such as consumer and career knowledge.

Does It Imply More Specific Learnings?

1. *Is it "big" enough or general enough to include more specific learnings?* Competencies should be so important to learning that they do not stand alone. So important that they are not ends in themselves but do, in fact, lead the learner to the significant underlying knowledge and skills. For example, language arts competencies should enable the learner to read and write on a more sophisticated level. Math competencies should make possible the more complex math operations.

2. *If it has been learned, can we naturally assume that other more specific learnings have been acquired?* For example, if a student can multiply two-digit numbers correctly, can it be assumed that he knows how to add? Yes, this assumption can be made because the skill of adding is an operation within the multiplication process.

Is It Teachable/Learnable?

1. *Are learners at an appropriate developmental stage to learn this?* This criterion addresses the question of how and when to sequence certain skills and concepts. Most courses of study make reference to the various phases of the curriculum process. They will indicate when a skill or concept is introduced, when it is reinforced, and when it is expected to be mastered. Competency items should, of course, be tested only at the mastery level. If the course of study has properly sequenced skills and concepts, it will automatically place the competencies in the grade level that represents the appropriate developmental stage for learning.

2. *Can it be taught in different ways?* Competency development should take into account that people learn in different ways. Recent efforts in learning style research clearly show that how a person is taught will affect the achievement level depending on the learning style of the person. Competency items should be made up of skills and concepts that can be taught in concrete ways for concrete learners, shown to a visual learner, or presented intellectually to a symbolic learner. By utilizing competency items that can be taught in different ways, a school ensures that competency can be demonstrated by all students regardless of their learning style.

Is It Measurable?

It is oftentimes assumed that all competencies are measured with paper and pencil tests. Paper and pencil tests are the cheapest and easiest to administer. They are the safest politically because they are the most traditional. However, they are not the only way to measure competency. Some of the other methods of measuring competency achievement are:

a. Observation of the learner
b. Student work samples
c. Interaction with the learner

All these methods could be used to measure competency achievement. Obviously, the more objective the test questions are, the more defensible they become. A school should realize that the competencies chosen to be used and how they are to be measured are not definitely right or wrong. Instead, they are defensible or nondefensible to some degree. Therefore, whatever means a school decides to use to measure the competency results should be as defensible as possible.

The selection of competency items from the course of study in the planning workshop is done through three tasks. They are as follows:

Task 1— Decide which required pupil performance objectives in the course of study should be competency items.

Task 2— Decide to what grade level each competency should be assigned for testing.

Task 3— Conduct an in-service session on strategies to gather staff input. Agenda topics would be: (a) how to go about arranging and scheduling the time for gathering staff input, (b) how to work with the principal to get staff meeting time, (c) how to conduct dialogue sessions to work toward consensus, (d) how to resolve conflict, and (e) how to consolidate the input into presentable form.

Task 1, the tentative selection of competency, was just discussed in detail. Task 2, placing the competency at the proper grade level for testing, should also have criteria on which to base decision making. The first criterion is the course of study. At what grade level(s) is the competency taught? More specifically, at what grade level is the competency introduced and reinforced, and at what grade level is full achievement expected?

Competency assessment, (used for instructional purposes only) should occur at the grade level the competency is introduced. Competency testings (used for student evaluation as well as instructional purposes) should occur at least one year after the competency is introduced in the course of study.

The most significant factor in placing competency items at a grade level is to ensure that the grade placement is consistent with the course of study. By doing this, instruction is enhanced and supplemented, not interferred with or altered.

It should be emphasized again that all decisions made in the planning workshop are tentative. This includes the grade placement of competencies. When the items are field tested, the improper grade placement will show up and can be corrected.

IDENTIFYING HIGH SCHOOL COMPETENCIES

Since secondary competencies should be identified by the course offerings, some special development problems surface. The most obvious one centers around the numerous course offerings. If you develop different competencies for every specific course, two things occur:

1. There will need to be too many workshops to make the process feasible, efficient, or effective.
2. There will be numerous repetitions of competencies in similar courses.

Therefore, it is helpful to the developmental process to group similar courses together for the purposes of identifying competencies. By doing this, you eliminate the two problems referred to in the previous paragraph.

To help illustrate how this could be done, a typical high school course offering for math and English will now be presented and grouped to make the developmental process manageable without losing educational effectiveness.

Identification of Competencies—Math 9-12 Groupings

I. General Math
- Math 1
- Basic Computation
- Applied Computation
- Applied Math
- Survey of Math
- Foundations of Math
- Basic Math
- Business Math
- Consumer Math
- Math 2

II. Algebra
- Pre-Algebra
- Algebra 1
- Algebra 2

III. Geometry

IV. Advanced Math
- Analytical Geometry
- Trigonometry
- Calculus
- Advanced Placement
- Advanced Math 1
- Advanced Math 2
- Pre-Calculus

By using these groupings, the competencies could be identified in four workshops instead of twenty-two. (The figure twenty-two represents the number of course offerings.) The similarities of the courses grouped together would represent the same or similar basic skills. Therefore, the effectiveness of the development process would not be adversely affected.

Identification of Competencies—Language Arts 9–12 Groupings

I. Reading
   - Developmental Reading 11/12
   - Reading Improvement
   - That's the Way It Was
   - Adventures Near and Far
   - Reading 9
   - Developmental Reading 9
   - Remedial Reading 9
   - Accelerated Reading
   - Tutorial Reading
II. – English Composition—College Prep
   - English 9
   - English 10
   - English 11
   - English 12
III. English Composition—General
   - English 9
   - English 10
   - English 11
   - English 12

By utilizing these groupings, the number of workshops could be reduced from 17 to 9.

The significant factor in grouping high school courses for competency identification is to group courses by teacher specialty. For example, it's okay to group Algebra I and Algebra II in the same workshop because any teacher comfortable in Algebra I will also be at home in Algebra II. However, it would be unwise to group Biology with Physics because the chances are good that the teachers in the workshops won't be competent in both subjects. One is a biological science, the other is a physical science.

The teacher consultants must be knowledgeable in all the subjects for which competencies are being identified. So make those course groupings similar.

======

ACTIVITY 7

Training Session on Gathering Staff Input

The last task of the planning workshop is vital to the developmental process. If done correctly, it enhances the possibility of consistency in the developmental process. If done incorrectly, or not done at all, it practically ensures that the developmental process will not be consistent.

The agenda topics for the in-service session on strategies for gathering staff input would be: (a) how to go about arranging and scheduling the time for gathering staff input, (b) how to work with the principal to get staff meeting time for staff input, (c) how to conduct dialogue sessions to work toward consensus, (d) how to resolve conflict, and (e) how to consolidate the staff input into presentable and workable form for later use in the feedback workshop.

As is obvious from the agenda, communication with the school principal is the key to gathering good staff input. Each principal is different. Each staff is different in how they approach staff meetings, in-service, and other staff activities. Some staffs meet as a total group. Some meet by grade levels or departments. Some meet in the mornings, some in the afternoon. Some don't meet at all on a regular basis. Each teacher consultant in the training session should be asked to verbally explain how matters such as this are normally handled in their school and how they plan to proceed. Based on the explanation, suggestions could be offered.

It is important to ensure that the method used in the planning workshop by the teacher consultants to arrive at decisions is also used with staff input sessions. That method is, of course, dialogue.

There are many possible approaches to conducting these dialogue input sessions. It could be one-to-one, teacher-consultant-to-staff member during a conference period, before or after school. It could be a grade level meeting. It could be departmental. Or the meeting could be by level (primary, intermediate, and so on). Of course, a total staff meeting could be used.

ACTIVITY 8

Staff Input Sessions

All the procedures explained in Activity 7 should be carried out in the staff input sessions. Only two additional factors should be considered. First of all, the teacher consultants should explain to the staff not only what objectives were judged to be competencies in the planning workshop but also *why*. That dialogue is important information and allows all staff to hear the rationale for each decision that was made. That information will affect their thinking, as it should. The teacher consultants are knowledgeable teacher leaders. Their planning workshop discussion is worthy of consideration.

The most difficult task of the teacher consultants is to consolidate the staff input into workable form for the feedback workshop. The dilemma is similar to that of a congressman. If the constituency is 80 percent for and 20 percent against an issue, it is easy to vote yes. But if the constituency is split 50-50 for and against, the decision is more difficult. The teacher consultants face this same dilemma if half the staff is in agreement with a competency but the other half is not. In those cases, the teacher consultants must make a decision and bring that position back to the feedback workshop.

In consolidating staff input, the teacher consultants must decide if they will present the majority opinion of the staff regardless of their own position—or if they are going to listen to staff input, but will make the final decision based on their own position. Either method can be defended. The rationale for simply carrying back the majority opinion is as old as democracy itself. If the teacher consultants use this approach, they should take special care in presenting the reasons for the decisions that were made in the planning workshop, thereby preserving the dialogue process.

If the teacher consultants are going to listen to staff input, but reserve the final position to themselves, they must maintain a defensible position and be willing to defend it to those of their staff who disagree. The rationale for this approach is based on two assumptions:

1. The teacher consultants were chosen because of expertise in the subject area and should, therefore, be capable of rational decisions.
2. The teacher consultants have been privy to the entire dialogue process and are, therefore, in the best position to make the decision.

ACTIVITY 9

Feedback Workshop

In structure, the feedback workshop looks identical to the planning workshop. The participants are the same, the agenda is the same. The purpose is slightly changed. The planning workshop's purpose was to tentatively identify competencies and train the teacher consultants to gather staff input. The purpose of the feedback workshop is to finalize the list of competencies. This finalization should be based solely on the proper inputs which are:

–Planning workshop results
–Staff input phase information
–Feedback workshop dialogue based on the first two inputs plus the teacher consultants' opinions.

At the conclusion of the feedback workshop, a school system should have a list of competencies at each grade level for the content areas desired.

ACTIVITY 10

Gathering Resources for Development/Selection of Competency Test Items

There are two basic questions involved in this activity. First, who should be involved in gathering the resources and, second, what are the sources of the resource material?

The question of who should be involved does not refer to a particular person or position in the school system. Instead, it refers to types of expertise. Someone with expertise in testing should be involved. Someone with expertise in the subject area should be involved. Someone with knowledge of curriculum and testing material sources should be involved. Someone with knowledge of the demographic and educational makeup of the school system should be involved.

Maybe one person has expertise in all these areas. If so, he or she could gather the resource material. More likely than not, a team of people will be needed to cover these four areas of expertise.

There are many sources of good resource materials from which to develop and select competency test items. Any source utilized must have validity and reliability which has been established either through field testing, success in implementation, or both. The sources that meet these criteria include school systems that have implemented competency-based education, commercial testing companies that have data banks of test items, and state department of education and other intermediate-type agencies that are responsible for large-scale leadership in competency-based education. Another good source is research-oriented foundations that carry a high credibility due to their research base. It's always comfortable to be able to say your program is based on national research.

Once the resources have been gathered, it is time for the person responsible for the feedback workshop to collate the materials and put them in working form before the workshop.

Each competency should have all the samples collated together so the teacher consultants can easily examine all the possible test items. The more sample items the better. The formula looks like this:

Many Sample Items = Less Time Required
Few or No Sample Items = More Time Required

ACTIVITY 11

Test Item
Development/Selection Workshop

The best format for this workshop is small groups. It is a task-oriented activity that requires close dialogue. Test item development and selection should follow this process. (See Figure 3-2.)

1. Select one of the sample items intact (requires no development). If this is not agreeable, then
2. Modify one of the sample items. If this is not agreeable, then
3. Combine two or more of the sample items. If this is not agreeable, then
4. Reject all the sample items and develop an original test item. This development includes the following components:
   –Directions
   –Test questions
   –Format

The teacher consultants should follow this process for each competency until test items have been developed for all competencies. Only one form of the test (Form A) should be developed. A second form (Form B) should not be developed until after the first field test. Following this procedure will save time and allow you to identify the bad items in the first field test before you develop Form B. One form is enough to identify bad competency items. Before the second field test, Form B should be developed and field tested.

The terms *Form A* and *Form B* are used to differentiate between two forms of the same test item. For example, let's assume that the math competency being tested is three-digit addition with carrying. Both Form A and Form B would measure the student's ability to perform three-digit addition with carrying. However, each form would use different problems. (See Figures 3-3 and 3-4.)

Later, during the implementation phase of competency-based education, the teacher will have two tests to measure each competency. Form A and Form B would be used alternately in assessing each student's achievement.

In view of the fact that test items are difficult to write, a good rule of thumb is to select test items from other sources, if possible, and develop test items from scratch if you must.

If selection of test items from other sources is the aim, then the quality of the test items relies on the quality of the sources. The curriculum leader's job is to gather good sources of tests. Commercial test materials are abundant and should be utilized. Teaching materials are also a good source for competency test items.

Listed below are some helpful hints to follow during the test item development process:

1. After teachers select or develop a test item, have other teachers take the test for a double check.
2. Put all test items on a form (see Form B for an example). This will simplify matters later when the test items are typed in final form.
3. The curriculum leader should have a list of acceptable verbs placed on the wall so that teachers who are writing or selecting the test items have quick access to them. Selection of the proper verb is the most difficult part of writing objectives or test items. A quick reference list will be appreciated by the teachers.

In order to have good correlation between curriculum and assessment, the pupil performance objectives found in the course of study (curriculum) must be specific and measurable.

If the pupil performance objectives are specific and measurable, it is easy to write or select test items. If the pupil performance objectives are not specific and measurable, it is not possible to have true competency-based education because the competency will not be criterion-referenced. The competency item must measure one pupil performance objective from the course of study, and only that one objective.

To ensure specific and measurable pupil performance objectives, they should be written to include the following three components;

1. Conditions
     For example:
          Given the name of a picture . . .
          Given a word . . .
          Given a sentence containing . . .
2. Expected Student Behavior
     For example:
          Student will identify . . .
          Student will write . . .
          Student will sound . . .
          Student will follow . . .
          Student will read . . .
          Student will match . . .
          Student will name . . .
3. Minimum level of acceptance
     For example:
          With 75% accuracy
          With 80% accuracy

Putting these three components together, a pupil performance objective could read:

> Given a passage (the condition) the student will read the passage and identify the main idea from a set of titles (the expected student behavior) with 75% accuracy (the minimum level of acceptance).

Refer to Figure 3-5 for a set of language arts pupil performance objectives containing these three components. A second use of this figure is to illustrate a sample set of basic skill competencies for a subject area, in this case, language arts.

Competency test item selection and competency test item development are two distinctly different processes. See Figure 3-6 for a comparison.

The positive reasons for having the educational staff develop the competency test items are: (a) it creates a format for an excellent staff development opportunity, (b) it produces staff ownership of the product, and (c) it produces the "purest" assessment document.

On the other hand, having the educational staff develop the competency test items is also time-consuming and carries the prerequisite of having sufficient human and material resources.

The positive reasons for selecting competency test items from an outside source are: (a) it can be done quicker and more efficiently than self-development, (b) selection of reputable test items will carry built-in validation and thus lessen the emphasis on field testing, and (c) it requires fewer local resources.

The drawbacks to selecting outside competency test items are that it does not produce staff development or staff ownership and requires alteration to create a match between the competency item and the testing measurement.

Figure 3-2

Competency Test Item _____
Grade Level _____
Course of Study Objective _____

Directions:

SAY: 1. Look at number 1. Cut out the word cards. Arrange the word cards in order to make a sentence that makes sense. Paste the word cards in order to make a sentence that makes sense on your answer sheet.

| 1. boy fast a ran | 1. a boy ran fast |

	Study of Test Items, Teacher Comments, and Statistics
Yes	Competency
see below	Quality of Test Item Good
see below	Appropriate Direction Vocabulary
see below	Appropriate Grade Level
	Change Grade Level to Even Test Distribution
	Single Competency Tested
	Sufficient Instruction Given Objective
	Other English

Comments and Suggestions:

(1) I concur with the teacher comments on this item indicating confusion with directions.
(2) These itemsd test more than one competency. Students unfamiliar with the vocabulary would find it necessary to decode as well as organize the words into a sentence.

To correct these difficulties you could:

(1) Move these test items to the second grade level.
(2) Keep the items at the first grade level but change the test item vocabulary to first grade sight words.

i.e. A boy ran fast.

(3) It would be ideal if the students could arrange word cards to put order to the words in the sentence. Such would eliminate the confusion that arises when students have to order by number. This could be accomplished if each student were given scissors and paste for this competency, a word list to cut, and a blank answer sheet on which to paste the words in order in sentence form.

Figure 3-3

<u>MATHEMATICS COMPETENCY TEST ITEM</u>   <u>FORM A</u>

NAME_____ DATE_____

COURSE OF STUDY OBJECTIVE #_____255-1_____

COMPETENCY TEST ITEM #_____90_____ GRADE_____6_____

DIRECTIONS: Work each addition problem.

1. Add

    7428
    8136
    +5624
    _____

    __X__ A) 21,188

    _____ B) 20,288

    _____ C) 21,178

    _____ D) 21,718

2. Add

    2617
    8590
    +3702
    _____

    _____ A) 14,809

    _____ B) 14,899

    __X__ C) 14,909

    _____ D) 15,090

3. Add

    1191
    5326
    +4040
    _____

    _____ A) 10,477

    _____ B) 10,450

    _____ C) 10,547

    __X__ D) 10,557

4. Add

    4169
    3829
    +5797
    _____

    _____ A) 13,670

    __X__ B) 13,795

    _____ C) 13,783

    _____ D) 14,673

Figure 3-4

MATHEMATICS COMPETENCY TEST ITEM   FORM B

NAME_____ DATE_____

COURSE OF STUDY OBJECTIVE #_____255-1_____

COMPETENCY TEST ITEM #_____90_____ GRADE____6____

DIRECTIONS: Work each addition problem.

1. Add

    7428
    8136
  +5625

  __X__ A) 21,189
  _____ B) 20,289
  _____ C) 21,179
  _____ D) 21,719

---

2. Add

    2619
    8590
  +3704

  _____ A) 14,813
  _____ B) 14,893
  __X__ C) 14,913
  _____ D) 15,093

---

3. Add

    1791
    5326
  +4040

  _____ A) 11,457
  _____ B) 10,150
  _____ C) 10,547
  __X__ D) 11,157

---

4. Add

    3169
    3828
  +5797

  _____ A) 12,670
  __X__ B) 12,794
  _____ C) 13,783
  _____ D) 13,763

Figure 3-5

LANGUAGE ARTS COMPETENCY-BASED EDUCATION
PUPIL PERFORMANCE OBJECTIVES

<u>Grade Level</u>

1. Given a picture or shape, the student will identify the same picture or shape from a set of pictures or shapes with 75% accuracy.   K

2. Given a letter of the alphabet, written in manuscript, the student will identify the same letter from a set of letters, written in manuscript, with 75% accuracy.   K

3. Given a set of shapes or letters, the student will identify the shape or letter that is different from the others with 75% accuracy.   K

4. Given the name of a picture, the student will identify the name of another picture that rhymes from a set of names of pictures with 75% accuracy.   K

or

 Given the name of a picture, the student will identify the name of another picture that rhymes with 75% accuracy.   K

5. Given a continuous horizontal dotted line, the student will follow that line with a pencil from left to right with 75% accuracy.   K

6. Given a continuous vertical dotted line, the student will follow that line with a pencil from top to bottom with 75% accuracy.   K

7. Given the name of a letter of the alphabet, the student will identify that letter from a set of letters written in lowercase manuscript with 75% accuracy.   K

8. Given the name of a letter of the alphabet, the student will identify that letter from a set of letters written in uppercase manuscript with 75% accuracy.   K

9. Given a set of pictures, the student will identify one of the pictures on the basis of size with 75% accuracy.   K

10. Given a set of pictures, the student will identify one of the pictures on the basis of position with 75% accuracy.   K

11. Given a word, the student will identify another word that rhymes with the given word from a set of words with 75% accuracy.   1

or

 Given a word, the student will identify another word that rhymes with the given word with 75% accuracy.   1

Figure 3-5
(Continued)

	Grade Level

12. Given a sequential segment of the alphabet, written in uppercase manuscript and containing one missing letter, the student will identify the missing letter from a set of letters written in uppercase manuscript with 75% accuracy. — 1

or

Given a sequential segment of the alphabet, written in uppercase manuscript and containing one missing letter, the student will identify the missing letter with 75% accuracy. — 1

13. Given the name of a letter of the alphabet, the student will write the uppercase and lowercase manuscript forms of that letter with 75% accuracy. — 1

14. Given a word orally, the student will identify the symbol representing the initial, medial, or final consonant sound in that word from a set of symbols representing consonants with 75% accuracy. — 1

or

Given a word orally, the student will identify the symbol representing the initial, medial, or final consonant sound in that word with 75% accuracy. — 1

or

Given a word orally, the student will identify the initial, medial, or final consonant sound in that word from a set of symbols representing consonants with 75% accuracy. — 1

or

Given a word orally, the student will identify the initial, medial, or final consonant sound in that word with 75% accuracy. — 1

15. Given the name of a picture whose sound symbols follow the cvc pattern, the student will identify the symbol representing the short vowel sound in the name from the set of symbols representing vowels with 80% accuracy. — 1

or

Given the name of a picture whose sound symbols follow the cvc pattern, the student will identify the symbol representing the short vowel sound in the name with 80% accuracy. — 1

or

Figure 3-5
(Continued)

<u>Grade Level</u>

Given the name of a picture whose sound symbols follow the cvc pattern, the student will identify the short vowel sound in the name from the set of symbols representing vowels with 80% accuracy.　　　　　　　　　　　　　　　1

or

Given the name of a picture whose sound symbols follow the cvc pattern, the student will identify the short vowel sound in the name with 80% accuracy.　　　　　　　　　　　1

16. Given the name of a picture whose sound symbols follow the cvcé or cvýc pattern, the student will identify the symbol representing the long vowel sound in the name from the set of symbols representing vowels with 80% accuracy.　　1

or

Given the name of a picture whose sound symbols follow the cvcé or cvýc pattern, the student will identify the symbol representing the long vowel sound in the name with 80% accuracy.　　　　　　　　　　　　　　　　　1

or

Given the name of a picture whose sound symbols follow the cvcé or cvýc pattern, the student will identify the long vowel sound in the name from the set of symbols representing vowels with 80% accuracy.　　　　　　　　　　1

or

Given the name of a picture whose sound symbols follow the cvcé or cvýc pattern, the student will identify the long vowel sound in the name with 80% accuracy.　　　　1

17. Given a word orally containing an initial consonant blend, the student will identify the symbol representing the sound of the blend in that word from a set of symbols representing blends with 75% accuracy.　　　　　　　　　1

or

Given a word orally containing an initial consonant blend, the student will identify the symbol representing the sound of the blend in that word with 75% accuracy.　　　　　　　1

or

Given a word orally containing an initial consonant blend, the student will identify the sound of the blend in that word from a set of symbols representing blends with 75% accuracy.　　　　　　　　　　　　　　　　　1

or

Figure 3-5
(Continued)

		Grade Level
	Given a word orally containing an initial consonant blend, the student will identify the sound of the blend in that word with 75% accuracy.	1
18.	Given a word orally containing an initial consonant digraph, the student will identify the symbol representing the sound of the digraph in that word from a set of symbols representing digraphs with 75% accuracy.	1
	or	
	Given a word orally containing an initial consonant digraph, the student will identify the symbol representing the sound of the digraph in that word with 75% accuracy.	1
	or	
	Given a word orally containing an initial consonant digraph, the student will identify the sound of the digraph in that word from a set of symbols representing digraphs with 75% accuracy.	1
	or	
	Given a word orally containing an initial consonant digraph, the student will identify the sound of the digraph in that word with 75% accuracy.	1
19.	Given a set of pictures depicting connective events, the student will number the pictures in correct sequence with 75% accuracy.	1
20-a.	Given a passage, the student will read the passage and identify the main idea from a set of titles with 75% accuracy.	1
b.	Given a passage, the student will read the passage and identify details about the passage with 75% accuracy.	1
21.	Given a list of words, the student will rewrite the words creating a meaningful complete sentence with 75% accuracy.	1
22.	Given a picture of an object with the singular form of the name of that object written below the picture, the student will write the plural form of the name below the pictures of several of the objects with 75% accuracy.	1
	or	
	Given the singular form of a word, the student will write the plural form with 75% accuracy.	1
23.	Given a sentence in which the first letter of the first word in the sentence is not capitalized, the student will identify the first word as needing to be capitalized with 75% accuracy.	1

Figure 3-5
(Continued)

	Grade Level
24. Given a word, the student will identify another word from a set of words that would come *after* the given word alphabetically according to the first letter of the word with 75% accuracy.	1
25. Given a lowercase letter of the alphabet written in cursive, the student will identify the same letter of the alphabet written in manuscript from a set of letters written in manuscript with 75% accuracy.	2
or	
Given a lowercase letter of the alphabet written in cursive, the student will identify the same letter of the alphabet written in manuscript with 75% accuracy.	2
or	
Given a lowercase letter of the alphabet written in cursive, the student will identify its counterpart written in manuscript with 75% accuracy.	2
or	
Given a lowercase letter of the alphabet written in cursive, the student will identify its manuscript counterpart with 75% accuracy.	2
26. Given an uppercase letter of the alphabet written in cursive, the student will identify the same letter of the alphabet written in manuscript from a set of letters written in manuscript with 75% accuracy.	2
or	
Given an uppercase letter of the alphabet written in cursive, the student will identify the same letter of the alphabet written in manuscript with 75% accuracy.	2
or	
Given an uppercase letter of the alphabet written in cursive, the student will identify its counterpart written in manuscript with 75% accuracy.	2
or	
Given an uppercase letter of the alphabet written in cursive, the student will identify its manuscript counterpart with 75% accuracy.	2

Figure 3-5
(Continued)

	Grade Level
27. Given a sequential segment of the alphabet, written in uppercase cursive and containing one missing letter, the student will identify the missing letter from a set of letters written in uppercase cursive with 75% accuracy.	2

or

Given a sequential segment of the alphabet, written in uppercase cursive and containing one missing letter, the student will identify the missing letter with 75% accuracy.	2
28. Given a word, the student will identify an antonym for that word from a set of words with 75% accuracy.	2
29. Given a word, the student will identify a synonym for that word from a set of words with 75% accuracy.	2
30. Given a word orally containing a final consonant blend, the student will identify the symbol representing the sound of the blend in that word from a set of symbols representing blends with 75% accuracy.	2

or

Given a word orally containing a final consonant blend, the student will identify the symbol representing the sound of the blend in that word with 75% accuracy.	2

.or

Given a word orally containing a final consonant blend, the student will identify the sound of the blend in that word from a set of symbols representing blends with 75% accuracy.	2

or

Given a word orally containing a final consonant blend, the student will identify the sound of the blend in that word with 75% accuracy.	2
31. Given a word orally containing a final consonant digraph, the student will identify the symbol representing the sound of the digraph in that word from a set of symbols representing digraphs with 75% accuracy.	2

or

Given a word orally containing a final consonant digraph, the student will identify the symbol representing the sound of the digraph in that word with 75% accuracy.	2

or

Figure 3-5
(Continued)

		Grade Level
	Given a word orally containing a final consonant digraph, the student will identify the sound of the digraph in that word from a set of symbols representing digraphs with 75% accuracy.	2
	or	
	Given a word orally containing a final consonant digraph, the student will identify the sound of the digraph in that word with 75% accuracy.	2
32-a.	Given a passage, the student will read the passage and identify the main idea from a set of titles with 75% accuracy.	2
b.	Given a passage, the student will read the passage and identify details about the passage with 75% accuracy.	2
c.	Given a passage, the student will read the passage and identify the proper sequence of an event in the passage in relationship to another event from the passage with 75% accuracy.	2
33.	Given a sentence in which proper nouns are not capitalized, the student will identify the proper noun as needing to be capitalized with 75% accuracy.	2
34.	Given a sentence in which the personal pronoun "I" is not capitalized, the student will identify the personal pronoun "I" as needing to be capitalized with 75% accuracy.	2
35.	Given a set of proper nouns including titles, one which is capitalized and one which is not capitalized, the student will identify the title which is capitalized correctly with 75% accuracy.	2
36.	Given a sentence containing no end punctuation, the student will identify the correct end punctuation for the sentence from a choice of end markings with 75% accuracy.	2
	or	
	Given a sentence containing no end punctuation, the student will identify the correct end punctuation for the sentence with 75% accuracy.	2
37.	Given a set of proper nouns including titles, one which is punctuated and one which is not punctuated, the student will identify the title which is punctuated correctly with 75% accuracy.	2
38.	Given a set of dates including month, day, and year, one which is punctuated correctly and one which is not punctuated correctly, the student will identify the date which is punctuated correctly with 75% accuracy.	2

**Figure 3-5
(Continued)**

		Grade Level
39.	Given a sequential listing of the days of the week with one day omitted, the student will identify the name of the missing day with 75% accuracy.	2
	or	
	Given a sequential listing of the days of the week with the name of one day omitted, the student will identify the name of the missing day with 75% accuracy.	2
40.	Given a sentence containing an action verb, the student will identify the action verb with 75% accuracy.	2
41.	Given a lowercase or uppercase letter of the alphabet orally, the student will write the letter in cursive form with 100% accuracy.	3
42.	Given a word, the student will identify another word from a list of words that combined with the first word will create a compound word with 75% accuracy.	3
	or	
	Given a word, the student will identify another word that combined with the first word will create a compound word with 75% accuracy.	3
43.	Given homonyms, the student will identify the homonym needed to complete the context of a sentence correctly with 75% accuracy.	3
44.	Given a word, the student will identify the base or root of that word from a set of base or root words and affixes with 75% accuracy.	3
45-a.	Given a passage, the student will read the passage and identify the main idea from a set of titles with 75% accuracy.	3
b.	Given a passage, the student will read the passage and identify facts about the passage with 75% accuracy.	3
c.	Given a passage, the student will read the passage and identify the proper sequence of an event in the passage in relationship to another event from the passage with 75% accuracy.	3
d.	Given a passage, the student will read the passage and identify a cause-effect relationship from the passage with 75% accuracy.	3
46.	Given a set of names of cities and states, one which is punctuated correctly and one which is not punctuated correctly, the student will identify the name of the city and state that is punctuated correctly with 75% accuracy.	3

Figure 3-5
(Continued)

	Grade Level

47. Given a sequential listing of the months of the year with one month omitted, the student will identify the name of the missing month with 75% accuracy. — 3

or

Given a sequential listing of the months of the year with the name of one month omitted, the student will identify the name of the missing month with 75% accuracy. — 3

48. Given a sentence containing a contraction, the student will identify the two words from which that contraction is composed with 75% accuracy. — 3

49. Given a list of words, the student will identify the noun in that list of words with 75% accuracy. — 3

50. Given a simple sentence, the student will identify the subject of that sentence with 75% accuracy. — 3

51. Given a set of two sentences, the student will identify the sentence in which the subject and verb agree with 75% accuracy. — 3

52. Given a word spelled four different ways, the student will identify the correct spelling of the word with 75% accuracy. — 3

53. Given a word, the student will identify another word from a set of words that would come *after* the given word alphabetically according to the third letter of the word with 75% accuracy. — 3

54. Given a sentence with a word having more than one meaning, the student will identify the meaning of the word as used in the given sentence with 75% accuracy. — 3

55. Given a table of contents, the student will identify information from the table of contents with 75% accuracy. — 3

56-a. Given a picture, the student will write three complete sentences describing the events in the picture from a personal point of view with 75% accuracy. — 3

b. Given a picture, the student will write three complete sentences following the conventions of sentence structure, grammar, capitalization, punctuation, and spelling with 75% accuracy. — 3

57. Given three directions presented orally and without repetition, the student will follow the directions with 75% accuracy. — 4

58. Given a word, the student will identify an antonym for that word from a set of words with 75% accuracy. — 4

Figure 3-5
(Continued)

		Grade Level
59.	Given a set of four sentences three of which contain the misuse of a homonym and one in which a homonym is used correctly, the student will identify the sentence in which the homonym is used correctly with 75% accuracy.	4
60.	Given a word, the student will identify the base or root of that word from a set of base or root words and affixes with 75% accuracy.	4
61.	Given a passage, the student will read the passage and identify the meaning of words underlined in the passage from context with 75% accuracy.	4
62-a.	Given a passage, the student will read the passage and identify the main idea from a set of titles with 75% accuracy.	4
b.	Given a passage, the student will read the passage and identify the proper sequence of an event in the passage in relationship to another event from the passage with 75% accuracy.	4
c.	Given a passage, the student will read the passage and identify a cause-effect relationship from a set of events in the passage with 75% accuracy.	4
63.	Given a sentence in which proper nouns are not capitalized, the student will identify the proper noun as needing to be capitalized with 75% accuracy.	4
64.	Given four sentences three of which contain the correct end punctuation and one of which contains incorrect end punctuation, the student will identify the sentence containing the incorrect end punctuation with 75% accuracy.	4
65.	Given a sentence, the student will identify the action verb in that sentence with 75% accuracy.	4
66.	Given a sentence, the student will identify the noun in that sentence with 75% accuracy.	4
67.	Given the parts of a friendly letter, the student will rewrite the letter putting the parts in proper order and following the conventions with relationship to the use of margins with 80% accuracy.	4
68.	Given a sentence in which one word in the sentence is incomplete, the student will identify the prefix from a set of prefixes that will complete the word with 75% accuracy.	5
69.	Given a sentence in which one word in the sentence is incomplete, the student will identify the suffix from a set of suffixes that will complete the word with 75% accuracy.	5

Figure 3-5
(Continued)

Grade Level

70-a. Given a passage, the student will read the passage and identify the main idea from a set of titles with 75% accuracy. 5

b. Given a passage, the student will read the passage and identify the proper sequence of an event in the passage in relationship to another event from the passage with 75% accuracy. 5

c. Given a passage, the student will read the passage and identify a cause-effect relationship from the passage with 75% accuracy. 5

71. Given a passage with the main idea underlined, the student will identify two sentences that support the main idea from a set of sentences with 75% accuracy. 5

72. Given a passage, the student will read the passage and identify two sentences of opinion concerning the passage and two sentences of fact concerning the passage from sets of sentences with 75% accuracy. 5

or

Given a passage, the student will read the passage and identify two statements that express an opinion about the passage and two statements that express a statement of fact about the passage with 75% accuracy. 5

73. Given a passage, the student will read the passage and identify the main character in the passage with 75% accuracy. 5

74. Given a set of incomplete and complete sentences, the student will identify the sentence that is complete in the set with 75% accuracy. 5

75. Given an index, the student will identify information using the index with 75% accuracy. 5

76. Given a presentation orally and without repetition, the student will answer questions about the presentation with 75% accuracy. 6

77-a. Given a passage, the student will read the passage and identify the main idea from a set of titles with 75% accuracy. 6

b. Given a passage, the student will read the passage and identify the proper sequence of an event in the passage in relationship to another event from the passage with 75% accuracy. 6

c. Given a passage, the student will read the passage and identify a cause-effect relationship from the passage with 75% accuracy. 6

Figure 3-5
(Continued)

	Grade Level

78. Given a passage, the student will read the passage and identify the topic sentence in the passage with 75% accuracy. **6**

or

Given a paragraph the student will read the paragraph and identify the topic sentence in the paragraph with 75% accuracy. **6**

79. Given a sentence, the student will identify the simple subject of the sentence with 75% accuracy. **6**

80. Given a sentence, the student will identify the simple predicate of the sentence with 75% accuracy. **6**

81. Given a sentence, the student will identify the complete subject of the sentence with 75% accuracy. **6**

82. Given a sentence, the student will identify the complete predicate of the sentence with 75% accuracy. **6**

83. Given a sentence, the student will identify the adjective in the sentence with 75% accuracy. **6**

84. Given an incomplete sentence and comparative forms of an adjective, the student will identify the comparative form that will complete the sentence correctly with 75% accuracy. **6**

85. Given four words three of which are spelled correctly and one of which is spelled incorrectly, the student will identify the word that is spelled incorrectly with 75% accuracy. **6**

86. Given a word, the student will identify another word from a set of words that would come *after* the given word alphabetically according to the fourth letter of the word with 75% accuracy. **6**

87. Given a dictionary entry for a word with more than one meaning, the student will identify the correct meaning of the word used in context with 75% accuracy. **6**

88-a. Given a passage, the student will read the passage and identify the main idea from a set of titles with 75% accuracy. **7**

  b. Given a passage, the student will read the passage and identify the proper sequence of an event in the passage in relationship to another event from the passage with 75% accuracy. **7**

  c. Given a passage, the student will read the passage and identify a cause-effect relationship from the passage with 75% accuracy. **7**

89. Given a passage, the student will read the passage and identify the setting of the passage with 75% accuracy. **7**

Figure 3-5
(Continued)

		Grade Level
90.	Given several forms of a noun, the student will identify the correct form of the possessive to complete a given sentence with 75% accuracy.	7
91.	Given two forms of the possessive pronoun, the student will identify the correct form to complete a given sentence with 75% accuracy.	7
92.	Given four forms of a verb, the student will identify the correct form of the verb to complete a given sentence with 75% accuracy.	7
93.	Given two words, the student will identify the adverb to complete a given sentence with 75% accuracy.	7
94.	Given a series of related statements, the student will number the statements in proper sequence with 75% accuracy.	7
95.	Given a set of guide words, the student will identify a word that would appear between the guide words alphabetically from a list of words with 75% accuracy.	7
96-a.	Given a set of facts, the student will write a newspaper article incorporating those facts with attention to organization, style, and vocabulary with 75% accuracy.	7
b.	Given a set of facts, the student will write a newspaper article incorporating those facts with attention to the conventions of sentence structure, grammar, punctuation, capitalization, and spelling with 75% accuracy.	7

Figure 3-6

COMPETENCY TEST ITEM

Development	Selection
–Staff development	–Efficient
–Staff ownership	–Quick
–"Purest" assessment	–Built-in validation
–Criterion-referenced	–Requires fewer local resources
–Time-consuming	–Requires alteration to create "match" between item and testing measurement
–Resources required:	–Problem with staff ownership?
–Human	
–Materials	

ACTIVITY 12

First Publication of Test Items

The test document should contain only one item per page. Since competency-based education is criterion-referenced, any analysis performed will be done by the item. Therefore, competency items need to be in a format that will allow the teacher to keep all number 1's together and so on. In addition, having one item per page allows for revision in the simplest manner. Good items will remain intact. Items in need of revision can be revised without having to republish acceptable items.

Publish only the number of tests needed for the first field test. As a result of the field test, revisions will need to be made. Obsolete competency-based education test items are expensive scrap paper.

ACTIVITY 13

Training Session for Teachers Who Will Administer First Field Test

The purposes of this session are attitude building, communication to produce understanding, and quality control through proper and consistent testing procedures. To accomplish these purposes, the teachers' training session should include instructions on the rationale for competency-based education, including:

–The administering of the tests (see Figure 3-7)
–The collecting of tests
–The scoring of tests
–The reporting of tests

Figure 3-7

TEACHER'S DIRECTIONS

COMPETENCY FIELD TEST

I. PRELIMINARY INFORMATION

   A. You are not required to read the directions exactly as they appear on the teacher's direction page. However, if you use different words make sure you do not change the intent of the directions.

   B. There is no time limit for the competency test items. Use common sense as to when the students have had enough time to complete the competency test item.

   C. You may give as many of the competency test items as you wish at one time. That is, you may give them one at a time, five at a time, ten at a time, etc.

II. ADMINISTERING THE COMPETENCY TEST ITEMS

   A. Administer the tests by the following steps:

      1. Hand out the competency test packet.

      2. Give them the directions for the first item as indicated on the teacher's direction sheet. (Remember, you can clarify or alter the directions if you feel it is necessary.)

      3. Give them ample time to answer the questions.

      4. Go on to the next item and continue the process until all the questions are answered. *Remember, you are not required to give all the competency test items in one setting.*

III. SCORING THE COMPETENCY TEST ITEMS

   A. Score each competency test item by writing "yes" at the top of the student's test paper if he demonstrated competency and "no" if he did not. (The percent correct needed for competency is found in Column B of Form A.)

IV. REPORTING THE RESULTS

   A. When the test has been administered and scored, please use Form A to report the number of students who demonstrated competency on each test item and the number of students who did not demonstrate competency on each item.

   B. Go to Form A for instructions and complete the form.

V. RETURNING THE COMPETENCY TEST ITEMS AND FORM A

   A. Return the completed competency test items and the completed Form A to your principal. This information will be used for test analysis.

   B. Keep in mind that this is a field test to determine the validity and reliability of the test items so that necessary revisions can be made.

THANK YOU FOR YOUR HELP AND COOPERATION!

ACTIVITY 14

First Field Test

TEACHER SELECTION

There could be two motives for selection. The first motive could be to select the persons most competent in administering tests. However, the curriculum leader may not know who those people are. In that case, choose the most competent teachers. They usually make the most competent test givers. The second motive could be to choose teachers, not on the basis of teacher competency, but on the basis of program needs. For example, the curriculum leader may want to broaden the base of teacher involvement or maybe involve teachers who have been negative toward competency development in the hopes that involvement will improve their attitude. Perhaps a combination of the two motives is called for—that is, broad teacher involvement without jeopardizing the competence level of test administration.

STUDENT SELECTION

The only significant factor here is to make sure that all levels of classrooms are represented (high, low, medium, heterogeneous). If the competency-based education program is going to be a part of all the schools' classrooms, make sure it is field tested in every type of classroom that the school is operating.

DISTRIBUTION AND COLLECTION OF TESTS

For field test purposes, item results are the significant data. Therefore, collect the results by item, not by student. Test papers should also be kept. They can be as valuable as the report form when analyzing the item results.

ACTIVITY 15

Factors to Consider in Analyzing Field Test Results

When it comes to testing, educators are used to analyzing results through the use of the group mean or average for the complete test. Also, the data is presented student-by-student, through the use of statistics. In competency-based education, the significant data from the field test is the demonstrated competence or noncompetence on each competency item.

When analyzing field test results (data), the following statistics should be used:

1. **The Mean.** If the schools expect nearly 100 percent of the students to demonstrate competency with intervention, then a mean of 80 percent without intervention is needed on the field test. However, the mean must have been established through a consistent mode.

2. **The Mode.** Once again, the mean must have been established through a consistent mode. For example, a mean of 80 percent that was the result of all scores being between 70 and 90 percent is indicative of a good competency item. However, a mean of 80 percent that was the result of scores from 20 to 100 percent is not necessarily indicative of a good competency item. Therefore, what is looked for in a field test is a competency item that has both a mean and a mode that is 80 percent or higher.

3. **High and Low Score.** This statistic is significant because it will give clues as to whether or not an item is too hard for the lower-functioning student or too easy for the higher-functioning students.

In addition to these statistics, teachers' comments should be encouraged, accepted, and integrated into the analysis. These comments should be considered as significant as the statistical data.

Also, all student test papers should be kept throughout the analysis process. They give clues as to why the students found the test items too easy, too hard, confusing, or whatever problem may have arisen.

ACTIVITY 16

Compiling First Field Test Results

This is a task that could be done by any competent person. Therefore, it could be delegated to whatever level of the organization has the time to perform the task. The statistical data should be entered in the proper column on Form A. (See Figure 3-8.) Teachers' comments should be consolidated. People oftentimes say the same things in different ways. Doing this makes the comments easier to incorporate into the analysis.

Figure 3-8

COMPILATION OF FIELD TEST RESULTS
FORM A
REPORTING SHEET

INTERMEDIATE MATHEMATICS

INSTRUCTIONS

A. Column A contains the competency test item number.
B. Column B indicates the percent of correct responses required to demonstrate competency. (At least 75% or 3 out of 4 responses must be correct.)
C. In Column C write the number of students who *demonstrated* competency on that competency test item.
D. In Column D write the number of students who *did not demonstrate* competency on that competency test item.
E. Column C plus (+) Column D should equal the number of students who took the competency test item.
F. *Important:* Put additional comments on the back of this form.

COLUMN A Item #	COLUMN AA High & Low Score in Percentage (%)	COLUMN B Percent (%) required for competency	COLUMN C Number of students demonstrating competency		COLUMN D Number of students not demonstrating competency	
1	100% 64%	75%	159	87%	24	13%

**Figure 3-8
(Continued)**

COLUMN A	COLUMN AA	COLUMN B	COLUMN C		COLUMN D	
Item #	High & Low Score in Percentage (%)	Percent (%) required for competency	Number of students demonstrating competency		Number of students not demonstrating competency	
2	93% 64%	75%	137	75%	46	25%
3	93% 39%	75%	124	68%	59	32%
4	97% 76%	75%	162	89%	21	11%
5	100% 95%	75%	181	99%	1	1%
6	60% 16%	75%	63	34%	120	66%
7	100% 100%	75%	182	100%	0	0%
8	100% 88%	75%	148	95%	8	5%
9	100% 88%	75%	148	95%	8	5%
10	100% 93%	75%	179	99%	2	1%
11	100% 96%	75%	179	99%	1	1%
12	100% 85%	75%	169	93%	11	7%
13	100% 94%	75%	178	99%	1	1%
14	100% 28%	75%	135	75%	44	25%
15	96% 83%	75%	161	90%	18	10%

ACTIVITY 17

Analyzing First Field Test Results

The purpose of the field test is to answer the following four questions. (See Figure 3-9.)

1. Is the competency valid?
2. Is the test item that measures the competency valid?
3. Is the competency being tested at the proper grade level?
4. Is adequate instruction on the competency occurring?

Figure 3-9
Field Test Analysis

Components	The Question	The Evidence
COMPETENCY	Is the competency valid?	– Mean score acceptable – Mode score acceptable – Mean score consistent – Found in course of study
TEST ITEM(S)	Is the test item that measures the competency valid?	– Measures only the skills involved in the competency – Format and layout of test not a factor in achievement
GRADE LEVEL	Is the competency being tested at the proper grade level?	– Correlates with course of study – Achievement level somewhere between 75 and 90%
INSTRUCTION	Is adequate or better instruction occurring?	– Consistent test results from classroom to classroom

The field test results give clues concerning each of these questions. Let's take each question and discuss how field test results give evidence needed to validate the competency.

1. Is the competency valid?

The main indicator is the mean or average score. If you have established that you want 80 percent of your students to be able to demonstrate competency without intervention and the field test mean is 87 percent, then the mean indicates the item is valid. However, the mean must also be consistent. For example, a mean of 80 percent that is the result of four scores of 60 percent and four scores of 100 percent does not indicate a valid competency. Why? Because only 50 percent of the students demonstrated competency without intervention and it had been previously indicated that 80 percent need to demonstrate competency without intervention. However, a mean of 80 percent that is the result of eight scores of 80 percent does indicate a valid competency. So you see, the mean not only must be at the level you have established but must also have been achieved through a consistency of scores.

In summary, a field test must validate a competency item through an acceptable mean that was achieved through consistency in scores and not as the result of extreme high and low scores.

2. Is the test item that measures the competency valid?

To answer this question, apply the following analysis:

a. Does the test question measure the competency?

b. Does the test question measure only the intended competency and not other competencies or questions?

c. Is the test format and layout a factor in whether or not the competency was demonstrated?

The answer to the first two questions should be yes, and the answer to the third question should be no.

In an attempt to illustrate the question of test item validity, take a look at the following competency exam.

Language Arts Competency Test Item

Course of Study Objective # ___105-9___

Competency Test Item # ___18___   Grade ___1___

Objective: Given a list of words, put them in order to make a complete sentence.

Directions: Number the words so that they will read as a complete sentence.

   1. Spot   fast   ran

   _____   _____   _____

---

2. dog   the   barks

______   ______   ______

3. Karen   the   hit   ball

______   ______   ______   _____

4. Spot   high   jumps

______   ______   ______

This test item does measure the competency. Therefore, it answers question (a) adequately. However, it does not answer questions (b) and (c) adequately because other competencies are involved. For example, the student has to know numbers in sequence in order to answer this question correctly. The student must also be able to correlate the proper number with the proper word and place the number in the proper place. Therefore, the student could fail this competency for any of the above reasons and there would be no way of determining which competency was lacking. Therefore, this is not a valid competency test item.

To make this test item valid, the directions could say:

Arrange the words to make a complete sentence, and write the complete sentence in the blank box after the number 1.

1. boy fast a ran	1.

3. Is the test item at the proper grade level?

If it is the consensus of the staff that the competency is a valid one, and that the test item is proper but the field test results are poor, then the test item is probably at the wrong grade level.

Poor results could mean two different things. If the scores are too low, then the item should be moved up to a higher grade level. If the scores are too high, then perhaps the item should be moved to a lower grade.

Some people would argue that there is no such thing as too high an average on the field test results. They would say that 100 percent achievement is the goal. And, of course, it is true that 100 percent is what you are looking for in a competency-based education program. But keep in mind that the field test results indicate achievement levels without the benefit of regular instruction, intervention, remediation, or any other kind of teaching procedure.

It can, therefore, be assumed that if all or a very high percent of the students demonstrate competency on an item on the first test, the item is too easy to be of much benefit to the instructional program.

Any competency-based program which demonstrates 95 percent or better achievement on the first testing will represent no challenge to too many of the students. Neither will it improve the instructional program because it will provide little or no diagnostic information.

An achievement level of 75 percent to 90 percent on the first testing indicates that the competency test item is placed at the proper grade level. If only 75 percent of the students get the item correct, the item does appear to represent an academic challenge. Therefore, it is beneficial to the instructional program because it renders diagnostic information. In addition, it is reasonable to assume that, through intervention, the number of students demonstrating competency can be raised to 90 percent or higher, thus achieving the goals of the competency-based program.

4. Is adequate instruction on the competency occurring?

If the field test results are consistently bad, then one needs to look at the competency or the test item or the grade level. But if the results are inconsistent, the problem most likely lies in the instructional program. Therefore, when this is the problem, the instructional shortcomings should be addressed. There are many possible problems. Among them are: (1) poor teaching methods, (2) poor teachers, (3) inadequate or poor learning materials, (4) lack of curriculum continuity, and (5) not enough emphasis on the competency.

ACTIVITY 18

Reporting First Field Test Results

A detailed report on the results of the first field test should be shared with the administration and teachers as soon as the analysis has been done. The statistical results, teacher comments and valid interpretations, and inferences should be presented in educational terminology.

The boards of education and the community should also be informed of the field test results. However, the format and the method of presentation will differ from that used in reporting to the administration and teachers. More explanation must accompany the report. Remember that most of these people are not professional educators and will need lay terminology in the report. It would also be wise to keep the report in capsule form.

Regardless of which group you are reporting results to, constantly emphasize that the competency-based education program is still in a rough, unfinished state, and that it will undergo further revision and refinement. This is important because some of the field test results will reveal weaknesses and problems with the competency-based education program. If a proper emphasis and explanation does not accompany the results, there is the probability that the program will suffer from criticism. Even worse, the program could be lost.

The purpose of reporting the first field test results is to set the rationale for the revision process. Everyone involved needs to know if a lot of revision is needed or if the field test results indicate little revision will be needed.

ACTIVITY 19

Test Item Revision Workshop

The purpose of the revision workshop is to revise the competency test items that were found to be deficient in the field test. This workshop should consider only the competencies that were deficient on the field tests and should not discuss those items that the field test revealed were adequate and acceptable. This workshop should also not deal with the revision of items based on any information other than the field test results. This workshop must resist the "on second thought" mentality. If the field test results were good, put the item to rest. Spend this valuable workshop time on the items that the field test revealed were deficient.

The materials that the participants need for this workshop are:

–The field tests analysis
–A copy of the competency test items to be revised

ACTIVITY 20

Second Publication of Test Items

This is a duplication of Activity 12 with a few additional considerations. Very important is the fact that, if the previous nineteen activities have been successful, this may be the last revision of the test items or at least, the last revision for most of the test items. Therefore, make sure the publication is done properly. For example, make sure that the page margins are correct and will allow for a loose-leaf format. Also, make sure that all the information you want and need is on the test items.

Refer to Activity 12 for other specifics concerning the publication process.

ACTIVITY 21

Training Session for Teachers Who Will Administer Second Field Test

This activity is a repeat of Activity 13. Refer to Activity 13 if you need to review the information.

ACTIVITY 22

Second Field Test

This activity is identical to Activity 14. Refer to Activity 14 for a review if needed.

ACTIVITY 23

Factors to Consider in Analyzing Field Test Results

This activity is identical to Activity 15. Refer to Activity 15 for a review if needed.

ACTIVITY 24

Compiling Second Field Test Results

This activity is identical to Activity 16. Refer to Activity 16 for a review if needed.

ACTIVITY 25

Analyzing Second Field Test Results

This activity is identical to Activity 17. Refer to Activity 17 for a review if needed.

ACTIVITY 26

Reporting Second Field Test Results

This activity is identical to Activity 18. Refer to Activity 18 for a review if needed.

If after Activity 26 further revision of the competency-based education test items is needed, the school system should go back to Activity 19 (Test Item Revision Workshop) and repeat activities 19 through 26 until the competency test items are accepted as valid and reliable.

ACTIVITY 27

Developing Classroom Management Procedures and Recordkeeping Systems for Competency-Based Education

Four outcomes are necessary for a management system to be effective. They are:

1. A recordkeeping system for the competency-based education program within a grade level.
2. A recordkeeping system for the carrying over of unmastered competencies from one grade level to the next.
3. A procedure to communicate the individual student's performance on the competency test items to the parent(s) or guardian(s).
4. An in-service plan for each school to instruct the teachers on how to use the competency-based education procedures and documents.

It is in the process of classroom management and student recordkeeping that competency-based education most often fails. The failure is due to the fact that recordkeeping becomes so cumbersome that the teacher spends more time recording information than he or she does teaching. Therefore, the key word in this process is *simplicity*. In order to achieve simplicity, the method of recording information and the style and number of documents must be kept to a minimum. The classroom management procedures must be kept as simple as possible. If this is accomplished, the classroom teacher will have more time to teach.

PRETEST

Best pretest procedures:

1. Administered early October.
2. Math administered in one session.
3. Language Arts administered in two sessions (flexible).
4. Use necessary physical measures to avoid copying.
5. Use monitors if available.
6. Severe disruptions: Problem children should be removed and given the test at a later time, one-on-one or in small group.
7. Flexibility to retest to raise percent should be available.

In order to achieve the goal of simplicity in student recordkeeping, various documents are recommended.

COMPETENCY-BASED EDUCATION PROGRAM COMPONENTS

Following is an annotated listing of the various components of the competency-based education program.

1. Documents
   a. Student Test Items—These tests should be packaged by item (1's together, etc.). There are thirty tests in each packet. Also, there are Form A's and Form B's. These student tests should be housed in the classroom of all teachers.
   b. Teacher Notebooks—These materials should be color coded, for example, gold (language arts) and orange (mathematics). They should be organized by grade level. Each teacher should have one of each at his or her grade level or subject. These notebooks contain a list of all pertinent competency items plus the teacher directions and answer sheets for each competency. (Forms A and B)
   c. Student Record or Management Card—This manila-colored oak tag is to be used to record each individual student's demonstrated achievement of the competencies. It is designed to be housed in the student's cumulative folder. (See Figures 3-10 and 3-11.)
   d. Competency Class Rosters—These optional forms are organized by grade level or subject. They are designed to help the teacher diagnose class needs and deficiencies. Each teacher needs only one roster per year. The form contains space for thirty students. (See Figures 3-12 and 3-13.)
   e. Form 1—This form is green and is designed to be the initial parent communication. It is organized by grade level and contains the competencies of that grade level or subject. (See Figure 3-14.)

Figure 3-10
Student Record Card

CLERMONT COUNTY BASIC COMPETENCY TESTS

Name _____
Last   First

*A.C.A. = All Competencies Accomplished.

Key: + Achieved
        − Needs Intervention

K Language Arts	Competency #	1	2	3	4	5	6	7	8	9	10	A.C.A.
	Pre-Test A B											
	Post-Test A B											
	Comments:											

K Math	Competency #	1	2	3	4	A.C.A.
	Pre-Test A B					
	Post-Test A B					
	Comments:					

First Language Arts	Competency #	11	12	13	14	15	16	17	18	19	20a	20b	21	22	23	24	A.C.A.
	Pre-Test A B																
	Post-Test A B																
	Comments:																

First Math	Competency #	5	6	7	8	9	10	11	12	13	14	15	A.C.A.
	Pre-Test A B												
	Post-Test A B												
	Comments:												

Second Language Arts	Competency #	25	26	27	28	29	30	31	32a	32b	32c	33	34	35	36	37	38	39	40	A.C.A.
	Pre-Test A B																			
	Post-Test A B																			
	Comments:																			

Second Math	Competency #	16	17	18	19	20	21	22	23	24	25	26	27	28	29	A.C.A.
	Pre-Test A B															
	Post-Test A B															
	Comments:															

Third Language Arts	Competency #	41	42	43	44	45	46	47	48	49	50	51	52	53	54	55	56a	56b	A.C.A.
	Pre-Test A B																		
	Post-Test A B																		
	Comments:																		

Third Math	Competency #	30	31	32	33	34	35	36	37	38	39	40	41	42	43	A.C.A.
	Pre-Test A B															
	Post-Test A B															
	Comments:															

School: _____
Teacher: _____

School: _____
Teacher: _____

School: _____
Teacher: _____

School: _____
Teacher: _____

School: _____
Teacher: _____

School: _____
Teacher: _____

School: _____
Teacher: _____

School: _____
Teacher: _____

Figure 3-11
Student Record Card

CLERMONT COUNTY BASIC COMPETENCY TESTS

Name _____ Last _____ First

*A.C.A. - All Competencies Accomplished.

Key: + Achieved
      - Needs Intervention

Fourth Language Arts

Competency #	57	58	59	60	61	62a	62b	62c	63	64	65	66	67	A.C.A.
Pre-Test														
Post-Test														
Comments:														

School: _____ Teacher: _____

Fourth Math

Competency #	44	45	46	47	48	49	50	51	52	53	54	55	56	57	58	59	60	A.C.A.
Pre-Test																		
Post-Test																		
Comments:																		

School: _____ Teacher: _____

Fifth Language Arts

Competency #	68	69	70a	70b	70c	71	72	73	74	75	A.C.A.
Pre-Test											
Post-Test											
Comments:											

School: _____ Teacher: _____

Fifth Math

Competency #	61	62	63	64	65	66	67	68	69	70	71	72	73	74	75	A.C.A.
Pre-Test																
Post-Test																
Comments:																

School: _____ Teacher: _____

Sixth Language Arts

Competency #	76	77a	77b	77c	78	79	80	81	82	83	84	85	86	87	A.C.A.
Pre-Test															
Post-Test															
Comments:															

School: _____ Teacher: _____

Sixth Math

Competency #	83	84	85	86	87	88	89	90	91	92	93	94	95	96	97	98	99	100	101	A.C.A.
Pre-Test																				
Post-Test																				
Comments:																				

School: _____ Teacher: _____

Seventh Language Arts

Competency #	88a	88b	88c	89	90	91	92	93	94	95	96a	96b	A.C.A.
Pre-Test													
Post-Test													
Comments:													

School: _____ Teacher: _____

Seventh Math

Competency #	102	103	104	105	106	107	108	109	110	111	112	113	114	115	116	117	118	119	120	A.C.A.
Pre-Test																				
Post-Test																				
Comments:																				

School: _____ Teacher: _____

Figure 3-12

COMPETENCY CLASS ROSTER Teacher: _____ School: _____ PRIMARY LANGUAGE ARTS Grade: Kindergarten Student Name	Item #	1 Identical Objects	2 Size, Shape, Position	3 Different Objects	4 Rhyme Objects	5 Left to Right	6 Top to Bottom	7 Lowercase Manuscript	8 Uppercase Manuscript	9 Identify Size	10 Identify Position	

Figure 3-13

COMPETENCY CLASS ROSTER School: _____ PRIMARY LANGUAGE ARTS Grade: Third Grade Year:	Item #	Cursive Letter From Dictation	Compound	Homonyms	Root Words	Main Ideas	Facts	Sequence	Cause-Effect	Comma	Months	Contraction	Nouns	Subjects	Subject-Verb Agreement	Spelling	Alphabetizing	Word Meaning	Table of Contents	Writing Sample Content	Writing Sample Mechanics
		41	42	43	44	45a	45b	45c	45d	46	47	48	49	50	51	52	53	54	55	56a	56b

Figure 3-14
Sample of Form 1 Letter to Parents

Third Grade

Dear Parents:

The Batavia Schools have a competency-based education program in language arts and mathematics. Listed are competencies that have been identified as basic to your child's grade level.

Third Grade Language Arts

41. Write as dictated upper- and lowercase cursive letters.
42. Recognize the compound form of two words.
43. Recognize the correct homonym.
44. Given a list of words, identify the root or base word.
45. a. After reading a given passage recognize the main idea.
    b. After reading a given passage recall facts.
    c. After reading a given passage recall the sequence of events.
    d. After reading a given passage recognize cause and effect relationships.
46. Recognize that a comma separates city and state.
47. Recognize months of the year in sequence.
48. Recognize the contracted form of two words.
49. Recognize nouns in a list of words.
50. Identify the subject of simple sentences.
51. Recognize simple subject-verb agreement in written sentences.
52. Identify written words that are spelled correctly.
53. Given a list of words in which the first two letters are the same, put the words in order alphabetically.
54. Recognize more than one meaning for a given word.
55. Use a table of contents to find information.
56. Write three complete sentences describing the events in a picture.

Third Grade Mathematics

30. Recognize the ones, tens, and hundreds place in a three-digit numeral.
31. Subtract a three-digit numeral from a three-digit numeral without regrouping.
32. Recognize the value of each digit in a four-digit number.
33. Add two two-digit numerals with regrouping.
34. Add two three-digit numerals without regrouping.

Figure 3-14
(Continued)

35. Add two three-digit numerals with regrouping.
36. Subtract two-digit numerals with regrouping.
37. Subtract a two- or three-digit numeral from a three-digit numeral with only one regrouping.
38. Multiply two numerals where the multiplier is 0 through 5.
39. Find the value of a given group of coins that totals up to $1.00.
40. Recognize the written time (hour, half-hour, quarter-hour) represented on a given clock face.
41. Recognize the correct symbol [<, =, >] that belongs between two given numerals when neither has more than three digits.
42. Solve word problems involving addition of two two-digit numerals.
43. Solve word problems involving subtraction of two two-digit numerals.

f. Form 2—This form is buff-colored. It is designed for the last parent-teacher conference. The purpose is to identify unmastered competencies for the student and parent as a basis for summer or home intervention. (See Figure 3-15.)

Figure 3-15
Sample of Form 2 Letter to Parents

Kindergarten

To the parents of_____

The items circled indicate basic skills that your child has not yet mastered. Please see the "Teacher Comments" below for further information.

Kindergarten Language Arts

1. Given a concrete object or a picture of an object, identify another object or picture that is the same.
2. Given concrete objects, pictures of objects, or letters, identify the one that matches the sample in size, shape, or position.
3. Given concrete objects, pictures of objects, or letters, identify the one that is different.
4. Recognize the sounds of the names of objects that rhyme.

Figure 3-15
(Continued)

5. Given a continuous dotted line moving from left to right, follow the line with a pencil.
6. Given a continuous dotted line moving from top to bottom, follow the line with a pencil.
7. Identify lowercase manuscript letters.
8. Identify uppercase manuscript letters.
9. Identify pictures, objects, or letters on the basis of size.
10. Identify pictures, objects, or letters on the basis of position.

Kindergarten Mathematics

1. Recognize the numbers 0 through 10.
2. Identify a circle, square, triangle, and rectangle.
3. Recognize the smallest or largest object in a group of objects.
4. Given a group of objects with one object different from the rest, recognize the object that is different.

Teacher Comments: _____

_____

_____

HOW SHOULD STUDENTS BE TOLD ABOUT COMPETENCY-BASED EDUCATION?

This should be handled by the classroom teacher in the same way that other important components of the educational program are handled. For example, teachers explain the need for regular attendance, doing homework, etc. The importance of the mastery of basic skills (competencies) should also be emphasized.

SAMPLE AGENDA FOR STAFF IN-SERVICE ON COMPETENCY-BASED EDUCATION

The following agenda is recommended for this valuable in-service. You may wish to alter the topics. It is presented to give you a frame of reference to begin your planning.

Agenda (sample)

Presentation of Program

1. Components of the program (hands-on process)
   -question and answer
   -how to use forms
   -how to store tests
2. Pretest Procedures
   -when?
   -how?
   -flexibility?
   -instructional emphasis!
3. Teachers' questions and comments

Use of the Student Card for the Basic Competency Test

1. Each student will have a card on which the teacher will record the student's name, the school, and teacher's name in the appropriate spaces.
2. On the appropriate language and math spaces, circle the pretest form, A or B.
3. On the pretest item numbers, record a + for each item passed and a − for each item that shows a need for intervention.
4. On the posttest space, record the form used. Only record those items passed during the year and at the end of the year put a − if the student was still unable to pass the test after intervention and retesting.
5. If a decision is made on color coding the recording of passing the items:
   Kindergarten—Black

   First Grade—Green

   Second Grade—Red

   Third Grade—Blue
6. At the end of the year, when you put the record cards in the cumulative folder, be sure to fill in the space marked A.C.A. ("All Competencies Accomplished") if the student has passed all the items at your grade level. Be sure to leave it blank if there are items which need to be carried over to the following year.

Use of Student Class List Rosters

A class roster is for use in the classroom as a quick means for the teacher to see who needs intervention and who has passed the basic competency.

A teacher may wish to check off those students who have passed the item or may wish to do the reverse—check off those students who have shown the need for some kind of intervention.

Passing a competency item means that the child scored three out of four when the test has four items. Also, passing means four out of five if the test has five items.

There is no limit to the number of times a student may be tested. After intervention, you may wish to wait a week and test one individual item to see if the student has maintained the knowledge. If not, then reteaching is done and the item is tested again. Be sure to use alternate items.

Figures 3-16 and 3-17 list the competencies for language arts and mathematics, K–7. Refer to these when completing the management cards.

Figures 3-18 through 3-20 show samples of a letter to workshop participants, a workshop information sheet, and an agenda.

Figure 3-16

PRIMARY LANGUAGE ARTS (K-3)

1. Identical Objects	K
2. Size, Shape, Position	K
3. Different Objects	K
4. Rhyming Objects	K
5. Left to Right	K
6. Top to Bottom	K
7. Lowercase Manuscript	K
8. Uppercase Manuscript	K
9. Identify Size	K
10. Identify Position	K
11. Rhyming Words	1
12. Alphabetical Order of Letters	1
13. Manuscript Letters	1
14. Consonant Sounds	1
15. Short Vowels	1
16. Long Vowels	1
17. Initial Consonant Blends	1
18. Digraphs	1
19. Sequence of Events	1
20. a. Main Ideas	1
b. Facts	1
21. Sentence Sense	1
22. Plural Nouns	1
23. Capitalization	1
24. Alphabetical Order of Words	1
25. Match Cursive Manuscript (Lowercase)	2
26. Match Cursive Manuscript (Uppercase)	2
27. Order of Cursive Letters	2
28. Antonyms	2
29. Synonyms	2
30. Final Consonant Blends	2
31. Digraphs	2
32. a. Main Ideas	2
b. Facts	2
c. Sequence	2
33. Capitalize Names	2
34. Capitalize "I"	2
35. Capitalize Titles	2
36. End Punctuation	2
37. Punctuation of Titles	2
38. Punctuation of Dates	2
39. Days of the Week	2
40. Action Verbs	2
41. Cursive Letters From Dictation	3
42. Compounds	3
43. Homonyms	3

PRIMARY LANGUAGE ARTS (K-3)
(continued)

44. Root Words	3
45. a. Main Ideas	3
b. Facts	3
c. Sequence	3
d. Cause-Effect	3
46. Comma	3
47. Months	3
48. Contractions	3
49. Nouns	3
50. Subjects	3
51. Subject-Verb Agreement	3
52. Spelling	3
53. Alphabetizing	3
54. Word Meaning	3
55. Table of Contents	3
56. a. Writing Sample Content	3
b. Writing Sample Mechanics	3

PRIMARY MATHEMATICS (K-3)

1. Numbers 1-10	K
2. Circle, Square, Triangle, Rectangle	K
3. Smallest, Largest Object	K
4. Different Objects	K
5. Tens and Ones	1
6. 0-100	1
7. Numbers by Fives	1
8. Numbers by Tens	1
9. One-Digit Addition	1
10. One-Digit Subtraction	1
11. Time to Hour	1
12. Numbers of Objects	1
13. Small to large	1
14. Number Sentences	1
15. $+, -, =$	1
16. Numbers by Twos	2
17. Coins	2
18. Value Coins	2
19. Add to Eighteen	2
20. Two-Digit Addition	2
21. Add Three One-Digit Numbers	2
22. Add Two Two-Digit Numbers	2
23. Subtract to Eighteen	2
24. Subtract Two-Digit Numbers	2
25. Value of Coins	2
26. Hour/Half-Hour	2
27. $<, =, >$	2

Figure 3-16
(Continued)

PRIMARY MATHEMATICS
(*continued*)

28. Word Problems Addition	2	36. Subtract Two-Digit Numbers	3
29. Word Problems Subtraction	2	37. Subtract Two-Digit Numbers, Regrouping	3
30. Ones, Tens, and Hundreds	3	38. Multiply	3
31. Three-Digit Subtraction	3	39. Coins to $1.00	3
32. Four-Digit Numbers	3	40. Hour, Half-Hour, Quarter-Hour	3
33. Add Two-Digit Numbers	3	41. $<, = >$	3
34. Add Three-Digit Numbers	3	42. Word Problems Addition	3
35. Add Three-Digit Numbers, Regrouping	3	43. Word Problems Subtraction	3

Figure 3-17

INTERMEDIATE LANGUAGE ARTS (4–7)

57. Following Oral Directions	4
58. Antonyms	4
59. Homonyms	4
60. Base/Root Words	4
61. Word Meaning From Context	4
62. a. Main Idea	4
b. Sequence	4
c. Cause-Effect	4
63. Capitalization Proper Nouns	4
64. Punctuation End Marks	4
65. Verbs	4
66. Nouns	4
67. Organizing a Friendly Letter	4
68. Prefix	5
69. Suffix	5
70. a. Main Idea	5
b. Sequence	5
c. Cause-Effect	5
71. Details	5
72. Fact-Opinion	5
73. Story Character	5
74. Complete Sentence	5
75. Index	5
76. Attend to an Oral Presentation	6
77. a. Main Idea	6
b. Sequence	6
c. Cause-Effect	6
78. Topic Sentence	6
79. Simple Subject	6
80. Simple Predicate	6
81. Complete Subject	6
82. Complete Predicate	6

INTERMEDIATE LANGUAGE ARTS
(*continued*)

83. Adjectives	6
84. Adjectives (comparative/superlative)	6
85. Spelling	6
86. Alphabetical Order	6
87. Correct Meaning in Dictionary Entry	6
88. a. Main Idea	7
b. Sequence	7
c. Cause-Effect	7
89. Story Setting	7
90. Possessive Nouns	7
91. Possessive Pronouns	7
92. Verb Form	7
93. Adverbs	7
94. Logical Order	7
95. Dictionary Guide Words	7
96. a. Writing Sample Content	7
b. Writing Sample Mechanics	7

INTERMEDIATE MATHEMATICS (4–7)

44. Place Value Five-Digit Number	4
45. Add Two Whole Numbers Any Order	4
46. Group Whole Numbers, Addition Problem, Any Order	4
47. Subtraction Reverses, Addition Whole Numbers	4
48. Multiple Two Whole Numbers, Any Order	4
49. Fractional Symbol	4
50. Recognize Fraction	4
51. Add Numbers, Three-Digit	4
52. Missing Addend	4

Figure 3-17
(Continued)

INTERMEDIATE MATHEMATICS
(*continued*)

53. Subtract Two-Digit Numbers, Regroup	4	
54. Product Two One-Digit Numbers, (0–9)	4	
55. Product Three One-Digit Numbers	4	
56. Product One-Digit Number, Two-Digit Number	4	
57. Product One-Digit Number, Three-Digit Number	4	
58. Product One-Digit Number, Multiple of Ten	4	
59. Product One-Digit Number, Multiple of 100	4	
60. Two-Digit Number × Two-Digit Number; Multiple of Ten	4	
61. Factors/Product	5	
62. Place Value Six-Digit Number	5	
63. Group Whole Number/Multiple	5	
64. Division Reverses Multiplication (Facts 1–9)	5	
65. Fractional Part, Set/Whole	5	
66. Numerator/Denominator	5	
67. Sum Three Addends (three digits each)	5	
68. Equation One Step + Word Problem	5	
69. Subtract Two Numbers (Three-Digit or less regroup)	5	
70. Multiply One-Digit Number by 10, 100, 1000	5	
71. Multiply Two-Digit Number by 10, 100, 1000	5	
72. Multiply Three-Digit Number by 10, 100 1000	5	
73. Three-Digit Number × Two-Digit Number (Multiple 10)	5	
74. Equation One Step × Work Problem (One-Digit)	5	
75. Missing Factor Multiple (0–9 Facts)	5	
76. Product Two Two-Digit Numbers	5	
77. One-Digit Number ÷ One-Digit Number	5	
78. Two-Digit Number ÷ Two-Digit Number	5	
79. Three-Digit Number ÷ Three-Digit Number	5	
80. Two-Digit Number ÷ Two-Digit Number (Multiple 10)	5	
81. Add Two Proper Fractions, Like Denominators	5	

82. Subtract Two Proper Fractions, Like Denominators	5
83. Parts Fractional Symbol	6
84. Equation Muliple Word Problem	6
85. Four-Digit Number ÷ One-Digit Number	6
86. Place Value Seven-Digit Number	6
87. Mixed Number	6
88. Mixed Number for Improper Fraction	6
89. Fraction in Lowest Terms	6
90. Sum Three Addends (up to four-digit)	6
91. Subtract Two Numbers (no more than four digits)	6
92. Equation + Word Problem, Whole Number	6
93. Three-Digit Number × Two-Digit Number	6
94. Two-Digit Number ÷ Two-Digit Number	6
95. Add Two Mixed Numbers, Like Denominators	6
96. Subtract Two Mixed Numbers, Like Denominators (no regroup)	6
97. Add Whole Number and Fraction	6
98. Add Whole Number and Mixed Number	6
99. Add Two Decimals (Same Number Decimal Places)	6
100. Subtract Two Decimals (Same Number Decimal Places)	6
101. Proper Use >, <, =, ≠, Math Sentence	6
102. Equivalent Fractions	7
103. Equation Subtract, Whole Number, Word Problem	7
104. Word Problem, Three-Digit Number × Two-Digit Number	7
105. Word From Numeral, Hundred-Thousandth	7
106. Numerical Name Word Form, Hundred-Thousandths	7
107. Mixed Number as Improper Fraction	7
108. Three Fractions for Whole Number	7
109. Lowest Common Denominator (Two Fractions Unlike Denominators)	7
110. Three- or Four-Digit Number ÷ Two-Digit Number (remainder)	7
111. Equation for Division Word Problem (Two-Digit Divisor)	7
112. Subtract Two Mixed Numbers, Like Denominators	7

Figure 3-17
(Continued)

INTERMEDIATE MATHEMATICS
(*continued*)

113. Multiply Two Factors (Fraction) Lowest Terms	7	117. Subtract Two Horizontal Written Decimals	7
114. Decimals for Fractions, Denominator of 10, 100, 1000	7	118. Decimal × Whole Number (Two-Digit)	7
115. Decimals as Fractions	7	119. Decimal × Decimal	7
116. Add Decimals (Five or Less)	7	120. Decimal ÷ One-Digit Whole Number	7

Figure 3-18

Dear Teacher Consultant:

I'm looking forward to working with you in the summer workshop on competency-based education, June 12, 13, and 14. Please refer to the enclosed syllabus which includes the pertinent information such as times, objectives, and daily agendas.

We have a very important job to do in this workshop. As you probably know, the primary competencies with accompanying test items have been developed and field tested. Now it is time to develop a classroom management procedure and a recordkeeping system. We want to make sure that we develop these procedures and documents in such a way that competency-based education enhances instruction and does not become a cumbersome, paper-shuffling nightmare.

That's our challenge. I think we're up to this challenge. Please bring all your knowledge, experience, and expertise with you. And don't forget your positive attitude.

See you on June 12. Thanks.

Sincerely yours,

Enc.

Figure 3-19

Summer Workshop

Competency-Based Education—Primary Grades (K–3)

(Classroom Management Procedures and Recordkeeping)

I. Dates—June 12, 13, 14

II. Enrollment—At least one key classroom teacher from each local school. Primary principals are also welcome as participants.

III. Location—Holly Hill Elementary School (located on Rte. 132 less than one mile north of Rte. 125)

IV. Purpose—To develop the classroom management procedures and recordkeeping systems necessary to properly implement competency-based education grades K through 3 in Reading, English Composition, and Mathematics

V. Workshop Objectives (Outcomes)

1. Become familiar with the competency test items.

2. Develop a recommended procedure for the administering of the pretests.

3. Develop a recommended procedure for the administering of the posttests.

4. Develop a recommended procedure for the housing of the test items.

5. Develop a recordkeeping system for the Competency-Based Education program within a grade level.

6. Develop a recordkeeping system for the carrying over of unmastered competencies from one grade level to the next.

7. Develop a recommended procedure to communicate individual student performance on the competency test items to parent(s) or guardian(s).

8. Develop an in-service plan for their school to instruct the teachers on how to use the procedures and documents developed in this workshop.

VI. Workshop Budget Items

1. Stipends for participants—$40.00 per day

2. Material (paper, pens, etc.)

3. Coffee, donuts, etc.

NOTES: 1. Funding source—Teacher Development Funds

Figure 3-20

AGENDA

Day 1—Tuesday, June 12

8:30–9:00	Coffee, donuts, introductions
9:00–11:00	In-depth study of competency test items (Outcome #1)
11:00–12:00	Pretesting Procedures (Outcome #2)
12:00–1:00	Lunch
1:00–2:30	Posttesting Procedures (Outcome #3)
2:30–3:30	Test housing procedures (Outcome #4)

Day 2—Wednesday, June 13

8:30–9:00	Coffee, donuts, conversation
9:00–12:00	Recordkeeping System (Outcomes #5 and #6)
12:00–1:00	Lunch
1:00–3:30	Parent Communication System (Outcome #7)

Day 3—Thursday, June 14

8:30–9:00	Coffee, donuts, conversation
9:00–12:00	School In-Service Plan (principals should be present for this session)
12:00–1:00	Lunch
1:00–3:30	Open

ACTIVITY 28

Publication of Final Competency-Based Education Documents

The competency-based education documents can be published through a commercial printer or through self-printing by the school. The decision as to which of these options to use depends upon a number of variables. For example, are there sufficient funds to employ a commercial printer? If so, will the printer guarantee delivery dates? This is absolutely necessary because of the instructional importance of the testing. If the answer to these two questions is yes, then a commercial printer is a viable option.

If the school has sufficient personnel and time to do their own printing, and if the quality of printing is acceptable, then printing your own competency-based education documents is a viable option also.

Whichever option is used, have one goal in mind—that the competency-based education process will never have to wait for printed material to be finished. Keep an inventory of materials sufficient to cover any request and need.

ACTIVITY 29

Development of Intervention Program

Intervention is a term which simply means *to reteach*. This reteaching of competencies to students who fail the pretest should be based on individual student needs and the resources available. A good classroom is a smorgasbord of learning opportunities. Intervention is not restricting the students to one or two offerings, but allowing them to experience the total smorgasbord. The smorgasbord should not be presented in just one learning mode. It should accommodate the auditory learner, the visual learner, the abstract learner, and so on.

DEFINITION OF INTERVENTION

Intervention is an alternative or supplemental action designed to remediate, reinforce, or support pupil learning relative to specified performance objectives.[1] Ultimately, intervention is an instructional action taken when a planned learning activity is judged to be wholly or partly inappropriate for helping a student achieve a desired level of competence.

CHARACTERISTICS OF INTERVENTION

Intervention is a process tailored to the individual needs of each student. It begins with an identification of competencies which have not been met. It requires an assessment of the student's prerequisite knowledge, learning capabilities, and particular needs. It entails a survey of available resources and constraints. And it results in the development and implementation of further instructional activities designed to achieve the desired competencies.

There is one assumption that underlies effective intervention. That assumption is that each school staff will assume the responsibility of developing specific intervention strategies to meet the needs of their students based on local textbook adoptions and available resources. Since the resources vary from school to school, the intervention options available will vary also. The curriculum leadership of a school district should provide the in-service opportunities for teachers and principals that will outline the intervention options of each school based on that school's resources. To plan intervention strategies for which there are no resources is futile and will result in staff frustration.

Even though the intervention strategies will vary from school to school, there are some principles of intervention planning and development that are uniform.

Let's start with teacher and administrative responsibilities.

Teacher Responsibilities

1. Identify competencies not met through assessment.
2. Develop and implement instructional actions designed to achieve competencies not met.

Administrative Responsibilities

1. Provide in-service to make teachers aware of their responsibility concerning intervention, emphasizing the fact that intervention actions are an integral part of effective learning sequences and not just added activities. Intervention actions allow the teacher to clarify intended learning outcomes and follow through in pursuing their accomplishment.
2. Evaluate the need for and provide, where possible, intervention programming, personnel, and materials.
3. Enlist support of parents in intervention.

With the assumption made and the responsibilities assigned, let's go to the planning aspect of intervention.

DESIGNING THE PROGRAM

District personnel will have to make decisions about appropriate alternatives to assist students in achieving performance objectives. Many students may have similar learning needs which can be met through class instruction, while one-on-one instruction may be necessary for other students. A district may have to consider the reallocation of resources to meet the learning needs of students.

A district may wish to consider the following options[2] to assist students in the achievement of performance objectives:

1. Classroom special needs group instruction consists of groups that are organized to develop a skill, provide a particular experience, or develop and extend a given objective. When the objective is achieved, the groups are dissolved and new

groups are formed to meet other needs. Time for the special needs groups can be found by altering or adjusting the regular classroom schedule.

2. Modification of learning materials within the classroom can be done by the classroom teacher. Students are assisted by the teacher who introduces different materials, modifies existing materials, and classifies materials for use in achieving specific objectives.

3. Adjustment of classroom instruction to the different learning styles of students is accomplished through teachers' identifying the strong learning modalities of students and adjusting instruction accordingly. Wooster[3] (1978) suggests that the teacher will need to ponder, observe, interview, and record notes concerning the following:

- Where does the student learn best?
- When does the student learn best?
- With whom does the student learn best?
- In what learning situations does the student respond well or poorly?
- To what teaching styles does the student respond best?

4. Personalization of classroom instruction in the content areas could begin with an informal assessment that could be constructed in any subject. The students' needs become the basis for the teaching activities. Content should be analyzed to locate the sections that are most important for achieving objectives. Assignment length could be varied, and different degrees of understanding could be required to correspond to student differences. Media should be used wisely to supplement instruction. Schedules should reflect a balance of individual, small group, and total group experiences.

5. Corrective classroom instruction is designed to meet the immediate needs of students. Skill problems should be detected in the early stages, preventive strategies administered, and regular, consistent correction and enrichment delivered to students.

6. Learning modules are self-instruction packages containing a set of learning experiences which may be purchased commercially or developed by teachers to meet specific needs. The modules are usually organized with a statement of rationale directed to the learner and objectives which state the expected learning results. A pretest to determine needs is followed by learning activities that help students attain the objectives. Posttesting then follows the completion of activities.

7. Programmed or computer-assisted instruction can consist of carefully constructed information units which are presented in a sequential manner. The learner is guided through the sequence until a specified performance level is reached. Care should be taken to select the materials that are designed for particular objectives.

8. Learning contracts are mutual agreements that may be entered into by the student, teacher, and parent. Contracts could be used to accompany library books, content reading assignments, and books in special interest areas. Contracts allow students to be exposed to content at an appropriate level of difficulty, to work independently at their own rates, and to spend appropriate amounts of time on relevant activities. Students could help design learning contracts. Objectives to be learned should be outlined, and the signatures of the participants affixed to the contract in order to add credibility to the process. Figure 3-21 is an example of a learning contract.

Figure 3-21

PLANNING

Learning Contract for an English Assignment

Name_____

Beginning
Date_____

Ending

Instructor_____

Date_____

I, _____ agree to do the
work described in this contract by the date indicated above. If I need any help, I will ask

_____, a fellow student,
or the teacher. If I still have difficulty, I will ask for a new contract.

CONTRACTED WORK:

Project_____

Themes_____

Worksheets_____

Other_____

Signatures

_____

Student

_____

Teacher

_____

Parent

COMMENTS:_____

_____

9. Diagnostic/prescriptive teaching could be effectively used in the regular classroom where students display a wide range of ability levels. The teacher will need to diagnose those levels in order to select activities for skill development. In the regular classroom, where class size makes diagnosis a time-consuming process, the teacher is constantly diagnosing the needs of students whether he or she is aware of it or not. The manner in which a student responds in discussion activities, the degree of independence the student exhibits during class, and the quality of a student's reporting all offer clues which aid the teacher in diagnosing needs.

Following diagnosis, the teacher and the student could cooperatively develop an instructional plan. Individual conferences could provide additional information and an opportunity for the teacher to check the student's progress.

Two types of records should be considered when using the diagnostic/prescriptive approach. The first is the teacher's record which serves to promote a balanced program and is an aid for planning and evaluating the student's activities. It should be kept as simple as possible and should include pertinent information regarding the student's difficulties, assigned activities, and progress. The second type is the student's record which the student could keep up-to-date. For younger students, recordkeeping could consist of listing books read or words learned. Older students could record information on charts or graphs.

10. The integration of performance objectives into the regular curriculum could be handled in the following manner:

- Provide a bank of suggested activities coded to each objective.
- Provide an inventory of resources and instructional materials coded to each objective.
- Appoint a member of the staff at each level to act as a resource person for specific performance areas.
- Encourage teachers to exchange classes for specific purposes.

11. Tutoring could assist a student who needs intensive instruction in specific objectives. It may be used to reinforce, review, or extend skills already presented in the classroom. Materials should focus on the objectives and on the student's learning style and interests. Tutoring may occur during a study hall period, before or after school, or during the school day.

The tutor could be a certificated teacher, teacher's aide, another student, parent, or volunteer. Matching a student to an adult or older student can offer intensive real world experience and provide expertise in special interest fields. Matching a student with a student of a similar age or older can increase the tutored student's motivation, encourage the student to interact, and provide him or her with the security of knowing someone who thinks, feels, and talks in similar ways. In peer tutoring, a student is paired with another student of the same age. In cross-grade or cross-age tutoring, upper-grade students work with lower-grade students.

12. Resource rooms are specially designated rooms which contain varied materials for all grade levels. They should be available to students who need opportunities to learn in specific subject areas. Students from several grade levels could be scheduled

into the resource room on a regular basis to work on objectives. The room serves as an extension of the regular classroom and will require staff cooperation and the coordination of instructional plans.

13. Supportive and remedial instruction could be provided by district support personnel in reading, mathematics, or writing. The setting would be similar to a classroom, and materials should be differentiated to meet individual student needs. Instruction should be designed to focus on identified objectives, and could be one-to-one, independent, or small group.

14. Home, school, and social agency work together when the teacher has used all available instructional alternatives at the school level and the student still has not achieved the performance objectives. The teacher may request additional support from the principal who may need to contact the school social worker, children's social services, school psychologist, or community guidance center to explore other alternatives. Working with the student's home, the social worker may enlist other support services that will focus on alleviating needs that may be hindering learning. Nurses and social workers are often able to gain support from parents that will help the student.

15. Independent study projects provide a means by which a teacher could differentiate instruction for students who need enrichment activities. The project could be planned cooperatively by the teacher and the student. A core of questions could be written with emphasis on higher cognitive processes (application, analysis, synthesis, and evaluation). After the student has completed introductory study, which usually involves knowledge and comprehension work, follow-up activities focusing on higher level thinking processes should be required.[4]

ACTIVITY 30

Staff In-Service

The competency-based education staff in-service should not be held until the principal and the teachers have had the opportunity to familiarize themselves with the competency-based education documents. Competency-based education is hard to explain verbally. A much more effective in-service would be a "hands-on" workshop which combines explanation with laboratory type activities. (See Figure 3-22 for agenda and content.) The competency items should not be new to the teachers because all teachers should have been involved with the selection. The test items may be new to the teachers who were not involved in the test item development or the field test. However, when you total the percentage of teachers who were involved in competency selection, test item selection, and field testing, it should cover a substantial number of the teachers. That fact makes the in-service task easier.

The in-service agenda should cover the following topics:

-Philosophy (aims and purposes)
-Policies
-Procedures for implementation
-Pretesting
-Intervention
-Posttesting
-Recordkeeping
 -Individual
 -Class
 -Carrying over if competencies not achieved (by individual)
 -Communication with parents and community

The staff in-service phase should conclude with a clinical in-service in which the teachers are supervised during the actual implementation of a small segment of the competency-based education program.

Figure 3-22

**COMPETENCY-BASED EDUCATION PROGRAM
STAFF IN-SERVICE**

Agenda

1) Distribution of CBE materials

 -Student test items
 -Teacher grade level packets
 -Parent communication letters
 -Recordkeeping documents
  -Manila folder
  -Class rosters
 -Principal packet

2) CBE Process

 -Preassessment
 -Instruction
 -Postassessment
 -Intervention
 -Postassessment
 -Testing—3rd and 7th

Figure 3-22
(Continued)

3) Scoring—CBE test items

4) Recordkeeping

    –Management card
    –Class rosters

5) Revisions

    –L.A.
    –Math

6) Home Communications

PRIMARY COMPETENCY-BASED TEST

Introduction

The competency-based educational program in language arts and math is designed to accomplish two major purposes:

1. Meet state educational standards.

2. Improve the instructional program in language arts and math by:

    –Verifying successful achievement of basic skills.

    –Providing intervention in cases of unsuccessful achievement of basic skills.

Giving Directions to Students:

Remember that it is permissible for a teacher to alter the directions for clarification purposes so long as the intent of the competency item is not changed.

Also, it is permissible to do a *sample item* before administering the competency items. The sample may be written on paper or the chalkboard.

Primary Language Arts Competency-Based Test
Scoring and Evaluation Instructions

Scoring:

All test items except #15, #16, #41, and #56 have four test questions. In order to demonstrate competency, a student must score at least 75% by answering three of the four questions correctly on all test items except those listed above.

Test items #15 and #16 have five test questions, one question for each of the vowel sounds. In order to demonstrate competency, a student must score at least 80% by answering four of the five questions correctly.

Test item #41 has twenty-four questions. Each question concerns a letter from the alphabet. The student must demonstrate 100% competency on this test item by answering all the questions correctly.

Figure 3-22
(Continued)

Test item #56 is designed in such a way that a student must demonstrate competency by scoring at least 75% in content and 75% in mechanics. This item is scored by marking the percentage points earned in each of the areas of evaluation on the student test sheet. The percentage points are then totaled to determine competency in content and mechanics.

Test items #20, #32, and #45 are designed in such a way that the questions numbered 1 on each of the four stories tests for main idea. To meet the 75% competency requirement for main idea the student must answer question 1 on three of the story samples correctly. If the student has missed more than one of the questions numbered 1 on the four story samples, he or she has not met the requirement for competency in determining the main idea, and intervention in this skill needs to take place. Likewise, the question numbered 2 on each of the four stories tests for details. To meet the 75% competency requirement for details, the student must answer question 2 on three of the story samples correctly. If the student has missed more than one of the questions numbered 2 on the four story samples, he or she has not met the requirement for competency in determining details, and intervention in this skill needs to take place. Test items #32 and #45 are designed in such a way that the question numbered 3 on each of the four stories tests for sequence of events. To meet the 75% competency requirement for sequence of events, the student must answer question 3 on three of the story samples correctly. If the student has missed more than one of the questions numbered 3 on the four story samples, he or she has not met the requirement for competency in determining the sequence of events, and intervention in this skill needs to take place. Test item #34 is designed in such a way that the question numbered 4 on each of the four stories tests for cause-effect relationships. To meet the 75% competency requirement for cause and effect, the student must answer question 4 on three of the story samples correctly. If the student has missed more than one of the questions numbered 4 on the four story samples, he or she has not met the requirement for competency in determining cause and effect relationships, and intervention in this skill needs to take place.

Primary Mathematics Competency-Based Test
Scoring and Evaluation Instructions

Scoring:

All math items have four questions. In order to demonstrate competency, a student must score at least 75% by answering three of the four questions correctly on all test items.

Recordkeeping

The Competency Class Roster is used to chart students' mastery of individual test items. A plus (+) may be used to show mastery. A minus (−) reflects the need for intervention.

The competency-based education Student Record Card is used to chart individual student mastery of math and language arts test items.

Figure 3-22
(Continued)

Within the appropriate language arts and math spaces, circle the test form being used: A or **B.**

Beneath the test item number, record a plus (+) for an item mastered and a minus (−) for an item requiring intervention.

Place a plus (+) in the space beneath A.C.A. when the student has achieved all competency items. Leave a blank if there are items which are unmastered and need to be carried over to the following year.

File individual record cards in the appropriate student cumulative folder, at the end of the year.

There are <u>Parent Letters</u>. Form 1 will be printed on green paper and will identify the competencies basic to the child's grade level. This letter should be shared with parents during the first Parent-Teacher Conference.

At the spring Parent-Teacher Conference, parents should receive Form 2, which is printed on yellow paper. Skills which have not been mastered should be circled.

Teacher comments might detail suggestions for intervention.

Parents not attending the conference should receive the parent letter in the report card or in the mail.

INTERMEDIATE COMPETENCY-BASED TEST

Introduction

The competency-based educational program in language arts and math is designed to accomplish two major purposes:

1. Meet state educational standards.
2. Improve the instructional program in language arts and math by:
   - Verifying successful achievement of basic skills.
   - Providing intervention in cases of unsuccessful achievement of basic skills.

Giving Directions to Students:

Remember that it is permissible for a teacher to alter the directions for clarification purposes so long as the intent of the competency item is not changed.

Also, it is permissible to do a *sample item* before administering the competency items. The sample may be written on paper or the chalkboard.

Intermediate Language Arts Competency-Based Test
Scoring and Evaluation Instructions

Scoring:

All test items except #67, #85, and #96 have four test questions. In order to demonstrate competency, a student must score at least 75% by answering three of the four questions correctly on all test items except those listed above.

Figure 3-22
(Continued)

Test item #67 asks the student to arrange the five parts of the friendly letter. In order to demonstrate competency, a student must score at least 80% or arrange four parts correctly. For the arrangement to be counted correct, the student must have observed the correct placement with respect to margins.

Test item #85 has five test questions pertaining to spelling rules. In order to demonstrate competency a student must score at least 80% by answering four of the five questions correctly.

Test item #96 is designed in such a way that a student must demonstrate competency by scoring at least 75% in content and 75% in mechanics. This item is scored by marking the percentage points earned in each of the areas of evaluation on the student test sheet. The percentage points are then totaled to determine competency in content and mechanics.

Test items #62, #70, #77, and #88 are designed in such a way that the question numbered 1 on each of the four stories tests for main idea. To meet the 75% competency requirement for main idea the student must answer question 1 on three of the story samples correctly. If the student has missed more than one of the questions numbered 1 on the four story samples, he or she has not met the requirement for competency in determining the main idea, and intervention in this skill needs to take place. Likewise, the question numbered 2 on each of the four stories tests for sequence of events. To meet the 75% competency requirement for sequence of events, the student must answer question 2 on three of the story samples correctly. If the student has missed more than one of the questions numbered 2 on the four story samples, he or she has not met the requirement for competency in determining sequence of events, and intervention in this skill needs to take place. The question numbered 3 on each of the four stories tests for cause-effect relationships. To meet the 75% competency requirement for cause-effect relationships, the student must answer question 3 on three of the story samples correctly. If the student has missed more than one of the questions numbered 3 on the four story samples, he or she has not met the requirement for competency in determining cause-effect relationships, and intervention in this skill needs to take place.

Intermediate Mathematics Competency-Based Test
Scoring and Evaluation Instructions

Scoring:

All math items have four questions. In order to demonstrate competency, a student must score at least 75% by answering three of the four questions correctly on all test items.

Recordkeeping

The Competency Class Roster is used to chart students' mastery of individual test items. A plus (+) may be used to show mastery. A minus (−) reflects the need for intervention.

Figure 3-22
(Continued)

The competency-based education <u>Student Record Card</u> is used to chart individual student mastery of math and language arts test items.

Within the appropriate language arts and math spaces, circle the test form being used: A or B.

Beneath the test item number, record a plus (+) for an item mastered and a minus (−) for an item requiring intervention.

Place a plus (+) in the space beneath A.C.A. when the student has achieved all competency items. Leave a blank if there are items which are unmastered and need to be carried over to the following year.

File individual record cards in the appropriate student cumulative folder, at the end of the year.

There are <u>Parent Letters</u>. Form 1 will be printed on green paper and will identify the competencies basic to the child's grade level. This letter should be shared with parents during the first Parent-Teacher Conference.

At the spring Parent-Teacher Conference, parents should receive Form 2, which is printed on yellow paper. Skills which have not been mastered should be circled. Teacher comments might detail suggestions for intervention.

Parents not attending the conference should receive the parent letter in the report card or in the mail.

ACTIVITIES 31 and 32

Policy Development and Adoption

DEFINITION OF TERMS

There are many terms used in competency-based education. There are many definitions of these terms. Therefore, a school can accept whatever definition fits their program. The important fact is that all concerned are using the same definition. Perhaps this discussion does not belong under policy development unless you consider defining terms as policy development. But it is very significant.

Rather than give sample definitions of terms, a discussion of competency samples is presented to illustrate the importance of the commonality of terms.

Example #1

> Competency—given a picture, the student will write three (3) complete sentences describing the picture at a 75% accuracy level.

Obviously, this competency involves the skill of writing. However, writing means different things to different people. What is important in evaluating the writing? Is form significant? How significant? Is content significant? How significant? Are both significant, but one more so than the other?

Some people would grade a third grade composition for content only. They would not be concerned about capital letters or punctuation. If the student made three observations about the picture that were accurate, they would consider the student competent. Others would not rate a student competent, no matter how accurate the content, unless the student demonstrated proper form, such as complete sentences, correct punctuation, and proper capitalization.

Hopefully, the point is now clear. Before this competency can be properly administered and evaluated, a definition of writing must be arrived at.

Let's look at one more example.

Example #2

> Competency—given four word problems involving subtraction, the student will select the correct answer in at least three out of four problems.

This is a math competency. However, as with most competencies, it involves reading. What if the student can answer the question if it is read to him, but, due to reading deficiencies, cannot answer the question *unless* it is read by someone else? The competency being evaluated is math. However, the competencies required to answer the question are both math and reading. Therefore, whichever way you go, make sure all teachers follow the same definition. That way the results are uniform, consistent, and thus more valid.

Defining all the terms will delay the competency-based education development process. But it will speed up and improve the implementation and evaluation process.

Any educational program that affects the status of students needs careful and prudent policies. Competency-based education will affect both retention and graduation. Therefore, for political and legal reasons, its policy development is vital. As illustrated by Figure 3-23, the policy development process should be ongoing. It should also begin early in the competency-based education developmental process.

While the educational components of competency-based education are being developed largely by the teachers with input coming from the administration, the policy component should be developed by the administration with input from the teachers. By dividing the leadership for the two processes in this way, the resources necessary for such a simultaneous process are available.

The policies necessary for effective competency-based education are not voluminous. In fact, one of the principles that should be followed in policy development is *simplicity*. The following list of topics will need policy development.

1. Promotion/Retention
2. Assessment/Testing
3. Student Transfer
4. Graduation
5. Handicapped Students
6. Vocational Students
7. Definition of Terms
8. Recordkeeping/Management System
9. Communication with Parents/Guardian

The remainder of this discussion of Activities 31 and 32 is devoted to the discussion of each of these policy topics. The significance of each topic, illustrating the necessity for policy development, will be presented along with recommendations.

PROMOTION/RETENTION POLICY

When the public thinks of competency, they think of standards. Higher standards, that is. Their expectation is that competency-based education will raise standards.

Figure 3-23

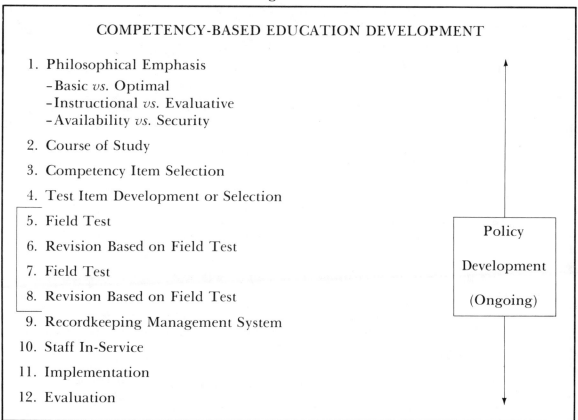

COMPETENCY-BASED EDUCATION DEVELOPMENT

1. Philosophical Emphasis
   - Basic *vs.* Optimal
   - Instructional *vs.* Evaluative
   - Availability *vs.* Security

2. Course of Study

3. Competency Item Selection

4. Test Item Development or Selection

5. Field Test

6. Revision Based on Field Test

7. Field Test

8. Revision Based on Field Test

9. Recordkeeping Management System

10. Staff In-Service

11. Implementation

12. Evaluation

Policy

Development

(Ongoing)

Educational standards affect promotion and retention. So on the one hand, the advent of competency-based education must affect promotion and retention to be taken seriously by the public. On the other hand, our knowledge of educational and human psychology tells us that to use competency-based education results as the sole criterion for promotion or retention would be a failure. The same problems that occurred when students were retained in grade solely for academic reasons without regard to ability, age, social development, maturation, and environment would resurface.

Whether anybody likes it or not, we are not all born equally in intelligence or aptitude. Whether anybody likes it or not, we can't have a 12-year-old in a classroom of 6-year-olds.

Therefore, policy on retention and promotion should attempt to accomplish two goals:

1. Help meet the public demand for quality education
2. Apply sound educational psychological principles to the promotion/retention policy

The difference between elementary (K–8) and secondary (9–12) curriculum organization requires separate policies for each level. (See Figure 3-24.)

Figure 3-24

I. PROMOTION POLICY RELATED TO COMPETENCY-BASED EDUCATION

ELEMENTARY (K-8) POLICY

Competency assessment and testing results will be utilized as one criterion, along with grades, social development, attendance, teacher input, principal input, parental input, and psychological data, to determine promotion or retention.

Guidelines

1. In cases where a student is promoted to the next grade and has not demonstrated achievement of all the competencies, all unmastered competencies will be carried over to the next grade.
2. Any student who demonstrates achievement of 90% or more in all competency areas cannot be retained on the basis of competency results.
3. Any student who does not demonstrate achievement of 90% or more in all three competency areas is not, based on competency results, deemed to be academically ready to be promoted to the next grade. Therefore, other criteria used for promotion/retention decisions must strongly indicate that the student should be promoted before such promotion takes place.
4. Any student who does not demonstrate achievement of 80% in all three competency areas should not be promoted to the next grade.

Figure 3-24
(Continued)

SECONDARY (9–11) POLICY

Students enrolled in courses which contain competencies in Reading, English Composition, or Mathematics must demonstrate achievement of all competency items contained within that course offering to receive credit for the course.

Guidelines

1. Any student who does not demonstrate achievement of 60% or more of the competency items contained within a course must reenroll in that course.

2. Any student who demonstrates achievement of 60% to 99% on the competency items contained within a course will receive an incomplete grade for the course. This incomplete grade will be erased when the student successfully demonstrates achievement of all the competencies.

II. GRADUATION POLICY RELATED TO COMPETENCY-BASED EDUCATION

No graduation policy statement is necessary because all graduating seniors in Ohio are required to take two years of math and three years of English, and the competencies will be contained within the courses. Therefore, if the student passes the courses, the competencies will have had to be successfully completed also.

At the elementary level, competencies can be developed by grade level. At the secondary level, competencies should be developed by the course. By doing it this way, the problem of what to do when a student meets all the course or unit requirements for graduation, but fails the competency tests, is avoided. By placing the competencies within Carnegie units, two positive factors are produced. First of all, the students themselves choose the level of difficulty of their personal competency by the courses they take. Secondly, this makes it more feasible to develop competencies that are realistic in relation to difficulty.

ASSESSMENT/TESTING

If the competency-based education program is going to have instructional emphasis, the assessment/testing policy must reflect this emphasis. In order to reflect this emphasis, the following principles must be emphasized in the policy. (See Figure 3-25.)

1. Multiple assessment/testing opportunities for the students
2. Use of item analysis in place of norm-referenced analysis
3. Correlation between the assessment/testing process and instruction; that is, grouping, curriculum, etc.

Figure 3-25

RECOMMENDED ASSESSMENT AND TESTING POLICY

1. Assessment Policy
   A. Sometime at the start of the school year, all the students will be given the competency test items. (Pretest) The results will be used to establish grouping and intervention with those students who do not demonstrate competency on particular items.

   The instruction and intervention will be based on item results, not normed results.

   B. After intervention, the student will be retested using Form B.
   C. The student can be retested as many times as necessary. The learning cycle for those not demonstrating achievement on the pretest will be:
   Intervention > Retest until achievement is demonstrated.

2. Testing Policy
   A. Competency testing will occur in grades 3, 7, and 10.
   B. All the third and seventh grade competency items will be given to all students regardless of their performance on the pretest and all subsequent posttests.
   C. Tenth graders enrolled in courses which contain competency items will be tested on all competency items regardless of their performance on the pretest and all subsequent posttests.

STUDENT TRANSFER

It is customary for schools to accept the grade level placement of the transferring school in the case of elementary students. It is also customary for high schools to accept successfully completed Carnegie units for students transferring into the school. The presence of a competency-based education program should not alter these customs.

At the elementary level, when a student transfers in during the course of a school year, an assessment on those grade level or course offerings should be done. If the assessment results indicate that a severe problem exists, appropriate measures should be undertaken to place the student at the proper grade level or in the proper course for his ability and achievement.

In view of the fact that a competency-based education program with instructional emphasis is an ongoing process, any attempt to implement the program in a short time frame defeats the instructional component and emphasizes testing, or evaluation, which is of course not desirable. Therefore, any formal policy development should emphasize the year-long process. The appropriate placement and instruction of transfer students should be accomplished without heavy competency-based education criteria. To require total adherence to the grade level requirements of the competency-based education program by a transfer student will sometimes place unreasonable demands on both the student and the teacher.

At the secondary level, incoming transfer students should be held accountable for the successful completion of the competencies. A prompt assessment of the student's capabilities and potential to meet the competencies should be made so that if a severe problem exists, a determination could be made as to an appropriate action. The two appropriate actions are: (1) intervention, and (2) placement in an easier course within the subject field.

GRADUATION AND COMPETENCY-BASED EDUCATION

No graduation policy, in relation to competency-based education, will be necessary if the competencies are placed within the course offerings, and if the successful achievement of the competencies is required to receive credit for the course.

By dealing with the problem of unsuccessful achievement of competencies in the course offerings, a school avoids the dilemma of having students meet all graduation requirements except the successful achievement of the competencies. It is difficult to explain, both educationally and politically, how a student could pass a course and not demonstrate achievement of the competencies contained within that course.

Keep in mind that the key issue in competency-based education and graduation policy is the official transcript, not the diploma. A diploma means nothing. A transcript means everything. A student's performance in relation to competency-based education should be recorded on the transcript. Then any prospective employer or university can see how the student performed in relation to competency-based education just as they can determine grades by subject, attendance, and other pertinent information. (Refer back to Figure 3-25.)

HANDICAPPED STUDENTS

Two different approaches can be taken with competency-based education and the handicapped student. The first approach is to develop a separate competency-based education program for handicapped students. Since there are many different handicaps that affect people, this would require many different competency-based education programs. Perhaps too many to be feasible. However, if this approach is taken, the same procedures and policies that are used for regular competency-based education programs could apply to handicapped competency-based education programs.

The second approach is to include handicapped students in the regular competency-based education program or exclude them from it on an individual basis.

If this second approach is taken, the policy[5] given in Figure 3-26 is recommended.

Figure 3-26

INTRODUCTION
COMPETENCY-BASED EDUCATION
FOR THE
HANDICAPPED

Competency-Based Education is a program designed to improve student instruction and achievement, diagnose learning problems, and assist teachers in planning instructional intervention. Components of competency-based education include preassessment, instruction, intervention, and postassessment. Ohio's "Minimum Standards for Elementary and Secondary Schools" require the development of a competency-based education program for all students. Effort should be made to accommodate the individual needs of all students in the CBE program. This document is designed to help teachers determine the participation of the handicapped student in the CBE program.

Advantages for handicapped students participating in CBE may include the following:

1. The CBE program provides a positive tool used to assess student strengths and weaknesses.
2. The CBE program can be viewed as <u>one</u> component of a multifactored evaluation.
3. The CBE program assists in developing Individualized Education Program goals and objectives.
4. The CBE program allows participating children an opportunity to gain a sense of acceptance and pride among their peers.
5. The CBE program provides the parents with evidence of their child's status in learning of basic skills.

Handicapped students may be exempted from participation in locally developed competency-based education program requirements. Consideration for exemption or inclusion in the competency-based program must be given on an individual basis and the decision written into the student's Individualized Education Program (IEP).

The decision to include or exempt a student will be made by the individualized education program team based on present educational performance levels, the specific special education and related services being provided, and participation in regular educational programs.

To assist special education teachers in decision making and implementation of CBE, this document provides guidelines for student participation, alternatives to consider for inclusion or exemption, the role of the special education teacher, and modifications in testing procedures.

Figure 3-26
(Continued)

POLICY FOR SPECIAL EDUCATION

COMPETENCY-BASED EDUCATION

Handicapped students, as defined in Ohio's "Rules for the Education of Handicapped Children," may be exempted from participation in the locally developed competency-based education program requirements. Consideration for exemption or inclusion in the competency-based program must be given on an individual basis and the decision written into the student's Individualized Education Program (IEP).

The determination that an individual handicapped student is exempted or included will be made using the following procedures:

1. The student's present levels of educational performance as indicated by the IEP will be reviewed. If mainstreaming has occurred, the student's performance in the regular class should also receive consideration. Communication between the regular education teacher(s) and the special education teacher is encouraged so that the special education teacher may be aware of the basic competencies covered in the regular class.

2. During the IEP meeting, a statement regarding participation in or exemption from the competency-based education program will be included on the IEP as part of the statement regarding the extent of participation in regular education programs. When appropriate, regular education teachers are encouraged to be participants at the IEP meeting.

3. If it is determined that the student will participate in the competency-based education program, any necessary modifications in the competency testing procedure will be indicated on the IEP.

4. If the student's participation in the competency-based education program is modified at any time during the school year, that modification must be determined by the IEP team and indicated on the IEP.

I. GUIDELINES FOR INCLUSION/EXEMPTION

During the IEP meeting, the participants will determine whether the special education student will be included or exempted from the CBE program.

In making this determination, attention should be given to the following considerations:

Ability level of the student
Academic level of the student
Functional skill levels in reading and math
Success/progress in the special education program
Frustration level of the student
Student's responsibility in completing work

Figure 3-26
(Continued)

Ability to do work independently in the classroom
Student's motivational level
Student's interest in participating in the CBE program
Student's ability/inability to function in formal testing situations
Teacher observation of the student in large-group/small-group learning
situations

II. ALTERNATIVES FOR INCLUSION/EXEMPTION

In order for a handicapped child to be considered a participant in the CBE program, he or she must participate in all four phases including preassessment, instruction, intervention, and postassessment. Special education teachers may use any of the materials of the CBE program such as the course of study, intervention techniques, and actual CBE tests. However, a handicapped child would not be a participant in the CBE program unless he or she is involved in each of the components of the CBE program.

In making a recommendation as to whether a special education student should be included/exempted from the CBE program, special education teachers may want to consider the following alternatives for his or her involvement:

A. If the special education student is mainstreamed for subject areas:

The child should be included in each of the areas of CBE (reading, math, and English composition) as a part of the regular class; that is, the child should participate in preassessment, instruction, intervention, if necessary, and postassessment. All components of the CBE program, including record-keeping are completed by the regular education teacher. The student's record is filed in his or her cumulative folder.

OR

The child should be included only if the child is mainstreamed and only in subject areas in which he is mainstreamed. The CBE program, including preassessment, instruction, intervention, and postassessment, is implemented by the regular education teacher.

OR

The child is included in the instructional phase of the CBE program but is not involved in the evaluative (testing) phase of the CBE program. Grade level instruction is completed by the regular education teacher. Since the student is not included in the assessment phase, the student is not a participant in the CBE program; therefore, no recordkeeping is required.

OR

The child could be included in the CBE program on a lower grade level. Instruction is completed by the regular education teacher. All components of the CBE program are implemented by the regular education teacher.

Figure 3-26
(Continued)

B. If the special education student is <u>not</u> mainstreamed in the content areas:

The child may be included in the CBE program on<u> the appropriate ability level of the child.</u> All components of the CBE program including preassessment, instruction, intervention, postassessment, and maintenance of student record cards will be implemented by the special education teacher.

OR

The child would <u>not take the test, nor would he or she be included in the CBE program.</u>

III. <u>ROLE DESCRIPTION</u>

The role of the special education teacher in the competency-based education (CBE) program <u>could</u> include one or more of the following activities:

1. Explain the relevance of the CBE program to special education students who may be involved in the program.
2. Act as a consultant for regular education teachers who may be administering CBE test items to special education students.
3. Recommend which special education students, if any, would be included in the CBE program.
4. Request that an IEP team meeting be convened to address changes in the child's participation in the CBE program.
5. Provide support for students involved in the CBE program.
6. Recommend the grade level at which the student will participate in the CBE program in the special education classroom.
7. Modify test administration for special education students.
8. Administer test items to selected special education students.
9. Record the results of the CBE testing on the child's individual record card as specifically indicated in "Alternatives for Inclusion/Exemption," Section A and B.
10. Communicate with the student's parents, informing them of the results of their child's assessment if their child is included in the CBE program.

IV. <u>MODIFICATIONS</u>

If it is determined that the student will participate in the CBE program, modifications to the procedures for <u>administering</u> the tests may be made; however, <u>the content of the test should not be modified.</u> Many teachers are aware of various modifications and may be implementing them in their classrooms.

**Figure 3-26
(Continued)**

Such modifications of the (CBE) program could include, but are not limited to one or more of the following:

A. In the regular classroom:
1. Provide simplified directions for students taking the CBE tests.
2. Repeat directions as often as requested by students taking the CBE tests.
3. Allow as much time as needed for students to complete test items.
4. Provide a testing environment free of distractions.
5. Administer the test in smaller groups or on an individual basis.

B. In the special education classroom:
1. Consider any and all strategies suggested in Section A.
2. Administer the test in the special education classroom to students who are being tested using a grade level or more lower than his or her age group.
3. Read the test items to students if the items are not specifically designed to test reading.
4. Reduce the number of competencies and/or test items tested on each page.
5. Allow for different types of responses: tape-recorded responses, typewritten, teacher-recorded, etc.

C. Suggested Specific Modifications

The following additional modifications may be made depending on the child's specific handicapping conditions:
1. Modify the procedures for <u>administering</u> the test and not the content of the the test.
2. Modify the involvement of developmentally handicapped students by using a lower-grade level of the CBE program.
3. Modify the CBE testing program by administering the test either orally or on taped cassettes, while the student follows along on the written test.
4. Provide the student with a study carrel for maximum performance in the testing environment.
5. Modify the presentation of CBE test items by using visual aids, such as large print, optacon, and braille.
6. Provide a modified answer sheet for the student, if needed.
7. Provide students with amplified taped cassettes, interpreter, etc., as needed.
8. Administer the test during the time of day most beneficial to the student.
9. Administer test items to students using shortened testing periods, as determined individually.

Figure 3-26
(Continued)

V. UTILIZATION OF CBE MATERIALS

The CBE program presents the special education teacher:

1. An opportunity to be informed of the scope and sequence of the curriculum of the regular classroom.
2. A criterion to be used in determining the Least Restrictive Environment (LRE)/mainstreamed placement of special education students.
3. A component for instructional planning.
4. A method to diagnose learning problems.

VOCATIONAL EDUCATION AND COMPETENCY-BASED EDUCATION

If the vocational curriculum is contained within a comprehensive high school, then no separate policy making is needed. However, if there is a vocational school off-site (campus) that provides vocational experiences for eleventh and twelfth graders, while the students remain part of the home high school, some specific policy development is called for. These policies should address the following key questions:

1. Will students who have not passed required courses containing competencies be admitted to the vocational school?
2. If so, who will become responsible for the remediation/intervention/retesting of these students?

If the vocational school has teachers in the academic areas where competencies are required, the problems are minimized because the vocational school can assume the complete administration of the program.

If they do not, then students should not be admitted to vocational school until they have fulfilled competency requirements in academic subjects not offered by the vocational school.

Recommended Policy

For vocational schools that have academic teachers:
–The administration of all aspects of the competency-based education program shall be the responsibility of the vocational school.
For vocational schools that do not have academic teachers:
–No student will be admitted until he or she has demonstrated achievement of all competencies in academic subjects not offered by the vocational school.

ACTIVITY 33

Informing the Public About Competency-Based Education

The key to effectively communicating competency-based education to the public is being able to explain the concept in lay terminology. That means *in plain English* without excessive educational jargon. Getting the public to understand competency-based education is easier when the program is being implemented. It is not so abstract. The public can see the program in operation. If they have children involved, the parent-teacher conferences and other school contacts will help communicate an understanding of the program. That is the reason this activity is placed here in the time line. It is the last developmental phase activity and is designed to continue through implementation and evaluation.

This ongoing communication process should tell the public the following things about competency-based education:

   –Why competency-based education was started.
   –What it hopes to achieve.
   –What the competency items include.
   –How the competencies were developed.
   –Who developed the competencies.
   –The implementation process.
   –Pretesting.
   –Intervention.
   –Posttesting.
   –The recordkeeping process.
   –What happens when students don't pass the competency items. (See Figure 3-27.)

This is one of the easier activities to accomplish. If the polls and studies of education are correct, the public perceives educational excellence as the prime need of schools and considers competency-based education a means of accomplishing this goal. Therefore, communicating the concept of competency-based education is usually a positive experience going in. All you have to do is keep it going. Sometimes that's hard, but at least it's easier than starting with a negative public attitude.

Figure 3-27

- **How Does It Work?**

  Students are tested at the beginning of the school year.

If students pass test:

Achievement is recorded. The students progress to more advanced instruction.

If students do not pass test:

The Clermont County Local Schools Have a **COMPETENCY-BASED EDUCATION PROGRAM**

reading   math   writing

- **What Is Competency-Based Education?**

  Students' basic skills are tested in the areas of Reading, English, Composition, and Math. Teaching is based on the results.

- **Who Is Involved?**

  Students in kindergarten through seventh grade are in the program. Students in Special Education programs may be exempted on an individual basis.

  Beginning in 1986 the program will be extended through high school.

- **Can these students read?**
- **Can these students write?**
- **Can these students work math problems?**

In the **CLERMONT COUNTY LOCAL SCHOOLS** **YES!**

One of the Reasons Is...

Figure 3-27
(Continued)

They *Deserve* the Best.

Are They Getting It?

Clermont County Office of Education

76 S. Riverside Drive

Batavia, Ohio 45103   (513) 732-3226

WE ARE PROUD OF OUR SCHOOLS

CLERMONT COUNTY LOCAL DISTRICTS

BATAVIA LOCAL
800 Bauer Ave. • Batavia, Ohio 45103
732-2343

BETHEL-TATE LOCAL
Bethel, Ohio 45106 • 734-2238

CLERMONT NORTHEASTERN LOCAL
5347 Hutchinson Rd. • Batavia, Ohio 45103
625-5478

FELICITY-FRANKLIN LOCAL
Felicity, Ohio 45120 • 876-2111

GOSHEN LOCAL
Goshen Rd. at S.R. 28 • Goshen, Ohio 45122
722-2222

WEST CLERMONT LOCAL
P.O. Box 177 • Amelia, Ohio 45102
528-0664

WILLIAMSBURG LOCAL
549 Main St. • Williamsburg, Ohio 45176
724-3077

Reteaching occurs.

Students are tested again.

If successful, achievement is recorded.

If not successful, reteaching and retesting continue until students pass the test.

• Why Are We Using a Competency-Based Education Program?

The Competency-Based Education Program is designed to accomplish three major purposes:

• to meet Ohio educational standards which require school districts to develop and use Competency-Based Programs.

• to improve instruction and student performance in Language Arts and Math.

• to make sure every student is taught and tested on the basic skills.

NOTES FOR CHAPTER 3

1. *Intervention, Minimum Standards Implementation Series,* Ohio Department of Education, 1983, page 3.

2. *Ibid.,* pages 9–12, 14, 15.

3. J. S. Wooster, *What to Do for the Gifted Few* (New York: D.O.K. Publications, 1978).

4. *Ibid.*

5. *Competency-Based Education for the Handicapped,* Clermont County Office of Education, Division of Special Education; compiled by Beverly Smith, Jamie Hopkins, Carol Ottman, Rose Lasita, Dan Stacy, April 1986.

CHAPTER 4

Implementation of Competency-Based Education

Two distinct instructional models, both based on different assumptions, form the basis of this chapter on implementation. These two models, first mentioned in Chapter 2, are the *verification model* and the *course of study model*. Which model you should use depends upon which assumptions fit the instructional philosophy of your school.

THE VERIFICATION MODEL

The verification model (refer back to Figure 2-8) consists of a five-step process. These steps are: (1) preassessment, (2) regular instruction, (3) postassessment, (4) intervention, and (5) postassessment.

Step 1:
Preassessment

The preassessment is conducted during the beginning of the first semester. It should take about one month to complete. This time will vary according to the grade level however. The lower the grade level, the longer the preassessment will take. Also, the more intelligent the student, the less time it will take. Therefore, this process could run from one day to two months depending upon the age and ability of the students being assessed. This process is done at the beginning of the year so that more school days are left for instruction based on the preassessment results.

To be successful, this process must be very flexible. The teacher must have no restrictions except a general time frame for completion. For example, the general time frame may be from September 15 through October 30. Within that time frame, the teacher must have the flexibility to assess items in any number and setting that matches the instructional schedule.

When using the verification model, the competency preassessment is given regardless of whether or not the competency item has been taught. Students who demonstrate achievement of the competency item will not be assessed again on that item unless the teacher wishes to check for retention. The last step of the preassessment process is to record successful achievement by competency item.

Step 2:
Regular Instruction

This step is rather self-explanatory. It simply means that the competency items are taught when prescribed by the course of study. The preassessment results should have a significant influence on how the competency items are taught and to whom. The amount of time and emphasis given to a particular competency should be greater for students who did not demonstrate achievement of the item during preassessment.

After a competency item has been covered during the regular instruction phase, a postassessment should occur. Common sense dictates how much time should expire between the end of instruction and the postassessment. Common sense also dictates how many competency items should be taught before a postassessment is given. As a general rule, five to ten competency items would be appropriate because using this number will measure retention and reduce the time necessary for assessment.

Step 3:
Postassessment

The postassessment process applies only to those students who did not demonstrate achievement on the preassessment. Successful achievement is recorded.

Steps 4 and 5:
Intervention and Postassessment

At the conclusion of the postassessment phase, the teacher is able to identify the students, if any, who are going to need intervention on competency items. Some of the students demonstrated competency on the preassessment without the benefit of instruction. Others demonstrated competency, after participating in regular instruction, on the postassessment. Students not demonstrating competency at this point obviously need some kind of special instruction or intervention.

At the conclusion of the intervention activities, a second postassessment is given. The cycle of intervention, postassessment, intervention, postassessment is then continued until the postassessment is successful.

Assumptions Upon Which the
Verification Model Is Based

1. Student may have achieved a competency without being taught it.

In the early grades, some students may already be competent in basic skills due to learning activities outside of school. The home may have provided this basic curriculum. Environmental influences, such as media, coupled with a high intelligence, may provide the competence. In later grades, the competence may be the result of the above-mentioned factors, plus school experiences. For example, students learning two-digit addition may quickly transfer that learning to three- or four-digit addition and thus, already be competent in skills beyond their grade level.

Whatever the reason for the "premature" competency, the preassessment will verify its presence.

2. If a student is already competent in a skill, three strategies will be followed— either the competency should not be taught, or it should be taught with less emphasis and time, or enrichment activities should be provided.

The decision as to which of these strategies to follow is determined by the retention factor. If the competency is one that does not need retention checks, then follow the strategy of not teaching. If, however, the competency is one that does need retention checks, follow the strategy of teaching with less time and emphasis.

Years of experience in teaching have clearly identified for educators the skills and concepts that tend to need reinforcement. These skills and concepts should be reinforced even for those students who demonstrate achievement of the competency. However, that teaching should be of less time and emphasis than for students who have not demonstrated achievement.

3. Preassessment results will be used for *grouping*.

This assumption is at the heart of the verification model. The whole reason for the preassessment is improved instruction, which takes place through the appropriate grouping of students based on preassessment results.

THE COURSE OF STUDY MODEL

The course of study model (refer back to Figure 2-9) differs from the verification model in that it eliminates the preassessment and begins with regular instruction which is followed by assessment, intervention, and postassessment. Since these terms have been defined under the verification model, there is no need to redefine them here.

Assumptions Upon Which the Course of Study Model Is Based

1. There is no need to assess student achievement on a competency until after it has been taught as part of the regular instruction.

This assumption implies that by observation, contact, or other informal means, the teacher is so confident that the student does not have the ability to pass the competency test that a preassessment would be a waste of time and resources. Such a decision might also be reached concerning the lack of readiness on the student's part to take any kind of test. This lack of readiness could be intellectual, emotional, or both.

2. It is not used for grouping.

This assumption indicates that any grouping being practiced will not need to be based on preassessment results, or that the grouping can be done without preassessment because the skill level of the students is so low that the preassessment is not necessary.

RECOMMENDED USE OF THE TWO MODELS

The course of study model is sometimes feasible for kindergarten and grades 1 and 2. The verification model is recommended for use from grades 3 through 12. The rationale for this thinking is based on the nature of people and the curriculum. At the primary grades, the following factors are sometimes present and make the use of the course of study model feasible:

1. Many of the students are not ready for any paper-and-pencil assessment due to both intellectual and emotional reasons.
2. The preassessment is less likely to give diagnostic results that are not obvious from observation.
3. It is a waste of instructional time and resources to give paper-and-pencil assessment when the results are predetermined.

The course of study model should be used with caution. Its utilization defies diagnostic principles. It should be used only when other diagnostic measures replace the competency-based education preassessment.

These assumptions are not valid after the primary grades. Therefore, the verification model, which includes preassessment, must be used for the intermediate and middle grades, and the high school level.

Competency-based education is effective only when it enhances instruction. When a preassessment enhances instruction, it should be used. When it interferes with instruction, it should not be used. For some primary students, the paper-and-pencil preassessment is not always necessary to use. For the remainder of students, the preassessment is a vital component of competency-based education.

COMPETENCY-BASED EDUCATION AND THE "TESTING MIND-SET"

For any school system implementing competency-based education, the biggest obstacle to overcome is the "testing mind-set." When people, both educators and laymen, think of competency, they think of testing and evaluation. In order to be successful with competency-based education, a new mind-set must be created. This mind-set must center around individual diagnosis, individual norms that are criterion-referenced, and a 100 percent achievement expectation. The following testing terms have no value in competency-based education: stanines, testing conditions, percentiles, bell curve, means, modes, standard deviation, specific testing directions, and so on.

The difference is, of course, in purpose. The purpose of competency-based education assessment is individual diagnosis and instruction based on this diagnosis. In addition, the diagnosis is item by item. Cumulative scores are not significant.

The changeover of a mind-set is difficult. Any time most teachers have given a paper-and-pencil test, it has been for evaluation purposes. Once you achieve the mind-set conversion, there is less anxiety involved because the teachers concentrate less on testing and more on emphasizing instruction.

A mind-set is a powerful force. It is established over a period of time. A mind-set, once established, is difficult to alter. Therein lies the greatest obstacle to competency-based education with instructional emphasis. The mind-set that competency means testing currently exists. No matter what terms or words are used in conjunction with the word "competency," the current mind-set converts it to "competency testing." Therefore, in order to achieve true and total competency-based education, this mind-set must be changed.

When competency-based education is first initiated, the mind-set is on the testing aspect. This makes it difficult for principals and teachers to confidently pursue the program with instructional emphasis. Questions involving test security and conditions will constantly arise. Only experience with the instructional emphasis will erode the "testing mind-set."

If every teacher who is responsible for implementing competency-based education could be extensively involved in the planning and development of the competency-based program, the mind-set conversion could be accomplished during the planning and development stages. However, since this is not possible, some teachers will be having their first extensive experience with competency-based education during the implementation phase.

The following strategies are effective in breaking down the "testing mind-set" and converting it to an "instructional mind-set":

1. Continually and consistently discuss competency-based education as an integral part of the curriculum-instructional cycle (course of study—instruction—assessment).
2. Continually and consistently discuss competency assessment and testing *only* in the total text of competency-based education.
3. Continually and consistently discuss the differences between assessment and testing.
4. Continually and consistently discuss the characteristics of a competency-based education program with instructional emphasis and contrast it with evaluation-oriented competency testing.
5. Continually and consistently utilize the teachers who were extensively involved in the planning and development of the competency-based education program in in-service and liaison activities.

Mind-Set Conversion Chart

FROM a test made up of many questions covering many skills and concepts	TO a test item assessing one skill or concept
FROM a test that measures overall ability or achievement	TO a test item that measures achievement of one skill or concept
FROM percentiles, stanines, and class rank . . .	TO competency (yes or no) on each individual competency item
FROM today is a test day for all the students	TO every day is an assessment day for some students
FROM means and modes	TO competency (yes or no) on each individual competency item
FROM group norms	TO individually criterion-referenced information
FROM valid and reliable testing conditions . . .	TO diagnostic assessment
FROM grading the entire test	TO grading items

COMPETENCY-BASED EDUCATION EVALUATION

Although competency-based education avoids group norms as a rule, the product evaluation calls for their use in the competency item analysis. At the end of the school year, it should be determined what percent of the students demonstrated achievement on each competency item.

Refer to Figure 4-1 to see how the competency item evaluation is done. Notice competency item #43. It evaluates the student's ability to recognize homonyms. A total of 1,072 students demonstrated achievement of this competency item. Six students did not demonstrate achievement of this competency item. This means that 99 percent of the third-grade students demonstrated achievement of this competency item.

These figures represent a positive evaluation of this competency item because it means that only six students out of 1,072 will have to carry over an unmastered competency to the next grade.

Figure 4-1

COMPOSITE REPORTING FORM

School: _____

PRIMARY LANGUAGE ARTS

Grade: Third Grade

Year: _____

Item #	41 Write Letter	42 Compound Words	43 Homonyms	44 Root Words	45a Main Ideas	45b Facts	45c Sequence	45d Cause-Effect	46 Comma	47 Months	48 Contractions	49 Nouns	50 Subjects	51 Subject-Verb Agreement	52 Spelling	53 Alphabetize	54 Word Meaning	55 Table of Contents	56 Writing
Composite																			
Achieved	1048	1057	1072	892	965	1005	860	938	1004	1047	1058	984	801	921	990	951	961	1066	831
Not Achieved	30	17	6	230	113	73	220	142	76	33	23	96	279	129	90	129	119	15	230
% Achieved	97	98	99	80	90	93	80	87	93	97	98	91	74	88	92	88	89	99	78

ACTIVITY 34

Pretesting

The purpose of pretesting is to establish which students need instruction in which competencies. It verifies achievement and identifies instructional needs. The pretest results should be used for grouping the students for instruction.

Even students who pass a competency item may receive instruction in the item for the purpose of reinforcement and thus, better retention. However, the level and intensity of this instruction should not be the same as it is for students who did not pass the pretest. For the student who passes the pretest, enrichment is called for. For the student who does not pass the pretest, regular instruction and/or remediation is called for.

PROCEDURE FOR ADMINISTERING THE PRETEST

1. In order to best utilize the test of basic skills, it is recommended that all students entering all grades be tested by the end of September.

2. During September, the classroom teacher should review the previous year's test scores to develop an intervention plan for students who have not achieved previous mastery.

3. Those students entering school from outside the testing program should be tested for the previous year's grade level when the teacher feels there is a need to establish some guidelines.

4. It is recommended that the classroom teachers do the pre- and posttests in their own classrooms. Makeup tests and testing of new students entering during the school year can be done by an aide on an individual basis.

5. It is recommended that the teacher directions for the test be reviewed by the grade level teachers; that they make the necessary changes in terminology according to the needs of that grade level; and that all directions for the tests be given uniformly.

6. The physical setup of the testing situation shall be conducive to maximum testing results. The setup and time line for testing should be developed and implemented by the classroom teacher.

7. Special education and handicapped students who are mainstreamed into the regular classroom would be expected to take the basic skills pre- and posttest of the given subject being mainstreamed.

PRETEST SPECIFICS

1. In-service (school).
2. Time—October (first week).
3. Informal instructions.
4. Break up test (be flexible).
5. Teachers should use their own discretion.
6. How much of the test to give is determined by the teacher, as long as the test is completed by deadline.
7. Test should be given by the classroom teacher.
8. Allow one-half of a day for recording test results and planning intervention.
9. Separate children (physically).

ACTIVITY 35

Intervention

All hierarchical levels of the school system must assume and carry out certain responsibilities if intervention is to be successful. The responsibilities will vary for each organizational level, as shown in Figure 4-2.

At the central office or district level, there are responsibilities in both line and staff function. Line functions include policy development, whereby the board of education (with input from the superintendent and staff) establishes the intended ends for the intervention program. Basically, this is the philosophical direction to be pursued and what evidence will be used to judge the program.

The staff functions are: (1) providing awareness and clarification of the concept of intervention, (2) explaining the definition, (3) interpreting any standards that are present, (4) defining the students to be served, (5) supplying strategies/alternatives, and (6) supplying resources.

At the school/principal level, three major functions are performed. They are:

1. Establishing the goals or focus of the intervention, which is determined through (a) needs assessments, (b) management team decision making based on needs assessment, and (c) instructional leaders' implementation of the goals/focus.
2. Developing in-service policy and providing in-service activities for the staff.
3. Documenting the school staff's participation in the in-service activities and adhering to the district goals/focus.

Figure 4-2

INTERVENTION IMPLEMENTATION MODEL

DISTRICT/CENTRAL OFFICE   POLICY DEVELOPMENT
PHILOSOPHICAL DIRECTION
AWARENESS/CLARIFICATION
STANDARD
DEFINITION
STUDENTS TO BE SERVED
STRATEGIES/ALTERNATIVES
RESOURCES

PRINCIPAL/SCHOOL   GOALS/FOCUS

-management team decision
-instructional leaders decision
-staff needs assessment

PROVISION FOR IN-SERVICE POLICY
 -mandatory
 -voluntary

DOCUMENTATION

-district focus
-school focus
-in-service/participants

TEACHER/STAFF   IMPLEMENTATION
DOCUMENTATION

-lesson plans
-evaluation component

At the teacher/staff level, implementation occurs in the classroom. Documentation of this implementation is achieved through lesson plans and the evaluation component.

The responsibilities for the central office and the principal are administrative in nature. They are also standard procedure for any curriculum or instructional program. They are vital to the success of the intervention program. However, they don't need detailed explanation. If the will is there, the ways to get it done are well documented.

However, the implementation of intervention at the teacher/staff level needs some detailed discussion. Teachers will tell you that school administrators are good at planning programs that teachers must carry out without specific implementation direction. So let's look at intervention in the classroom.

LEVELS OF STUDENT PERFORMANCE

Following is a suggested process for dealing with the varying levels of student performance. This suggested process establishes three levels of performance and shows the teacher how to intervene with each level. Figure 4-3 shows teaching strategies for the three levels of student performance, which are:

1. **Developing**—Those students who demonstrate very little or no mastery of the pupil performance objectives skills/concepts, lack enabling skills, and may need additional and/or remedial instruction.

2. **Partial**—Those students who demonstrate some mastery of the skill/concept but need additional instruction or practice as mastery emerges.

3. **Mastery**—Those students who demonstrate total mastery of the skill/concept and would benefit from alternative learning strategies.

Some suggested procedures for teaching to the three performing levels are:

1. Decide on activities to use (pool); assign students to the various groups, and communicate activities and expectations to students.
2. Explain to students how clustering arrangement will work, how to proceed independently, when to ask questions and where to get the follow-up activity (for example, what is an acceptable noise level or movement around the room).
3. Sketch a room arrangement that could facilitate three cluster areas, determine where materials are to be kept for each cluster area, and decide where the teacher will meet a group of students.
4. Make use of an overhead projector or chalkboard to list activities for each group.
5. Have an ongoing activity that students can do individually when they finish the assigned activity.
6. Set up class time to facilitate meeting with each cluster and providing direction as needed.
7. Determine how to assess each activity.

In addition to addressing the varying levels of student performance, teachers can also utilize many different instructional materials, such as:

Texts	Newspapers	Films
Teacher's manuals	Reference books	Filmstrips
Workbooks	Brochures	Slides
Worksheets	Pamphlets	Cassette tapes
Supplemental texts and books	Handouts	Audiotapes
	Posters	Transparencies
Magazines	Videotapes	Maps

Figure 4-3*

DEVELOPING	PARTIAL	MASTERY

A. TEACHING ENABLERS
　1. skill
　2. content
　3. experience
B. REDUCE LEVEL OF DIFFICULTY
C. POSTPONE AND MOVE ON

D. ALTERNATIVE STRATEGIES
E. ADDITIONAL PRACTICE
F. RETEST MISSING SKILLS
G. POSTPONE AND MOVE ON

H. PARALLEL/ENRICHMENT
I. ACCELERATION
J. PEER TUTORING
K. INDEPENDENT STUDY

<u>DEVELOPING</u>

1. Task analysis of content, determine what prerequisites may be missing, provide direct instruction for these
2. Determine students' developmental level for concept, provide instruction at that level
3. Teach needed study skills to students
4. Teach students how to read text
5. Develop folders with problems at various levels of skill development

<u>PARTIAL</u>

1. Utilize any of developing strategies as appropriate and adjust
　a. content-terminal or pupil performance objective skill rather than enabling
　b. time allotted
　c. volume of work
　d. amount of teacher direction
　e. level of student self-direction
　f. nature of the product
2. Diagnose student assignments and assign only those questions/problems needed by students

<u>MASTERY</u>

Enrichment
1. Assign more sophisticated problems to solve at higher levels of thinking
2. Have students apply process to real life problem or simulation
3. Have students develop their own problems or applications
4. Provide interest centers based on special learning skills
5. Utilize contracts for personal goal setting

6. Give fewer examples/problems at any one time
7. Reduce level of difficulty to point where student can succeed
8. Provide models for students to follow
9. Work on student motivation
10. Teach students how to break down word problems
11. Provide students with math facts/charts
12. Allow students to use calculators
13. Vary student response mode
14. Vary learning modality

POSTPONE AND MOVE ON

3. Arrange practice problems in ascending order of difficulty, have students work until mistakes begin in order to identify point of intervention
4. Have students work in dyads or triads to analyze each other's error patterns
5. Develop chart or grid showing projects/activities for entire unit or chapter
6. Develop learning centers equipped with self-instructional, self-checking activities
7. Utilize pairs/triads, volunteers to aid instruction
8. Let students develop packets of additional practice activities
9. Have students write description of what they have learned or of how to do problems
10. Retest only those pupil performance objectives that apply
11. Retest using a different modality
12. Develop non-paper/pencil assessment

POSTPONE AND MOVE ON

6. Seek out mentors in the community for very advanced secondary students
7. Have students develop problems, games, bulletin boards, etc. to teach concepts to others
8. Students attend pull-out program

Acceleration
1. Pretest students, place at appropriate level in the curriculum
2. Upon completion of objective, students move on to next chapter, units
3. Assign problems from higher grade level related to skills presently taught
4. Summer programs such as Midwest Talent Search for students to study advanced material
5. Students attend college and high school simultaneously
6. Advanced placement courses

Peer Tutoring
1. Mastery students tutor each other
2. Mastery students tutor partial or developing students
   a. through direct instruction
   b. through materials that mastery students develop

Independent Study
1. Allow student to proceed through a unit or chapter on his or her own
2. Develop district policy for an independent study for an entire course

*Developed by Columbiana County Schools, Lisbon, Ohio; Judith March and Karen Peters. Used with permission.

Globes

Learning packets

Teacher notes

Computer software

Language master

Computer management feedback activities

Student-made materials

Community resource file

Calculators

Resource speakers (from business, industry, such as a math surveyor)

Reading specialists

Games

Learning centers

Field trips

Real life materials

Home/Simulation

Educational TV

Buddy system

Study guide

Instructional manual for parents

Intervention won't reach its potential without good communications among teachers, parents, and community. Here are some imperative communication measures:

Parent/Teacher conferences

Letters

Telephone calls

Home visits

P.T.O. meetings

Radio and TV

Newspaper

Parent newsletters

Volunteer programs

"Family Involvement" activities

Progress reports

Interims

Speakers bureau

Instructional guide

Brochures

Various classroom management techniques can be used to enhance intervention. Among them are:

- Establishing a basic time line for instruction
- Planning for a variety of grouping patterns
- Facilitating several activities at one time
- Deciding which pupil performance objectives to cover each grading period
- Pacing instruction at different levels
- Time-on-task
- Organizing the room effectively
- Deciding the amount of time needed to review
- Deciding the amount of time to reteach
- Team teaching
- Resource people—Senior citizens
- Field trips
- Independent study
- Grade level meetings—teacher sharing
- Organization for independent study

- Departmentalization
- Computer aid
- Self-contained classrooms

Strategies that assist student learning and thus, intervention include:

Assertive discipline

T.E.S.A.

Developing self-concept

Providing for different learning styles

Grouping for specific needs

Modifying materials

Study skills instruction

Teaching problem-solving strategies

Demonstration

AV presentations

Field trips

Experiments

Questioning

Discussions

Brainstorming

Seminars

Interviewing

Role playing

Debates

Adjusting assignment length

Thinking skills

Gaming

Committees

Buzz sessions

Volunteer tutoring

Peer tutoring

Resource people

Student team learning

Simulations

Goal setting

Student contracting

Mastery learning

Partnerships

Interns

Guided observations

Some instructional alternatives to consider in intervention are:

Mastery learning

Diagnostic/Prescriptive learning

Parent/Peer tutoring

Computer-assisted instruction

Chapter I reading

Learning activity packets

Sustained silent reading

Read-Aloud program

Recreational reading

Additional assignments

Dramatization

Taped lessons

Oral tests

Team teaching

Drill and practice

Corrective reteaching

Independent study

Interest inventory

Learning centers

Learning contracts

Reading recovery

Writing process

Simulations

Boardwork

Gaming

Summer school

Manipulatives

Retention

Environment

Individual packets

Content area—Reading/ Math

Learning levels

Balance time-on-task between acquisition of skills and application of skills

Learning modalities

Saturday school

Gifted programs

Figure 4-4

NEEDS ASSESSMENT

INSTRUCTIONAL MATERIALS ALTERNATIVES	COMMUNICATION	CLASSROOM MANAGEMENT TECHNIQUES	STRATEGIES THAT ASSIST STUDENT LEARNING	INSTRUCTIONAL ALTERNATIVES
Learning Packets	Parent/Teacher Conference	Grouping	Modify Materials	Learning Contract
Computer Software	Letters	Time-on-Task	Learning Styles	Independent Study
Reference Books	Calls	Pacing Instruction	Problem Solving	Chapter I
Cassette Tapes			Demonstration	Reading Recovery
Magazines			Questioning	Tutoring
Videotapes				Manipulatives
				Retention

In doing the district or school needs assessment, the groupings of intervention actions could be used to guide the needs assessment process. Figure 4-4 shows how a needs assessment might look.

The principal should document intervention goals and activities. Figure 4-5 shows a form to document goals. Figure 4-6 could be used to document intervention in-service activities.

The teacher needs to document intervention activities also. Figure 4-7 is a weekly lesson plan form with a space provided at the bottom to record intervention activities.

Figure 4-5

DOCUMENTATION
DISTRICT/SCHOOL _____
_____
SCHOOL YEAR
FOCUS/GOAL(S) _____

Figure 4-6

DOCUMENTATION

DISTRICT/SCHOOL_____

STAFF DEVELOPMENT/IN-SERVICE AND RESOURCE STAFF	DATES	PARTICIPANTS

Figure 4-7

DATE_____
MONDAY
TUESDAY
WEDNESDAY
THURSDAY
FRIDAY
INTERVENTION

SOMETHING OLD, SOMETHING NEW . . .

If you've read this intervention section carefully, you are probably saying to yourself, "This is nothing new, this is what good teaching has always been." You are right. This *is* what *good* teaching has always been. It is not what all teaching has been. And most certainly, it has not been documented and communicated to parents.

It is also true that this section on intervention contains ideas that are supported in the research on good teaching practices. Maybe what we need is to define good teaching through standards, policy, and in-service activities. Competency-based education provides, through the intervention process, all three of these components.

What is important is that competency-based education can provide a conceptual framework from which good teaching practices can be fostered and maintained, and that is what separates competency-based education from competency testing.

INTERVENTION ALTERNATIVES AND STRATEGIES

To help illustrate how intervention might operate within a specific course, the following intervention alternatives and strategies for *reading* are presented. The same kind of process could be followed in other subject areas.

I. Address the development of a good self-concept.
   A. Premises:
      1. What a child thinks he or she is and is able to achieve determines much of his or her behavior and achievement.
      2. One of the most important skills for improving self-concept and achievement is encouragement.
      3. Nothing succeeds like success.
   B. What the educator can do.
      1. Demonstrate approval by praising that which the student does well, be it academic or nonacademic.
         a. Praise verbally.
         b. Praise nonverbally.
            – By facial expression.
            – By written awards and notes. (See Figure 4-8.) A sample note might be: "You did a great job in leading the playground activity today. Some of your classmates commented on your leadership skills. Thanks."
            – By telephone calls to parents and guardians. (See Figure 4-9.)
      2. Focus on the student's strengths, providing opportunities for academic success and building further knowledge and skills on successes.
      3. Help students recognize that they will not always be successful in skill acquisition but that they can depend upon you for the support that will help them become successful.
      4. Create materials that will provide students with opportunities to better understand themselves and others and improve their self-image.
         a. Classroom self-concept activities.
         b. Parent/child self-concept packets.
      5. Develop a good rapport with students. (See Figure 4-10.)
II. Identify individual learning styles and stages.
   A. Premise—Individuals tend to demonstrate a perceptual preference for learning that is dependent upon the strength they demonstrate in the use of one of their senses.

Figure 4-8

Figure 4-9

TEACHER/PARENT TELEPHONE CONTACT

NAME OF STUDENT_____ DATE/TIME_____

GRADE_____ TEACHER_____

SUMMARY OF CONVERSATION_____

_____

_____

_____

_____

_____

_____

_____

Figure 4-10

Developing Good Teacher-Student Rapport*

Here are some comments from sources that really count in building good teacher-student rapport.

The following are quotes from adolescents who were interviewed by prospective teachers at North Texas State University.

- "_____ always finds time to have individual conferences with each student. I think she cares about me."

- "In _____ class we fill out information cards at the beginning of school, and he finds out what we are involved in besides his class. He considers this information in making project assignments, in class activities, and group work."

- "_____ is aware of what I am doing outside her English class. She often asks me how I am doing in marching or concert band, and she remarks after a concert how much she enjoyed it. That makes me appreciate and work harder in her English class."

- "I really like _____ because she always includes a personal note on test papers. It makes me feel I really count. There is nothing worse than getting back papers with only a grade on them."

- "It is really neat what _____ does in his class. He takes individual pictures of each student and has a bulletin board reserved for 'Very Important Persons.' Each person appears at least once during the year, and it really gives you a special lift to know a whole bulletin board is devoted to you, your achievements, and goals."

- "_____ is my favorite teacher because she gives me things I can do. I know I'm not the best student in the class, but it's no fun to fail. I would rather succeed at a lower level than fail at something I can't do."

---

*Taken from an article written by Lloyd P. Campbell, associate professor of secondary education, University of North Texas, published in the March, 1978 issue of *Phi Delta Kappan*. Used with permission.

B. What the educator can do.
   1. Identify the student's perceptual learning style preference.
   2. Provide a variety of activities for each objective that offer students the opportunity to learn by using their perceptual learning style preference.
C. Conduct tests for visual, auditory, or kinesthetic learning style preference. *Caution:* These tests are merely indicators of preference for learning. Students often know how they learn best and can simply tell you that they have a

preference. If you provide directions that can be seen and heard and if you provide a variety of activities in teaching objectives that appeal to different learning styles, students will gravitate to those that are best for them.

1. Test a small group of students at a time.
2. List the students' names, observe and record observations next to their names.
3. Note V for visual, A for auditory, and K for Kinesthetic.
4. Watch for the following reactions:
   a. Visual learners will usually close their eyes or look at the ceiling as they try to recall a visual picture.
   b. Auditory learners will move their lips or whisper as they try to memorize.
   c. Kinesthetic learners will use their fingers to count off items or write in the air, on their palms, or on the table.
5. Begin the test by telling your students that you are giving them a test to determine in what way they learn best.
6. Explain that we learn all three ways and that the test will determine which way is the easiest for them to learn. Remind them that there is no "best" way.
7. You may wish to ask someone to serve as an observer with you.
8. Remember to record the reactions previously mentioned in (4) as well as the results of your tests in helping determine the student's learning style preference.

D. Conduct a test for visual preference.
   1. List five words on the board appropriate to the students' reading level.
   2. Leave the list for one minute.
   3. Erase.
   4. Ask for the list.
   5. Have the students repeat the words to you without the others hearing.
   6. First and most accurate responders will be visual learners.
   7. For nonreaders, place five objects on a tray. Follow the same procedure as for readers.

E. Conduct a test for auditory preference.
   1. Select five different words appropriate to the students' level.
   2. Pronounce the words. Do not write them.
   3. Allow thirty seconds between each word.
   4. Have the students repeat the words to you without the others hearing. Choose the students in the order in which they volunteer.
   5. First and most accurate responders will be auditory learners.

F. Conduct a test for kinesthetic preference.
   1. Select five different words from those used previously.
   2. Pronounce the words. Do not write them.
   3. Have the students write the words as you say them.
   4. Have the students rewrite the words beside the first list.
   5. Have the students turn the paper over and rewrite the words from memory.
   6. Those with correct lists will be kinesthetic learners.

7. For nonreaders, have the students handle five different objects from those presented in the test for visual preference. Remove the objects and have the students name the objects.

III. Address the development of a good attitude toward reading.
    A. Understand personal interests.
        1. Premise—Interest evokes effort.
        2. What the educator can do.
            a. Talk to students informally about their interests and use this knowledge in suggesting materials for independent reading that will appeal to their interests.
            b. Hold personal private conferences for the same purpose.
            c. Create oral, written, or collage-type interest inventories to ascertain information about students. (See Figures 4-11 through 4-13.)

Figure 4-11

PERSONAL INVENTORY
(Elementary—Oral or Written)

DATE_____

Name_____ Date of Birth_____

Address_____ Telephone_____

What kind of work does your father do?_____

What kind of work does your mother do?_____

How many brothers do you have?_____ Older_____ Younger_____

How many sisters do you have?_____ Older_____ Younger_____

What is the name of your favorite book or story?_____

_____

What kind of stories do you like to hear?_____

_____

Do you go to the public library?_____ Do you have a library card?_____

What are the names of some of the books which you own at home?_____

_____

Figure 4-11
(Continued)

Name two of your favorite television shows: _____

_____

_____

What do you like to do after school? _____

_____

What is your favorite thing to do on Saturday? _____

_____

What are your favorite games? _____

_____

Name two of your favorite animals: _____

_____

Do you like to read or be read to? _____

Figure 4-12

PERSONAL INVENTORY
(Middle/High School—Written)

DATE _____

Name _____ Date of Birth _____

Address _____ Telephone _____

Father's Occupation _____

Mother's Occupation _____

Number of Brothers _____ Ages ____ ____ ____ ____ ____

Number of Sisters _____ Ages ____ ____ ____ ____ ____

Figure 4-12
(Continued)

How much do you like to read? (Put a check mark in the correct space.)

_____ Very Much

_____ Some

_____ Not Very Much

_____ Not At All

What was the title of the last book you read? _____

What is the title of the best book you ever read? _____

About how many books did you read in school last year? _____

Do you have a library card? _____

How many books did you check out from the public library during the summer?

_____

Do you read the newspaper? _____

Put a check mark by the parts of the newspaper you like to read.

_____ Front Page

_____ Editorials

_____ Sports

_____ Comics

_____ Advice Column

_____ Movie, Television, and Radio Information

Do you read comic books? _____ Name the ones you like best: _____

_____

What magazines do you read? _____

_____

Name your three favorite television shows: _____

_____

_____

What was the name of the last movie you saw? _____

What has been your favorite movie? _____

What is your favorite subject in school? _____

What sports do you like? _____

Figure 4-12
(Continued)

What type of music do you listen to?_____

Who is your favorite recording artist or group?_____

What do you usually do after school?_____

What do you like to do best on Saturday?_____

What kind of hobbies or collections do you have?_____

_____

Do you have special interests such as electronics, mechanics, etc.? If so, what are they?

_____

What clubs or groups do you belong to?_____

What living person do you admire most?_____

What do you like to do during summer vacation?_____

_____

Of the following kinds of books, which ones would you like to read for pleasure? (Put a check mark by the types you like.)

- _____ Sports
- _____ Adventure
- _____ Historical Novels
- _____ Problems of Teenagers
- _____ Biographies or Autobiographies
- _____ Mysteries
- _____ Westerns
- _____ Science Fiction
- _____ Nature or Animal Stories
- _____ Romantic Stories
- _____ War Stories
- _____ Spy Stories
- _____ Stories About Young Adults or Teenagers
- _____ Humorous Stories

Please list any others:_____

Figure 4-13

PERSONAL INVENTORY
(Collage)

DIRECTIONS: Collect as many pictures as you can including photographs and pictures cut from magazines and newspapers that tell about you and the things you like. Use these pictures to design a collage that will describe you as a person. Paste your pictures on the cardboard provided. Try to find pictures to tell about each of the things listed below. If you are unable to find pictures for every category, print your interest on a small piece of paper and paste that on your collage.

TRY TO INCLUDE THE FOLLOWING:

1. A picture of your family and pets

2. The titles of some of your favorite books

3. Articles from your favorite sections of the newspaper

4. Titles of your favorite magazines

5. Titles of your favorite television shows

6. Titles of movies you have seen

7. Pictures of sports you like

8. Pictures of your favorite recording artists or group

9. Clothes you like

10. Pictures of hobbies, collections, or special interests you have

11. Things you like to eat

12. Things you like to do in your spare time

13. People you admire

14. Places you have been or would like to go

15. Jobs you think you might like to do in the future

B. Balance time-on-task between acquisition of skills and application of skills.
   1. Premise—Children learn to read by reading, not by filling out workbook pages. The skills learned to advance reading must be practiced and applied to stories and books.
   2. What the educator can do.
      a. Provide at least an equal amount of class time, if not more, for reading of books and stories. (See Figure 4-14.)

Figure 4-14

READATHON*

In an effort to encourage reading, middle school language arts students will be participating in an in-class READATHON on Tuesday, October 30. The money earned will purchase new paperback books for Mrs. Martin's classroom reading library. Participants will have the opportunity of selecting the books. If you would be interested in sponsoring your child in this endeavor, please complete the information below. Students will be reading in twenty-minute consecutive sessions. You will be sponsoring them for a given amount for every twenty minutes they read. The READATHON will not exceed fourteen twenty-minute periods or fourteen times the amount of money you are willing to give for the twenty-minute period. (EXAMPLE: If you sponsor 10¢ and the student reads for 14 periods, you would owe $1.40) Thank you for your support.

Sincerely,

Language Arts Teacher

I am willing to sponsor _____ in the language arts READATHON.

SPONSOR'S NAME	AMOUNT TO BE PAID FOR EVERY 20-MINUTE PERIOD STUDENT READS	TO BE FILLED OUT BY TEACHER ONLY	
		# OF PERIODS READ	AMOUNT EARNED

*From an unpublished manuscript by Carolyn D. Martin (Batavia, Ohio: Clermont County Schools, 1986). Used with permission.

      b. Read and become familiar with children's and young adult's literature and authors in order to build quality classroom libraries; interest children in books and motivate children to read for pleasure.

      c. Read to students.

      d. Develop literature units that teach, reinforce, and enrich skills while applying them.

C. Provide time for sustained silent reading (S.S.R.).[1]

    1. Premise—Children who are able to sustain themselves without interruption in silent reading for a given period of time improve their ability to read and comprehend.

    2. What the educator can do. (See Figure 4-15.)

      a. Provide time for S.S.R. (school-wide or individual classroom)

      b. Model reading behavior during S.S.R.

      c. Provide time to discuss books read during S.S.R.

Figure 4-15

Sustained Silent Reading

Primary Sustained Silent Reading Guidelines

1. Put fifty to sixty children's picture books in a pile.

2. For twenty minutes or so, the teacher takes books from the pile, reads a page or two orally and puts the books back in the pile.

3. The teacher reads one book in its entirety.

4. The children are then given one minute to choose a book and are asked to sustain their reading for one minute.

5. While the students read, it is very important for the teacher to read also.

Intermediate Sustained Silent Reading Guidelines

1. Discuss with your students how important silent reading is. It is a practice session that will develop their stamina and make them much better readers. It is the best way to improve their reading skills.

2. Take time to talk with kids about coming to class prepared for silent reading. Stress that silent reading practice is most effective when they read one book at a time. They shouldn't be switching back and forth in books. Such disruption keeps them from remembering what is going on in their book and ultimately destroys their reading enjoyment. Tell them that for these reasons it is their responsibility to bring their books to class. Along with this theme, it is appropriate to mention what will happen to them if they take another student's book. Some kids, rather than admit that they don't have a book that day, will grab a book out of the box that belongs to another student.

Figure 4-15
(Continued)

3. If the student has temporarily lost or forgotten his book (and he is not a chronic loser or forgetter), it helps to have alternative reading material—old *Scope* magazines, regular magazines, a newspaper. It is actually better for the student not to begin another book just for the sake of having something to read. If the book is in his locker, it is sometimes best to just let him get it.

GUIDELINES FOR SILENT READING TIME

- Students may select what they wish to read. Once they decide, they may not switch during that particular Sustained Silent Reading, unless they finish the book they are in. An adequate amount of time for browsing is very important. The teacher functions to help guide students in their selection.

- Students are to read something they enjoy and something that is easy for them. (Rule-of-thumb test: Have students open the book to any full page of print, read down it, count words they do not know. If more than five on one page, then book is too hard for student.)

- The teacher should be a model of reading. Students are influenced by seeing adults read novels with relish. (Clean ones, guys!) Talk about your book. Act like you don't want to put it down.

- Stress the enjoyment of reading. Students are too accustomed to endlessly reading and answering questions. They'll be shocked if they are allowed to merely read and enjoy what they read.

- It helps to have book markers available. It also helps to have an area in your room where students can leave their books overnight. (Have them write their names on their book markers.)

- Occasionally students who don't have books may be permitted to do homework. However, if this becomes routine, students who have a lot of homework may deliberately leave their reading books in their lockers.

- To turn off the requests to visit the nurse, rest room, office, etc., one technique is to require students to produce a "death" certificate to get out of silent reading. As in any classroom situation, there are times when such requests are appropriate or necessary.

- Try to establish some regular habits:
  a. Students get their books as soon as they enter the room, settle themselves, and begin to read. They are not to get up.
  b. A student with an individual problem is to come up to you and discuss it with you in a whisper—no hollering across the room, "I ain't got no book."
  c. Students may get up during silent reading only if they finish their book. They may then go directly to their folder and quietly record the book on their reading chart.

Figure 4-15
(Continued)

d. Chronic "I don't have my book" complainers can be a problem. This complaint may signal serious reading problems, negative attitude, or inability to select books on a level which will produce success. Regardless of the origin of the problem, you still have to deal with it.

GOALS OF SUSTAINED SILENT READING

1. All administrators should model pleasure reading behavior for young adults as a means of demonstrating reading as a lifelong pleasurable experience. Students expect teachers to read—they know it is part of the job. But it is important for the students to know that the principal, secretary, custodian, aides, and other administrators present in the building during the Sustained Silent Reading period are engaging in pleasure reading. This is an important role model for the students. Modeling good reading behavior has been proven statistically to have uncovered students who previously did not enjoy reading and to have motivated them to begin doing so.

2. Because it is important that administrators not in the classroom make students aware that they are reading during Sustained Silent Reading, all administrative personnel should endeavor to let the students see them carrying their book, magazine, or newspaper. Also, they should make a concerted effort to strike up a conversation with students concerning each other's reading material. Preferably, this conversation should take place outside the classroom, that is, in the hallways, cafeteria, playground, etc.

3. It is important that classroom teachers make students aware of administrators who are reading in the building. For example, students should know that the office is closed because the principal and secretary are reading and that any student, teacher, or administrator who enters the office will be offered reading material for the duration of the silent reading period.

D. Read to students.
   1. Premise—Reading aloud to students motivates them to read, improves their ability to read with expression and phrasing, increases their vocabulary, and helps develop the concept that reading is a worthwhile pleasurable experience.
   2. What the educator can do.
      a. Expose students to a variety of genres and high quality literature.
      b. Model good expression and phrasing.
      c. Motivate students to read other books by the same author.
      d. Demonstrate that reading is a pleasurable activity.

E. Establish a school environment that encourages reading.
   1. Premise—Children and young adults tend to emulate those values adults model and deem important.
   2. What the educator can do.
      a. Provide school-wide S.S.R. and model good reading habits.
      b. Celebrate reading through activities such as the school-wide readathon, National Book Week, and Right-to-Read Week.
      c. Invite authors to visit the school.
      d. Establish a link with a local children's bookstore.
      e. Provide book fairs.
      f. Encourage creative library activities and programs that encourage children to read.
F. Provide a well-developed source of quality literature and resource staff with knowledge concerning children's and young adults' literature.
   1. Premise—Students will develop an interest in books if excellent materials are available and resource persons with knowledge in the area of children's and young adults' literature share their knowledge and enthusiasm for literature with students.
   2. What the educator can do.
      a. Attend workshops and conferences on children's and young adults' literature.
         - College and university opportunities
         - International Reading Association
         - National Council of Teachers of English
      b. Subscribe to magazines and periodicals that recommend quality literature.
         - *School Library Journal*
         - *The Horn Book*
         - *The Web*
      c. Read children's and young adults' literature.
G. Involve parents in interaction actions.
   1. Premise—The child learns best when there exists a cooperative effort between the home and the school.
   2. What the educator can do.
      a. Communicate with parents.
         - Letters
         - Telephone
      b. Invite parents to participate in book fairs, educational in-service opportunities, and informational programs.
      c. Send home parent/student interaction packets.
IV. Identify individual reading levels.
   A. Premise—Children read at several different levels. Informal Reading Inventories can help a teacher determine at which reading levels a student will most likely be able to read without help, at which levels a student will need help, at which levels a student will meet frustration, and at which levels a student will

understand what is read aloud to him. Informal Reading Inventories should be considered useful as indicators only.

B. What the educator can do—Administer Informal Reading Inventories to ascertain a student's approximate independent, instructional, frustration, and capacity reading levels

1. Independent level—At this level the child can read alone or with minimum help. The child is able to pronounce 99 percent of the words read and comprehends with 90 percent accuracy. The child reads expressively, observing punctuation, and responds to questions in language equivalent to the author's.

2. Instructional level—At this level the child can read with teacher guidance. The child is able to pronounce words read with 85 to 95 percent accuracy and comprehends with 75 percent accuracy. The child is challenged by unfamiliar words but can meet challenges with teacher help.

3. Frustration level—At this level the material is too difficult for the child to succeed. The child is able to pronounce less than 85 percent of the words accurately and comprehends with less than 50 percent accuracy. The child demonstrates signs of tension and fatigue and often refuses to read.

4. Capacity level—At this level a child understands material read aloud to him or her. After hearing a selection the child should be able to accurately answer questions about the reading and is often able to supply additional information about the reading from his or her own experience.

V. Understand the developmental stages in the reading process and the developmental stages in skill acquisition.

A. Readiness

B. Vocabulary development

C. Word attack skills

1. Phonetic analysis
2. Structural analysis
3. Contextual analysis

D. Comprehension

1. Literal
2. Interpretive
3. Critical
4. Creative

E. Literary knowledge

1. Elements
2. Forms
3. Devices

F. Study skills

VI. Correlate basal activities to competency objectives.

VII. Develop a file of activities for each competency objective.

VIII. Provide supportive and remedial instruction.

IX. Provide tutoring options.

A. Peer

B. Cross-age

C. Parent

D. Volunteer

X. Utilize Bloom's Taxonomy

Bloom's taxonomy of cognitive objectives provides a framework from which to intervene. It provides the teacher with different levels of difficulty or complexity from which to work with the student. Success by the student at the higher levels of cognition is a good indicator that intervention is working.

Following is a chart of Bloom's Taxonomy of Cognitive Objectives[2] that defines what teacher and student do at the various cognitive levels and a classification of question cues.[3]

Area of Taxonomy	Definition	What Student Does	What Teacher Does
Knowledge	Recall of specific bits of information	Responds Absorbs Remembers Recognizes	Directs Tells Shows Examines
Comprehension	Understanding of a communicated material without relating it to other material	Explains Translates Demonstrates Interprets	Demonstrates Listens Questions Compares Contrasts Examines
Application	Using methods, concepts, principles, and theories in new situations	Solves novel problems Demonstrates use of knowledge Constructs	Shows Facilitates Observes Criticizes
Analyses	Breaking down a communication into its constituent elements	Discusses Uncovers Lists Dissects	Probes Guides Observes Acts as a resource
Synthesis	Putting together constituent elements or parts to form a whole	Discusses Generalizes Relates Compares Contrasts Abstracts	Reflects Extends Analyzes Evaluates
Evaluation	Judging the value of materials and methods given purposes, applying standards and criteria	Judges Disputes	Accepts Lays bare the criteria Harmonizes

BLOOM'S Sequential Classification of Question Cues:

Knowledge	(memory questions) These are mainly recall or fact kinds of questions.
Question Cues:	Tell—list—describe—who—when—where—which—what—do you remember—state—does—define—identify—did you know—relate
Comprehension	(translate) Student has to have some knowledge. The difference here is that the student is required to restate the information in his own way.
Question Cues:	Change to different symbol or medium—tell in your own words—describe how you feel about—relate—interpret—compare and contrast—what is an analogy to—when can you extrapolate from that—discover and explain—what does it mean—what are the relationships
Application	(problem solving) Requires the student to explain.
Question Cues:	Demonstrate—use it to solve—where does it lead you—how can you use it
Analysis	(problem solving) Requires the student to break down the information into parts.
Question Cues:	How—reason—why—what are causes—what are consequences—what are the steps of the process—how would you start—arrange—specify the conditions—which are necessary for—which one comes first, last—what are some specific examples of—list all the problems, solutions
Synthesis	(productive-divergent thinking, originality and imagination) Requires high degree of original thinking and ingenuity from the student.
Question Cues:	Create—devise—design—how many hypotheses can you suggest—think of all the different ways—how else—what would happen if—think of as many as possible
Evaluation	(judgments, logical accuracy, consistency, and other internal criteria) Requires quantitative and qualitative judgments.

Question
Cues: Compare criteria with standard accuracy of communication—
             indicate logical fallacies in arguments—compare a work with the
             highest known standard in field.

Intervention is the one phase of competency-based education that is already in place in all good schools. It is nothing more than teaching different ways with different materials for different students. If you already have it, use it. If you don't have it, you need it. There are identifiable reasons why students don't learn. One of the reasons is that the classroom curriculum is restrictive and thus, in conflict with how they learn. That can be corrected. When it is corrected, or where it is not a problem, intervention is occurring.

ACTIVITY 36

Posttesting

Ideally, posttesting should correspond with the course of study. Posttesting should occur one to two weeks after the competency has been taught in the sequence of the course of study. This practice causes no disruption due to testing because the competencies would be tested anyway as a part of the regular instruction and evaluation process. Remember that students who pass the pretest do not have to take the posttest for competency-based education recordkeeping. However, the teacher may wish to administer the posttest to these students to assess retention.

SOME HINTS ON POSTTESTING

1. For posttesting, teachers should make sure that they alternate using Forms A and B.
2. At a local school district, the basic skills being taught at a grade level could be divided into grading periods; posttests given at the end of the grading period could be used as an indicator for intervention procedure in the next grading period.
3. Posttest at the beginning of the last nine weeks.

ACTIVITY 37

Keeping Records
Management Simple

The key to the success of the competency-based education program is making it feasible for classroom teachers to administer. The teachers must feel that the competency-based education program augments and enhances their teaching and does not distract from their instructional efforts. The competency test items must be available to the teacher quickly. That can best be assured by having them housed in the classroom. Record folders which make it easy and quick to record demonstrated achievement of competencies must be provided. Accessibility of the test items and efficient means of recording the results will make the competency-based education program feasible for the teachers to administer and, thus, increase the possibility of a positive attitude toward competency-based education on the part of the classroom teacher. Needless to say, a positive attitude on the part of the teaching staff is vital to the success of the competency-based education program.

Madeline Hunter has often said, "Education needs less time devoted to paper shuffling and more time devoted to teaching."[4] I agree. Therefore, the key concept in this program is simplicity—make the management system as brief as possible.

MANAGEMENT PROGRAM COMPONENTS

The following is an annotated listing of the various components of the competency-based education program.

a. **Student Tests**—These tests are packaged by grade level for each student. They are glued along the left side of the page so as to create a padding effect. All the test items for that grade level are included in the pad. These student tests should be housed in the classrooms of all teachers.

For each competency item, there is a Form A and a Form B pad. One Form A pad should be produced for every student. Form B pads are produced only for the classroom teachers. If a student needs to utilize Form B, simply remove the test item needed from the pad and copy it as many times as needed. By following this procedure, the school system can save money by cutting down on paper costs. Many students will demonstrate competency on Form A and will not need to be tested with Form B. Therefore, if you make a Form B for every student, many will not be used. Since the test items are quite cumbersome, having only the number of Form B's that are needed helps eliminate unneeded paper.

b. **Teacher Notebooks**—These materials are organized by grade level. Each teacher should have one of each at his or her grade level. These notebooks contain a list of all competency items plus the teacher directions and answer sheets for each competency. (Both Forms A and B.)

c. **Student Record Card**—This manila-colored oak tag board is to be used to record each individual student's demonstrated achievement of the competencies. It is designed to be housed in the student's cumulative folder. (Refer to Figure 3-10, page 88, and Figure 3-11, page 89.)

d. **Competency Class Rosters**—These optional forms are organized by grade level. They are designed to help the teacher diagnose class needs and deficiencies. Each teacher needs only one roster per year. The form contains space for thirty students. (Refer to Figure 3-12, page 90, and Figure 3-13, page 91.)

e. **Form 1**—This form is green and is designed to be the initial parent communication. It is organized by grade level and contains the competencies of that grade level. (Refer to Figure 3-14, page 92.)

f. **Form 2**—This form is buff or yellow. It is designed for the last parent-teacher conference. The purpose is to identify unmastered competencies for the student and parent as a basis for summer or home intervention. (Refer to Figure 3-15, page 93.)

COMPETENCY-BASED EDUCATION AND TECHNOLOGY

The goal of technology in competency-based education should be to save time. That should be the only goal. Teachers are the people who most need this timesaving device. Technology will also save administrators time in working with their responsibilities in competency-based education. However, the goal should focus on timesaving, for that is the only reason to involve technology in competency-based education.

There are computers and scanners that can do anything in the competency-based education process that teachers can do by hand. Furthermore, once teachers learn to use the technology properly, they can do it faster.

In the competency-based education process, teachers perform the following functions:

- administer the tests to one or more students
- grade tests of individual students
- do an item analysis for each student
- do an item analysis for the total class
- record the results on a class roster
- record the results on the student record card

All these functions can be performed on a scanner. Let's take each function and show how it can be performed on the scanner. (The scanner forms shown in Figures 4-16 through 4-19 are courtesy of National Computer Systems, Inc., and are reproduced with their permission.)

Administering the Test to One or More Students

Instead of answering on the test itself, the students would record their answers on an answer sheet such as the one shown in Figure 4-16.

Grading Tests of an Individual Student

To use scanner scoring, the teacher takes a blank answer sheet and darkens the circle of the correct response. Then, the teacher feeds the answer key through the scanner. This operation tells the scanner the correct responses for each item. Finally, the teacher feeds the student answer sheet through the scanner, which scores the student's test by marking the incorrect responses.

If the teacher gave the same competency items to many students, he or she simply feeds all the students' answer sheets through the scanner.

Item Analysis for Each Student

By looking at the answer sheet, the teacher can see which items the student missed. There will be a check by each incorrect response.

Figure 4-16

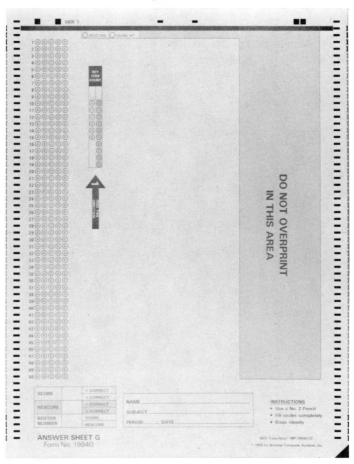

Item Analysis for the Total Class

After feeding all the individual students' answer sheets through the scanner, the teacher can then feed an item analysis answer sheet through the scanner. (See Figure 4-17.) The scanner will tabulate how many students answered each item incorrectly.

Record the Results on a Class Roster

Figure 4-18 shows a class roster that the scanner will record. The students are numbered, so each student's answer sheet must be fed through the scanner in the proper numerical order—not by name.

Figure 4-17

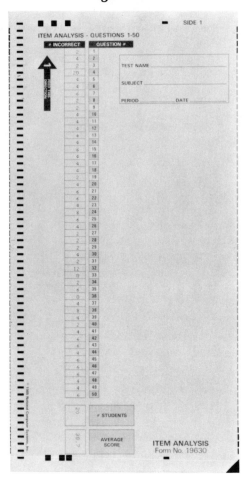

Record the Individual Student Results on a Student Record Card

A form like the one shown in Figure 4-19 could be used to take the competency test items. Instead of marking items on the test sheet, the student would circle in the answers on this form. Notice that the first competency tested at this grade level in math is round decimal numbers. Test items 1, 2, and 3 measure the skill.

The student pictured in Figure 4-19 answered all three test items correctly. Now drop down to items 26, 27, and 28 which all measure subtraction of whole numbers and numbers in mixed numeral form. The three checks beside the numbers indicate that the student missed all three of these questions.

Figure 4-18

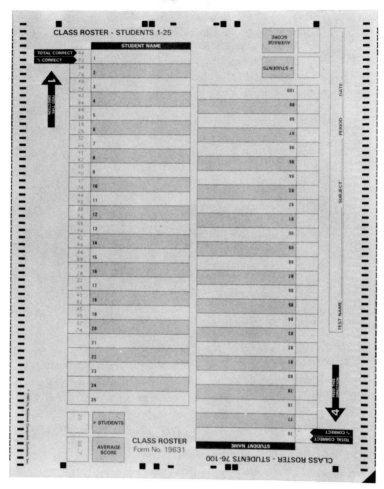

The student would continue taking the competency items on this form until all the checks disappear, which means that the student has demonstrated competency on all the items.

The form is then placed in the student's cumulative folder as a permanent record of the student's performance in the competency-based education program.

EVALUATING THE USE OF SCANNER SCORING IN COMPETENCY-BASED EDUCATION

In evaluating the use of scanner scoring in competency-based education, considerations other than timesaving must be addressed. The most significant consideration

Figure 4-19

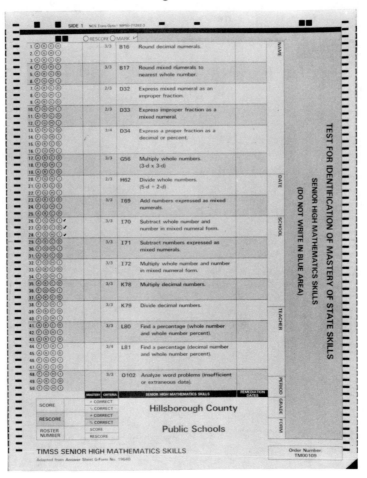

is, has the instructional emphasis of the competency-based education program remained intact? In other words, is the preassessment process still being used to diagnose the needs of students, and is instruction being planned to meet these needs?

These questions are asked because the use of scanner scoring can turn the competency-based education program into a testing program only. This conversion can occur very quickly; the availability of scanner scoring is a temptation to test all at once and grade all at once.

Scanner scoring for competency-based education will present some problems. The first is the resistance to technological change which always occurs. To combat this resistance, make scanner scoring an option for the teachers. Some teachers won't want it. Some teachers will not be able to use it effectively. For those teachers, it is a waste of time. So keep it an option for those who can benefit from its use.

A second problem is that the generic answer sheet won't perfectly match the format and numbering system of the individualized competency-based education program. If the students can't be taught to use the generic answer sheets without jeopardizing their performance, only two actions are feasible. They are: (1) develop personalized answer sheets, or (2) do not use scanner scoring.

In the final analysis, the evaluation of scanner scoring for competency-based education is really quite simple. Does it save teachers time without changing the goals, emphasis, and processes of the competency-based education program?

If the answer is yes, then scanner scoring should be offered as an option and will be a success. If the answer is no, then scanner scoring should be abandoned.

NOTES FOR CHAPTER 4

1. See Robert A. McCrachen and Marlene J. McCrachen, *Reading Is Only the Tiger's Tail* (San Rafael, California: Leswing Press, 1972)

2. As set forth in *Taxonomy of Educational Objectives: Cognitive Domain, Handbook I,* by B. S. Bloom (New York: David McKay, 1956).

3. S. Kaplan, *Student Resource Guide* (Inglewood, California: Inglewood Unified School District).

4. Madeline Hunter, *The Master Teacher* (El Segundo, California: T.I.P. Publication, 1985).

CHAPTER 5

Evaluation of Competency-Based Education

ACTIVITY 38

Evaluating the Competency-Based Education Program

There should be two types of evaluation, process and product. Product evaluation is the most objective. It should be based on how well the products of the program fared. In the case of competency-based education, the products are:

-the competencies
-the test items
-the grade level placement of the test items
-the recordkeeping documents
-the statistical data on the students
-the statistical data on the competency items
-the communication documents

Each of these should be evaluated based on:

-input from the educational staffs who implemented competency-based education
-input from students
-input from parents/community

The process evaluation should consist of an assessment of the following competency-based education processes:

-pretesting
-intervention
-posttesting
-communication among and between grade levels
-communication with parents
-recordkeeping process

Each of these should be evaluated based on:

–input from the educational staffs who implemented competency-based education
–input from students
–input from parents/community

Although competency-based education avoids group norms as a rule, the product evaluation calls for their use in the competency item analysis. At the end of the school year, it should be determined what percent of the students demonstrated achievement on each competency item.

Refer back to Figure 4-1, page 137, to see how the competency item evaluation is done. The competency item which this chart indicates needs close analysis is item #50, which asks the students to pick out the subjects in sentences.

The achievement level is 74 percent, which is the lowest achievement level of any of the third-grade competency items. The reason it is a topic of concern is that 279 students are going to carry over an unmastered third-grade competency into the fourth grade.

In statistical terms, 74 percent achievement is not an alarming figure. But in competency-based education terms, it needs to be addressed because the accumulation of unmastered competencies is harmful to the instructional program for obvious reasons. Additional information is needed to evaluate this competency. Therefore, it is appropriate to turn to the teachers and principals and ask these questions: "Is the 74 percent a cause for concern? Why would subjects have the lowest achievement rate? Is it expected?"

The answers to these questions would be as follows: "No, 74 percent achievement on subjects is not a cause for alarm. It is a difficult concept that needs reinforcement. The competency program does continue to assess subjects throughout the competency-based education program. Therefore, the student will be exposed to this competency again."

So long as achievement figures remain in the range of 70 to 80 to 90 percent, it can be assumed that, based on the data, the competencies are appropriate, the test items effective, and the grade level placement of items accurate.

However, in view of the fact that competency-based education is an instructional and not an evaluative program, information other than objective data is needed. This information is the subjective evaluation of the people involved in the program. These people should be asked to respond to questions in two general categories, the products or instruments of the competency-based education program, that is, the competency test items, the recordkeeping documents, and the communication documents, and the competency-based education process itself. Process is a broad term meaning everything that happens while competency-based education is being implemented. Specifically, it means the processes of preassessment, regular instruction, postassessment, intervention, communication among and between grade levels and with parents, and utilizing the recordkeeping system.

Figures 5-1 and 5-2 represent the kinds of questions that need to be addressed to gather the competency-based education product and process evaluation. The responses to these questions should be gathered through paper-and-pencil survey, and presented and discussed at a dialogue workshop. At this workshop, two types of input should be accepted—comments and recommendations. Comments can represent any number of people from one to the entire group. They should be recorded and distributed to the entire staff for their consideration.

Recommendations are accepted only if they receive a consensus from the entire group. Recommendations that are accepted represent a change of program or policy. See Figure 5-3 which illustrates how this dialogue workshop is conducted and shows examples of comments and recommendations.

CORRELATING COMPETENCY-BASED EDUCATION TEST RESULTS WITH STANDARDIZED TEST RESULTS

One of the temptations of school systems with competency-based education programs is to verify the value of the competency-based education program by checking standardized tests results. If the results on the standardized tests improve, the competency-based education program can then be given the credit. Such a use of competency-based education test results should be avoided except on test items which appear on both tests (competency-based education and standardized—norm-referenced) and measure the same skill or concept. The motivation for competency-based education should be based on the need to identify critical skills and the desire to organize and administer the instructional program to ensure the maximum possible achievement. If standardized test scores go up as a result of competency-based education, then you have another good public relations tool. However, it should not be the motivation for competency-based education nor the means of evaluating competency-based education.

ACTIVITY 39

For Revision, Repeat All Steps

The biggest difference between development and revision is that revision has the benefit of all the experience gained through development.

Figure 5-1

Competency Based Education (CBE)—Survey of Principals Involved

For several years now, much professional thought and energy has been devoted by the principals toward the development of courses of study and CBE objectives and testing. We believe that this effort displays high quality and feel that it is now time to begin taking a look at how CBE is working and what effects it may be having.

We appreciate your willingness to take the time to read this survey and are looking for your most candid thoughts and opinions. We would like to use the information you provide for planning in-service and making CBE as convenient and effective as possible.

CBE, YOUR STAFF, AND YOUR SCHOOL

How has CBE affected the instructional program of your school?

In what ways has use of CBE materials helped student learning?

How has CBE affected your management of your school?

How would you describe your staff's feelings about CBE?

Comment on successes and problems of each phase of the CBE program.

Pretest/Assessment:

Figure 5-1
(Continued)

Intervention:

Posttest/Assessment:

CBE AND YOU

Please describe the time demands that CBE has made on you and your reactions to this:

Please suggest in-service topics for the future:

CBE AND RECORDKEEPING

How would you evaluate the CBE recordkeeping procedures/materials?

– Your suggestions for improvement:

The following are some reasons for the recordkeeping. Please circle those pertinent to you:

Planning Instruction
Curriculum Improvement
Measuring Student Performance
Grouping of students

Figure 5-1
(Continued)

–Please list other uses you can think of:

CBE AND PARENTS

What parent reaction/response to CBE have you become aware of?

Do parents understand CBE?

–What suggestions do you have for improving parent understanding of CBE?

. . . AND FINALLY

What are your overall judgments and/or comments concerning CBE? (If there is anything else you would like to let us know, write it here.)

Figure 5-2

To: Teacher Representative for Competency-Based Education

From: Assistant Superintendent, Curriculum/Instruction

Topic: Meeting to Evaluate CBE Program

You have been involved in the planning, development, and implementation of the competency-based education program. This year the implementation phase (K–3) was initiated. Now it is time to evaluate the program and make the changes that the evaluation indicates are needed.

Figure 5-2
(Continued)

Therefore, you and other teacher representatives from all seven (7) of the Clermont County Local Schools will meet on June 11, from 8:30 A.M. until 12:00 noon at Holly Hill Elementary School to evaluate the Primary CBE program.

Between now and the end of school, please talk to your fellow staff members about the CBE program. Please find enclosed sample questions to help you gather input. Do not feel restricted by them. They are meant to be helpers. *Please do not give out written surveys.* One reason for conducting the evaluation in this manner is to avoid paperwork for the teachers. Try to get the information you need verbally or in other informal ways.

However, please come to the meeting knowledgeable concerning how your staff feels about the program. We want to make sure that all teachers have the opportunity for input.

To help with your expenses, a stipend of $20 will be paid for this half-day workshop.

Thank you for your interest in making your school the best it can be.

See you on June 11.

Sincerely,

Competency-Based Education (CBE)—Teacher Input Gathering Instrument

As you gather responses to the questions, record them in space provided at the end of each question.

CBE AND INSTRUCTION

In what ways has CBE enhanced or interfered with your teaching methods?

Has use of CBE provided you with any information which you have not had before to help your teaching? (If so, which information?)

Figure 5-2
(Continued)

In what ways has CBE enhanced or interfered with your teaching methods?

How accurately do the CBE objectives, with which you have been working, reflect/match the curriculum for your grade level?

CBE AND ASSESSMENT/TESTING

What is your overall feeling about the test items?

Are there any test items you feel should be changed? Which ones? How?

CBE AND YOU

Please describe the time demands that CBE has made on you and your reactions to this:

Please suggest ways or in-service topics to help make CBE less time-consuming, if you feel this is a problem:

CBE AND RECORDKEEPING

What comes to mind when you think of the CBE recordkeeping procedures/materials?

Figure 5-2
(Continued)

–Your suggestions for improvement:

The following are some reasons for the recordkeeping. Please circle those pertinent to you:

Planning Instruction
Curriculum Improvement
Measuring Student Performance
Grouping of Students

–Please list other uses you can think of:

CBE AND PARENTS

What parent reaction/responses to CBE have you experienced?

Do parents understand CBE?

–What suggestions do you have for improving parent understanding of CBE?

. . . AND FINALLY

What are your overall judgments and/or comments concerning CBE? (If there is anything else you would like to let us know, write it here.)

Figure 5-3

TO: Primary Principals

FROM:

TOPIC: Pertinent Information from the Primary Teachers' Competency-Based Education Evaluation

The teachers' input was of two kinds—comments and recommendations. Comments were unrestricted. Recommendations were heard, but accepted only if a clear consensus was present.

Needless to say, this report does not contain all comments, but represents what were, in my opinion, the most pertinent.

Recommendations

1. Kindergarten and first grade teachers should be given more time to give the preassessment.
2. Writing sample in the third grade should become two competencies, *form and content*. The student could be competent in one without being competent in the other. Make the starter words a complete sentence.
3. Every faculty should have an in-service at the beginning of the program each year.
4. A set of directions and informational clarifiers should be developed and be included at the beginning of each teacher packet.
5. Test items should not be on the back of a page.
6. Eliminate standardized tests in the third grade.
7. Put competency-based education on computer for intervention and makeup testing.
8. Reduce size of manila folder.

Comments

1. Many test items need format changes. These are too numerous to mention. Examples are coins, clock hands, change words from horizontal to vertical position, etc.
2. There was a discussion on the repetition caused by using both competency-based education and reading programs such as "scantron" or other basal text materials.
3. Recordkeeping procedure good.
4. Parent communication forms good.

Figure 5-3
(Continued)

COMPETENCY-BASED EDUCATION
TESTING EVALUATION MEETING

I. POSITIVE INPUT ON CBE PROGRAM

II. CONSTRUCTIVE INPUT ON CBE COMPONENTS

    A. CLASS ROSTER
    B. STUDENT MANAGEMENT CARD
    C. PARENT LETTER
    D. BROCHURE
    E. TEACHER MATERIALS/IN-SERVICE NEEDS
    F. TEST PACKAGING
    G. ANSWER SHEET

III. CONSTRUCTIVE INPUT ON INDIVIDUALIZED TEST ITEMS

    A. LANGUAGE ARTS
    B. MATH

Content _____

School _____

Grade Level _____

Teacher _____

Principal _____

Date _____

CBE TEST EVALUATION MEETING

I. Positive Input:

    CBE Test _____

    _____

    _____

    CBE Test Revisions _____

    _____

    _____

Figure 5-3
(Continued)

II. Constructive Input on CBE Components:

   A. Class Roster _____

       _____

      Needed Corrections _____

   B. Student Management Card _____

       _____

      Needed Corrections _____

   C. Parent Letter _____

       _____

       _____

   D. Brochure _____

       _____

       _____

   E. Teacher Materials/In-Service _____

       _____

       _____

   F. Test Packaging _____

       _____

       _____

   G. Answer Sheet _____

      At Which Grade Level _____

       _____

       _____

III. Constructive Input on Individualized Test Items

_____ Item #   _____ Format   Comments

        _____ Directions   _____

        _____ Type   _____

        _____ Spacing   _____

        _____ Front/Back   _____

        _____ Spelling   _____

Figure 5-3
(Continued)

_____ Item # _____ Content   Comments

_____ Pictures   _____

_____ Clarity   _____

_____ Validity   _____

_____

_____

_____ Teacher Answer Sheets   Comments
Needed Corrections

_____

_____

_____

_____

_____

CHAPTER 6

"Running the Roadblocks": Making Competency-Based Education Work

One of the practitioner's pet peeves about theory or theoretical thinking is that theorists usually don't speak to practical problems. To the practitioner, a theory is a useless entity until it is practiced. When it is practiced, theory oftentimes encounters problems that were not addressed in the theory. Of course, if the theory is valid, it can and will overcome the problems. However, it seems to me that the process of overcoming these "roadblocks" is enhanced if the possible problems are articulated simultaneously with the theory.

Therefore, this chapter will address the kinds of opposition that competency-based education with instructional emphasis is likely to encounter. If the theory behind competency-based education with instructional emphasis is sound, and if these oppositions can be successfully negotiated, it can be assumed that competency-based education with instructional emphasis will be successful.

ROADBLOCKS ENCOUNTERED BY EDUCATIONAL PROGRAMS

Educational programs usually run into three kinds of opposition. They are:

1. Obstacles—which "stand in the way or oppose."
2. Constraints—"a restriction or limitation caused by other processes."
3. Facades—"a fake, superficial, or artificial effort."

Competency-based education with instructional emphasis will encounter all three of these kinds of opposition. It will be helpful if each of these terms is broken down into specific descriptors. It will also serve the purpose better if the discussion is limited to the major obstacles, constraints, and facades to competency-based education with instructional emphasis. To list all the obstacles, constraints, and facades to anything would be laborious and ludicrous as well as nearly impossible. It would certainly be boring.

The major obstacles to competency-based education with instructional emphasis are:

1. That competency-based education with instructional emphasis is not really competency-based education because the program is not the sole criterion for graduation or promotion.
2. That it is not compatible with the modern philosophy of education needed for the current knowledge explosion and technical advancement.
3. That it is not compatible with the theories of individualization.
4. That it is too costly.
5. That local school districts do not have the human or material resources to accomplish competency-based education with instructional emphasis.

The major constraints to competency-based education with instructional emphasis are:

1. It is a duplication of other recordkeeping procedures (such as basal text management systems).
2. It is a duplication of standardized testing.
3. The teachers don't have time to properly implement the program due to:
   –other duties
   –too many scheduled programs

The major facades to competency-based education with instructional emphasis are:

1. Teacher attitudes and behavior which are convenient means to avoid accountability. It has already been stated under constraints that time is a problem. It always is in any quality program. Constraints are legitimate concerns. The attitude being pursued here is a facade. It is not legitimate. However, some teachers use the lack of time as an excuse to not implement competency-based education with instructional emphasis properly when, in fact, it is not a problem. People use facades that closely resemble obstacles or constraints. That is the only way they can get away with them.
2. Traditional teaching practices and modes that do not include preassessment. This facade involves the basic attitudes that the teacher knows what students can and cannot do, or what students know and do not know, without any preassessment. Also inherent in this attitude is that curriculum is based on grade level and is basically uniform. Therefore, instruction is content-based and convergent, rather than student-based and thus, divergent.

STRATEGIES FOR OVERCOMING THE ROADBLOCKS

Identifying the obstacles, constraints, and facades to educational programs is not too difficult. They hit the practitioner between the eyes on a regular basis. After a couple of decades, the practitioner knows all of them "by heart." How to overcome them will spark considerably more interest. So let's run those "roadblocks," one at a time.

Overcoming Obstacles

Obstacle #1: Competency-based education with instructional emphasis is not really competency-based education because the program is not the sole criterion for promotion and/or graduation.

The biggest obstacle to competency-based education with instructional emphasis is the common perception that it means competency testing only. This perception is the result of the early efforts in competency which centered not only on testing but specifically on minimum competency testing.

In addition, those early efforts usually involved a large scale effort, such as the statewide minimum competency testing program in states such as Florida. These testing programs were periodic, not ongoing, and were used mostly at the secondary level as an additional requirement for graduation.

It is difficult to understand why anyone would view competency this way. These earlier efforts have accomplished nothing that the standardized tests were not already doing. That's why they have failed thus far.

The real potential of competency-based education lies in the instructional realm developed and implemented at the local level so that the true curriculum can be assessed and achievement verified.

Since competency-based education with instructional emphasis does have a testing phase, the public, and some educators, automatically assume that two results will occur from the testing phase: (1) that group norms will be figured, publicized, and analyzed, and (2) that students must pass the competency tests to be promoted or to graduate.

Because of this perception, it is also felt that any competency program that does not control promotion/retention and graduation is a weak effort without sufficient clout to be meaningful. Until this perception is changed, competency-based education with instructional emphasis cannot gain the staff and public support it needs to be successful.

Therefore, the obstacle is twofold. First of all, to get the school community to *understand* that competency-based education involves more than assessment and testing. And secondly, get the school community to *accept* that promotion and/or retention is a multifactoral decision that competency results strengthen through more data. However, it should not supplant the process.

In attempting to get the school community to understand that competency-based education is more than testing, emphasize and explain that testing programs only identify or verify shortcomings and strengths. After these shortcomings have been verified, it is the instructional program that offers the avenue for improvement.

In attempting to get the school community to accept the results of competency-based education with instructional emphasis as one criterion rather than the total criteria for promotion decisions, it is comforting to know that educational research is supportive. People learn at different rates and at different speeds. We can't put everybody on the same track. To attempt to make total competency achievement necessary for promotion to another grade level would cause the same problems as the previous practice of failing students without regard to age and other sociological factors.

The key to overcoming this obstacle does not lie within the intellect. It lies within your "gut." You've got to have the "guts" to take these issues on. If you do, you will have all the evidence, that is, research, experience, and common sense, on your side. You've got to be willing to stand up to the traditional, oversimplistic view of education. This view involves the belief that only recently have we graduated students who are not academically at the twelfth grade level. This is, of course, erroneous. It also involves the belief that all people are relatively equal in intellectual ability, which is erroneous also.

In combating this view, don't be afraid to take the stance that the educational process is complex. Defend the position that competency is individually based and that the important question is how a student does in relation to his or her own ability.

Obstacle #2: Competency-based education with instructional emphasis is not compatible with modern educational philosophy due to the knowledge explosion and technological advancement.

It is because of the knowledge explosion that competency-based education with instructional emphasis is such a viable concept. It is true that schools cannot teach it all anymore, if they ever could. This fact only makes fundamental skills more vital. Instead of striving for comprehensive content coverage, schools should concentrate on basic skills which will give the student the tools necessary to become a lifelong learner. The verification of the accomplishment of these skills is absolutely necessary. Competency-based education with instructional emphasis will accomplish this.

Obstacle #3: Competency-based education with instructional emphasis is not compatible with individualization of instruction.

This obstacle would be insurmountable if optimal competency was being practiced. Optimal competency would be confining to the individualization of instruction. Basic competency is not. Any student is going to be involved with the learning of basic skills. Any flexibility needed after the learning of basic skills will not involve competency and will therefore be available.

Obstacle #4: Competency-based education with instructional emphasis is too costly.

Overcome this obstacle by refusing to discuss the cost of competency in isolation. It should be considered in the total context of the organizational budget. In that way, competency can be considered equally with all other budget items. Then, as the priorities are established, competency will be funded as the school's priorities dictate. The significant point is that the question concerning competency funding has been changed from, "Do we fund competency?" to "At what level do we fund competency?"

When the ongoing funding has been established, it is assured that competency will have a place in the budget. Some years, when money is tight, the budget may not be sufficient. But the belt tightening that occurs will occur to all the school programs. That's only fair. Being an integral part of the budget means that competency won't be a part of the "frills" cutbacks.

Obstacle #5: Local school districts do not have the human or material resources to successfully accomplish competency-based education with instructional emphasis.

The obstacle will be present only if the school district does not have a high curriculum/instruction priority and orientation. What does that mean? It means that if the superintendent or his central office administrators do not give curriculum and instruction any attention, time, or money, then there exists little or no orientation to the educational facet of the school operation. It means that if the school principals are good managers, but not instructional leaders, then the competency program will suffer.

If a school system does not have the human resources to successfully accomplish competency-based education with instructional emphasis then the real obstacle is a personnel problem. The administrators are not educational leaders. If they aren't willing or able to become educational leaders, then that problem should be addressed.

Every school has teachers. The same statements can be made about them as were just made about administrators.

If the teachers don't have the desire or the ability to establish competencies, select test items, or do the other educational tasks necessary to implement competency-based education with instructional emphasis, then a more important problem is present. That is, of course, staff incompetency. That problem can be attacked at the in-service or the evaluation process, whichever is called for.

The basic message here is that a school system with competent and motivated administrators and teachers has the resources necessary to plan, develop, and implement a competency-based education program. Conversely, any school system that does not have competent administrators and/or teachers admittedly does not have the human resources to plan, develop, and implement competency-based education. But big deal! This kind of school system cannot produce any quality educational program.

If this obstacle is present, the obstacle is not to competency-based education with instructional emphasis, but to quality education, period. Something should be done, but the absence of competency-based education is not that something. To admit to this obstacle is to admit to self-incompetence. No thanks.

Overcoming Constraints

Constraint #1: Competency-based education with instructional emphasis is a duplication of other recordkeeping procedures (such as basal text management systems).

This is the most legitimate teacher complaint concerning competency-based education. The duplication occurs in the testing phase. The solution is simple. If there is a duplication between the competency test and the basal text, require the use of only one testing measure. If the teacher wishes to use multiple test items, it should be permissible, but not required.

To be successful, competency-based education must enhance instruction. To require duplication of testing will only hinder instruction. It will take up too much instruction time and cause morale problems among the staff.

To ensure that the use of any testing item other than the competency items is valid, do a correlation of the learning objectives between the competency-based education program and the basal text. Make sure they are measuring the same outcome.

Constraint #2: Competency-based education is a duplication of standardized testing.

This constraint is present only where there is no understanding of the purposes of standardized testing and/or competency-based education testing and the differences between them. The purposes of standardized testing are program evaluation through comparative data and individual evaluation through comparative data. It is based on a national curriculum. The purposes of competency-based education testing are: (a) to verify individual student's achievement or nonachievement of the critical skills and concepts of the local curriculum, and (b) to provide diagnostic information for instructional planning and grouping. It is based on the local curriculum.

Through in-service activities and other communication means, the differences in the purposes of these two testing processes should be emphasized. Once people understand their differences, they can see the value of both.

Constraint #3: Teachers do not have the time to properly implement competency-based education with instructional emphasis due to: (a) other teaching duties, and (b) other nonteaching duties.

This constraint involves judgment about priorities. There is no claim that competency-based education is not valuable, just the claim that because of other things, there is no time for it. So the real problem is that of too much to do in the time provided.

If, in fact, this is true, then the time management solution should consider all the tasks that the teacher is being asked to perform and eliminate the ones that are providing the least contribution to the teaching and learning process.

If competency-based education is among the tasks that are contributing least to the teaching/learning process, then it should be curtailed. But if it is contributing well, then some other tasks will have to go.

The key to responding to this constraint is to consider competency-based education in conjunction with all teaching tasks and let it stand on its merit. Teachers need more time for teaching, and if used properly, competency-based education is an integral part of that teaching.

Overcoming Facades

There is no need to reiterate the facades to competency-based education. Remember that facades are fake, superficial. They are not legitimate. Don't legitimize them by giving them an extended audience. Pursue the facade long enough to see if the facade might really be an obstacle or a constraint. If it is, it must be dealt with because obstacles and constraints are legitimate. However, if it is a facade, expose it for what it really represents. Smoke it out and then dismiss it quickly.

People pursuing facades are involved in negative, nonproductive behavior. People pursuing obstacles and constraints are involved in positive, productive behavior. Pursue the solution to obstacles and constraints. Use one of two strategies with facades. Either expose them or ignore them. And, by the way, do it quickly. These are not worth a lot of your time.

A FINAL WORD

The positive aspect of confronting obstacles and constraints is that responding to them improves the competency-based education program in three ways. Response to these problems:

1. Improves both the efficiency and the effectiveness of the program.
2. Puts the program in a constant state of being open to improvement.
3. Provides a mechanism for the improvement of the program from the bottom up.

Regardless of how well the planning, development, and implementation are done, competency-based education will develop obstacles and constraints. The positive and continual response to them enhances the probability that the program will be in a continual state of improvement.

Language Arts
Competency Test Items

Grades K-7

NOTE

Some of the following competency test items may not be self-explanatory, especially at the primary grade level. Teacher directions for these primary test items are frequently given orally; thus they do not appear on the student's test form.

In these instances, refer to Figure 3-5 on pages 60 to 72, which lists the student Pupil Performance Objectives that correspond to these test items and numbers. Correlating the Pupil Performance Objectives with the competency test items gives a clearer understanding of the test items and the directions needed for their use.

As noted earlier in the text, it is recommended that teachers use two forms, Form A and Form B, for each competency test item. Since each student is given more than one opportunity to pass the test, and since these testing opportunities may occur close together (sometimes only a few days apart), a second form for testing the competency is desirable. For a detailed description of how the assessment and testing is done, refer to Chapter 2, pages 36 to 37, and to Chapter 4, pages 138 to 167.

LANGUAGE ARTS COMPETENCY TEST ITEM

COURSE OF STUDY OBJECTIVE #_____   FORM _____ (A or B)

COMPETENCY TEST ITEM #<u>1</u>   GRADE K

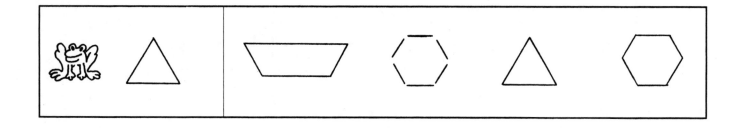

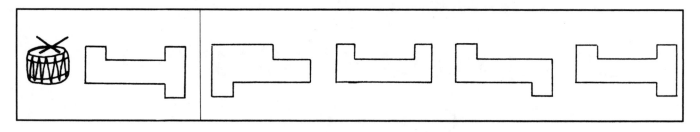

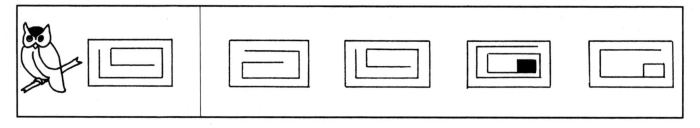

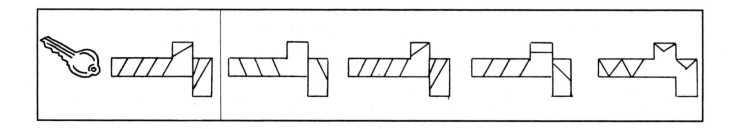

Name _____

Number correct _____ % correct _____

COURSE OF STUDY OBJECTIVE #_____   FORM _____ (A or B)

COMPETENCY TEST ITEM #2   GRADE K

	n	m	h	n	t

	t	f	t	k	l

	P	O	G	A	P

	B	P	R	B	D

Name _____

Number correct _____% correct _____

LANGUAGE ARTS COMPETENCY TEST ITEM

COURSE OF STUDY OBJECTIVE # _____

COMPETENCY TEST ITEM #3

FORM _____ (A or B)

GRADE K

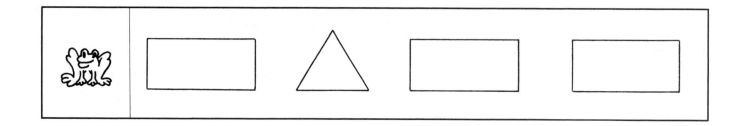

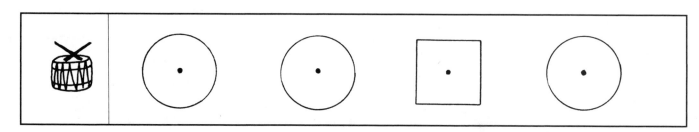

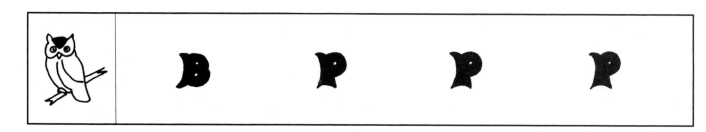

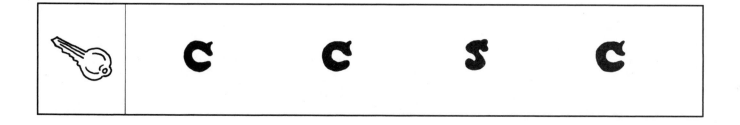

Name _____

Number correct _____ % correct _____

LANGUAGE ARTS COMPETENCY TEST ITEM

COURSE OF STUDY OBJECTIVE # _____

FORM _____ (A or B)

COMPETENCY TEST ITEM #4

GRADE K

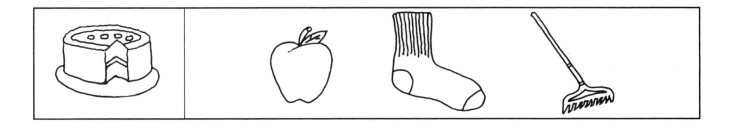

Name _____

Number correct _____ % correct _____

COURSE OF STUDY OBJECTIVE # _____   FORM _____ (A or B)

COMPETENCY TEST ITEM #5   GRADE K

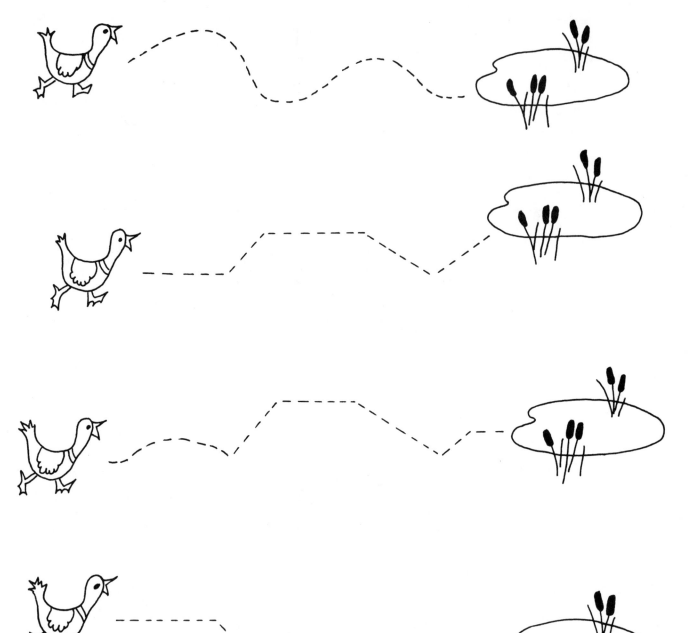

Name _____

Number correct _____% correct _____

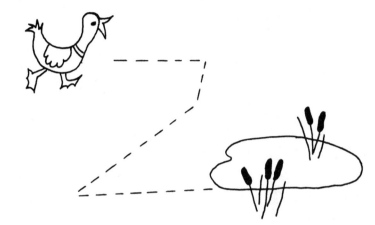

Name _____

Number correct _____% correct _____

🐸	n	v	m	w

🥁	x	y	n	v

🦉	h	d	k	e

🔑	y	t	q	l

Name _____

Number correct _____ % correct _____

COURSE OF STUDY OBJECTIVE # _____   FORM _____ (A or B)

COMPETENCY TEST ITEM #8   GRADE K

| | P | F | D | E |

| | Q | P | R | D |

| | V | X | M | W |

| | Z | N | W | R |

Name _____

Number correct _____% correct _____

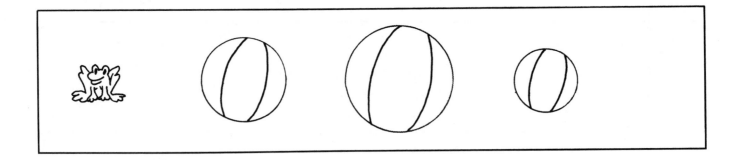

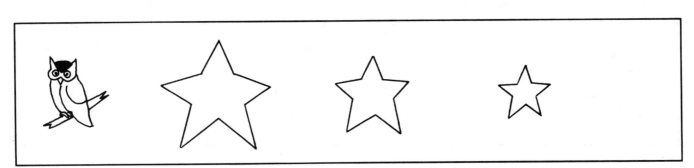

Name _____

Number correct _____% correct _____

LANGUAGE ARTS COMPETENCY TEST ITEM

COURSE OF STUDY OBJECTIVE # _____   FORM _____ (A or B)

COMPETENCY TEST ITEM #10   GRADE K

Name _____

Number correct _____% correct _____

LANGUAGE ARTS COMPETENCY TEST ITEM

COURSE OF STUDY OBJECTIVE # _____   FORM _____ (A or B)

COMPETENCY TEST ITEM #11   GRADE 1

| 1. <u>star</u> | fox | bed | car |

| 2. <u>lamp</u> | fan | stamp | boat |

| 3. <u>suit</u> | fan | pig | fruit |

| 4. <u>kite</u> | light | horn | pig |

Name _____

Number correct _____% correct _____

LANGUAGE ARTS COMPETENCY TEST ITEM

COURSE OF STUDY OBJECTIVE #_____   FORM _____ (A or B)

COMPETENCY TEST ITEM #12   GRADE 1

1. | M N O __ Q R |

    D   S   P   T

2. | __ I J K L M |

    E   H   N   P

3. | B __ D E F G |

    A   R   O   C

4. | S T U V __ X |

    Y   Q   W   Z

Name _____

Number correct _____% correct _____

COURSE OF STUDY OBJECTIVE # _____

COMPETENCY TEST ITEM #13

FORM _____ (A or B)

GRADE 1

1. _____

2. _____

3. _____

4. _____

Name _____

Number correct _____ % correct _____

LANGUAGE ARTS COMPETENCY TEST ITEM

COURSE OF STUDY OBJECTIVE # _____

FORM _____ (A or B)

COMPETENCY TEST ITEM #14

GRADE 1

© 1987 by Prentice-Hall, Inc.

1.　　　　r　　　　d　　　　g　　　　b

2.　　　　m　　　　p　　　　n　　　　s

3.　　　　b　　　　m　　　　d　　　　p

4.　　　　s　　　　t　　　　c　　　　l

Name _____

Number correct _____% correct _____

LANGUAGE ARTS COMPETENCY TEST ITEM

COURSE OF STUDY OBJECTIVE # _____

FORM _____ (A or B)

COMPETENCY TEST ITEM #15

GRADE 1

1.    a   e   i   o   u

2.   a   e   i   o   u

3.    a   e   i   o   u

4.   a   e   i   o   u

5.   a   e   i   o   u

Name _____

Number correct _____ % correct _____

LANGUAGE ARTS COMPETENCY TEST ITEM

COURSE OF STUDY OBJECTIVE # _____   FORM _____ (A or B)

COMPETENCY TEST ITEM #16   GRADE 1

1.    a   e   i   o   u

2. 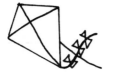   a   e   i   o   u

3.    a   e   i   o   u

4.    a   e   i   o   u

5.   a   e   i   o   u

Name _____

Number correct _____% correct _____

COURSE OF STUDY OBJECTIVE # _____   FORM _____ (A or B)

COMPETENCY TEST ITEM #17   GRADE 1

© 1987 by Prentice-Hall, Inc.

1.	fl	br	bl	sl

2.	sm	sn	sp	st

3.	gr	dr	pr	tr

4.	sk	sl	st	sm

Name _____

Number correct _____ % correct _____

1.   th   sh   wh   ch

2.   wh   sh   ch   th

3.   wh   th   sh   ch

4.   sh   th   wh   ch

Name _____

Number correct _____% correct _____

1.

_____   _____   _____

- - - - - - - - - - - - - - - - - -   - - - - - - - - - - - - - - - - - -   - - - - - - - - - - - - - - - - - -

_____   _____   _____

2.

_____   _____   _____

- - - - - - - - - - - - - - - - - -   - - - - - - - - - - - - - - - - - -   - - - - - - - - - - - - - - - - - -

_____   _____   _____

Name _____

3.

4.

Name _____

Number correct _____% correct _____

COURSE OF STUDY OBJECTIVE #_____   FORM _____ (A or B)

COMPETENCY TEST ITEM #20A   GRADE 1

Tom likes to read books. He has big books and little books. He has funny books. He has books about pets. He has books about people. He reads all kinds of books.

1. Circle the best name for this story.

>   Pets

>   Tom's Books

>   Funny Stories

2. Tom likes to _____.

>   run

>   play

>   read

Name _____

My friend is six. We like to play. We jump rope. We play ball. We ride bikes. We have fun.

1. Circle the best name for this story.

   My Bike

   My Ball

   My Friend and I

2. My friend and I _____.

   read

   play

   sing

Name _____

Jan went to a farm. She saw a cow. She saw ducks in a lake. A hen sat on some eggs. A horse ate some grass. Jan liked the farm.

1. Circle the best name for this story.

   Jan Visits a Farm
   Jan Visits a Zoo
   Jan Visits a City

2. Jan saw a _____.

   pig
   cow
   dog

Name _____

COURSE OF STUDY OBJECTIVE #_____   FORM _____ (A or B)

COMPETENCY TEST ITEM <u>#20D</u>   GRADE 1

It began to snow. The children were happy. They wanted to play in the snow. They wanted to ride on sleds. They wanted to throw snowballs. They wanted to make a snowman.

1. Circle the best name for this story.

   A Rainy Day
   A Sunny Day
   A Snowy Day

2. It began to _____.

   snow

   rain

   sleet

Name _____

Question #1 A–D	Question #2 A–D
Main Idea	Facts
Number correct _____%_____	Number correct _____%_____

LANGUAGE ARTS COMPETENCY TEST ITEM

COURSE OF STUDY OBJECTIVE # _____   FORM _____ (A or B)

COMPETENCY TEST ITEM #21   GRADE 1

A.   dog   is   the   big
_____

_____

1.   boy   the   games   likes
_____

_____

2.   friend   my   happy   is
_____

_____

3.   made   I   a   cake
_____

_____

4.   blue   is   bike   my
_____

_____

Name _____

Number correct _____% correct _____

© 1987 by Prentice-Hall, Inc.

1.

pig

2.

frog

3.

bat

4.

drum

Name _____

Number correct _____ % correct _____

COURSE OF STUDY OBJECTIVE #_____   FORM _____ (A or B)

COMPETENCY TEST ITEM #23   GRADE 1

1.   the dog is black.

2.   my friend is funny.

3.   games are fun to play.

4.   milk is good to drink.

Name _____

Number correct _____% correct _____

LANGUAGE ARTS COMPETENCY TEST ITEM

A.   <u>see</u>   play   top

1.   <u>come</u>   down   blue

2.   <u>over</u>   look   put

3.   <u>from</u>   get   can

4.   <u>ten</u>   run   up

Name _____

Number correct _____% correct _____

1.

$\mathscr{u}$

w   u   m   x

2.

$\mathscr{q}$

g   p   q   z

3.

$\mathscr{d}$

f   b   d   j

4.

$\mathscr{m}$

h   n   b   m

Name _____

Number correct _____% correct _____

COURSE OF STUDY OBJECTIVE # _____   FORM _____ (A or B)

COMPETENCY TEST ITEM #26   GRADE 2

1. $\mathcal{S}$

T   I   S   H

2. $\mathcal{R}$

S   U   T   R

3. $\mathcal{B}$

D   P   B   H

4. $\mathcal{M}$

Y   N   W   M

Name _____

Number correct _____% correct _____

1.

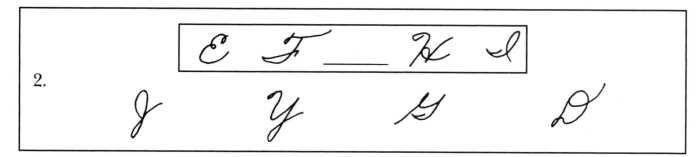

2.

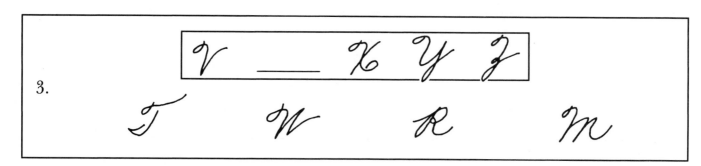

3.

4.

Name _____

Number correct _____ % correct _____

1.   __happy__

    wet   sad   give   fast

2.   ___out___

    is   go   in   over

3.   ___old___

    bad   new   next   from

4.   __hot__

    now   day   tall   cold

Name _____

Number correct _____% correct _____

LANGUAGE ARTS COMPETENCY TEST ITEM

COURSE OF STUDY OBJECTIVE #_____   FORM _____ (A or B)

COMPETENCY TEST ITEM #29   GRADE 2

1.   ___little___

    big   down   small   open

2.   ___pretty___

    beautiful   ugly   stop   work

3.   ___begin___

    last   start   help   end

4.   ___fast___

    slow   sad   large   quick

Name _____

Number correct _____% correct _____

1.   ld   ng   nd   lk

2.   ft   ng   sm   st

3.   nk   nd   ld   lk

4.   ld   nd   ft   st

Name _____

Number correct _____% correct _____

1.   ch   sh   th   ck

2.   ck   ch   sh   th

3.   ch   th   ck   sh

4.   sh   ch   th   ck

Name _____

Number correct _____% correct _____

Our class went on a trip to the zoo. We saw many animals. The animals lived in cages and behind bars. We ate our lunch on the grass. We all bought ice cream to eat going home on the bus.

1. Circle the best name for this story.

   Zoo Animals
   Class Trip to the Zoo
   The Bus Ride

2. The children ate their lunch _____.

   at home
   on the bus
   at the zoo

3. What happened after the children bought ice cream?

   They went home.
   They saw the animals.
   They ate lunch.

Name _____

Jack smelled smoke. He saw that an old red building was on fire. He raced to a phone and called the firefighters. The firefighters sprayed water on the building. Soon the fire was out. The firefighters thanked Jack.

1. Circle the best name for this story.

> Jack Reports a Fire
> The Fire Truck
> An Old Red Building

2. Jack raced to the _____.

> firehouse
> burned building
> phone

3. What happened before Jack saw the building on fire?

> Jack called the firefighters.
> Jack smelled smoke.
> Jack raced to the phone.

Name _____

Something shiny on the sidewalk caught Jan's eye as she walked home. It was a lovely gold ring. Jan picked it up. She took the ring to the police station. A man came for the ring the very next day. After a police officer gave the man the ring, the man left something for Jan. It was a dollar.

1. Circle the best name for this story.

   The Police Officer

   The Police Station

   A Reward for Jan

2. Jan found a _____.

   penny

   ring

   dollar

3. What happened after Jan gave the ring to the police?

   A man gave Jan a dollar.

   Something caught Jan's eye.

   Jan found a dollar.

Name _____

When we went camping, the first thing we did was put up our tent. Then we took a long hike. When we returned from the hike, we built a fire. We were all getting hungry, so we roasted hot dogs. Later, we sat around the fire telling stories. Then we went to bed.

1. Circle the best name for this story.

> The Long Hike
> Our Camping Trip
> Ghost Stories

2. The hike made us _____.

> hungry
> angry
> sad

3. What happened after the campers built a fire?

> They set up their tents.
> They went for a hike.
> They roasted hot dogs.

Name _____

Question #1 A-D	Question #2 A-D	Question #3 A-D
Main Idea	Facts	Sequence
Number correct	Number correct	Number correct
____ % ____	____ % ____	____ % ____

1. May bill come to the park?

2. We made a picture for jane.

3. The name of my kitten is buffy.

4. The dog jumped on tim.

Name _____

Number correct _____% correct _____

1. Don and i will ride in our new car.

2. Pat was lost and i found her.

3. Jim and i saw a light in the old house.

4. For my birthday, i got a dog.

Name _____

Number correct _____% correct _____

COURSE OF STUDY OBJECTIVE # _____   FORM _____ (A or B)

COMPETENCY TEST ITEM #35   GRADE 2

1.   dr. Jones   Dr. Jones

2.   ms. Black   Ms. Black

3.   Mr. Brown   mr. Brown

4.   mrs. Baker   Mrs. Baker

Name _____

Number correct _____% correct _____

LANGUAGE ARTS COMPETENCY TEST ITEM

COURSE OF STUDY OBJECTIVE #_____

FORM _____ (A or B)

COMPETENCY TEST ITEM #36

GRADE 2

1. Can snakes hear

.   ?

2. Children like to play

.   ?

3. The boy ran to the store

.   ?

4. Did it snow last night

.   ?

Name _____

Number correct _____% correct _____

COURSE OF STUDY OBJECTIVE #_____   FORM _____ (A or B)

COMPETENCY TEST ITEM #37   GRADE 2

1.   Mr Fox   Mr. Fox

2.   Dr. White   Dr White

3.   Ms. Day   Ms Day

4.   Mrs Hill   Mrs. Hill

Name _____

Number correct _____% correct _____

LANGUAGE ARTS COMPETENCY TEST ITEM

COURSE OF STUDY OBJECTIVE #_____

COMPETENCY TEST ITEM #38

FORM _____ (A or B)

GRADE 2

1.   February, 16 1982   February 16, 1982

2.   April 20 1984   April 20, 1984

3.   July 7, 1972   July 7 1972,

4.   September 30 1980   September 30, 1980

Name _____

Number correct _____% correct _____

LANGUAGE ARTS COMPETENCY TEST ITEM

COURSE OF STUDY OBJECTIVE # _____   FORM _____ (A or B)

COMPETENCY TEST ITEM #39   GRADE 2

1.

| Monday | Tuesday | _____ | Thursday | Friday |

Sunday   Wednesday   Saturday

2.

| _____ | Monday | Tuesday | Wednesday | Thursday |

Friday   Thursday   Sunday

3.

| Friday | _____ | Sunday | Monday | Tuesday |

Saturday   Wednesday   Thursday

4.

| Tuesday | Wednesday | _____ | Friday | Saturday |

Sunday   Monday   Thursday

Name _____

Number correct _____% correct _____

1. The boy ran home.

2. The frog jumped into the water.

3. The man painted the house.

4. The girl beat the drum.

Name _____

Number correct _____ % correct _____

LANGUAGE ARTS COMPETENCY TEST ITEM

COURSE OF STUDY OBJECTIVE #_____

COMPETENCY TEST ITEM #<u>41</u>

FORM _____ (A or B)

GRADE 3

1. _____

2. _____

3. _____

4. _____

5. _____

6. _____

7. _____

8. _____

9. _____

10. _____

11. _____

12. _____

13. _____

14. _____

15. _____

16. _____

17. _____

18. _____

19. _____

20. _____

21. _____

22. _____

23. _____

24. _____

Name _____

Number correct _____% correct _____

1. <u>snow</u>

   cold   wet   man   sky

2. <u>in</u>

   out   side   of   near

3. <u>base</u>

   ball   bat   glove   yard

4. <u>play</u>

   fun   out   jump   ground

© 1987 by Prentice-Hall, Inc.

Name _____

Number correct _____ % correct _____

1. The _____ is hot.

       son   sun

2. We _____ the game.

       won   one

3. _____ are beautiful animals.

       Dear   Deer

4. Mother put _____ candles on the cake.

       ate   eight

Name _____

Number correct _____% correct _____

1.	unhappy	happy	un	hap

2.	kindness	ness	kind	kin

3.	return	re	urn	turn

4.	fearless	ear	fear	less

Name _____

Number correct _____% correct _____

In Portugal, they have a day called the Festival of the Trays. On this day, 600 girls wear trays on their heads. The trays look like hats. On top of each tray is a basket that holds up a huge tower of bread. In fact, the towers of bread are often as tall as the girls are!

The girls march into the city. There they give the bread to the poor. It is a day in Portugal when everyone gives thanks that there is enough food for all.

1. Circle the best title for this story.

    People of Portugal   Festival in Portugal   Hats of Portugal

2. During the Festival of the Trays, the baskets are piled with _____.

    fruit   vegetables   bread

3. After the girls march into the city they give food to _____.

    the poor   animals   the rich

4. The Festival of Trays is held to _____.

    honor the girls of Portugal
    give thanks for food
    have a vacation

Name _____

Spiders do not try to bite people. If you touched a spider by mistake, it might take a little nip out of you. But that is because you look so big, and it is trying to defend itself. Most spiders do not have poison. The black widow has some. You could get sick if you touched one, and it bit you. People don't die from it. A tarantula is another poisonous spider. It is so afraid of people that it hides most of the time.

Spiders can all do something wonderful. They give off silky threads from their stomachs. Many spiders, but not all, build webs with these silky threads. The webs have many different patterns. Some are only a few centimeters wide, and others stretch for many meters. Spiders use their webs to catch insects.

1. Circle the best title for this story.

    Tarantula   Facts About Spiders   Black Widow

2. Most spiders do not have _____.

    silky threads   legs   poison

3. After they spin their webs, spiders _____.

    spin new webs
    wait to catch insects
    go to sleep

4. A spider will bite you because _____.

    it is trying to defend itself
    it hates people
    it is a mean insect

Name _____

Elizabeth Anderson was born in 1836 in a small town in Suffolk, England. When she was 24 years old, she decided that she wanted to become a doctor. There were very few women doctors at that time.

Since no medical schools would take her, she studied on her own at London hospitals and with private teachers. She worked very hard.

In 1865 she received a license to practice medicine. She worked at St. Mary's, a small London clinic. In 1870 she received a Doctor of Medicine degree in Paris. She returned to London as Dr. Anderson and started a school of medicine there for women.

1. Circle the best title for this story.

    Woman Nurse   Famous Teacher   Woman Doctor

2. Elizabeth received her Doctor of Medicine degree in _____.

    1836   1870   1865

3. After she received her Doctor of Medicine degree, she _____.

    returned to London and started a school
    went to work at St. Mary's
    studied at hospitals in London

4. Elizabeth started a school of medicine for women because _____.

    she wanted to get rich
    it was difficult for women to get into medical schools
    several women asked her to start a school

Name _____

LANGUAGE ARTS COMPETENCY TEST ITEM

COURSE OF STUDY OBJECTIVE #_____

FORM _____ (A or B)

COMPETENCY TEST ITEM #45D

GRADE 3

Janet Lynn is a famous figure skater. Janet has been on skates since she was two and one-half years old! One day when her parents were going skating, they could not find a babysitter for little Janet. They took her along and let her skate, too! They were amazed to find out that in no time at all, Janet taught herself to skate forward and backward!

Right from the start, Janet loved skating. So her parents found ice skating teachers for her. But Janet became so good that she soon needed better teachers. When she was only in second grade, she moved away to a larger town to be near good teachers. Janet decided she wanted to skate in competition with other skaters. Her parents hired a coach to work with her daily. Eventually, Janet became a world-famous figure skater.

1. Circle the best title for this story.

   Skating Classes   Famous Skater   Skating Coach

2. Janet learned about skating from _____.

   her friends   her parents   a magazine

3. After her parents hired a skating coach, Janet began to skate _____.

   backward   in competition   forward

4. Janet became a famous skater because _____.

   she rested
   she worked hard
   she moved to a larger town

Name _____

Question #1 A–D
Main Idea
Number Correct _____%_____

Question #2 A–D
Facts
Number Correct _____%_____

Question #3 A–D
Sequence
Number Correct _____%_____

Question #4 A–D
Cause-Effect
Number Correct _____%_____

LANGUAGE ARTS COMPETENCY TEST ITEM

COURSE OF STUDY OBJECTIVE # _____

FORM _____ (A or B)

COMPETENCY TEST ITEM #46

GRADE 3

1.   Fairfield, Ohio   Fairfield Ohio,

2.   Macon Georgia   Macon, Georgia

3.   Rockville Maryland,   Rockville, Maryland

4.   Kent, Washington   Kent Washington

Name _____

Number correct _____ % correct _____

COURSE OF STUDY OBJECTIVE # _____   FORM _____ (A or B)

COMPETENCY TEST ITEM #<u>47</u>   GRADE 3

1. | February _____ April May June

    July March January

2. | November December January _____ March

    April September February

3. | July August _____ October November

    September December June

4. | March April May June _____

    August July February

Name _____

Number correct _____% correct _____

1. <u>There's</u> one of the books I read.

    there was   there is   there does   there will

2. <u>She'll</u> get a gift from me.

    she would   she has   she will   she did

3. <u>They have</u> camped for years.

    they'd   they'll   they've   they're

4. <u>He will</u> leave for the party soon.

    he'd   he's   she'd   he'll

Name _____

Number correct _____% correct _____

1.   blue   small   pretty   bird

2.   barn   dig   gave   like

3.   speak   hear   shoe   climb

4.   green   apple   sticky   bumpy

Name _____

Number correct _____% correct _____

1.   Tim climbed the ladder.

   Tim   ladder   climbed   the

2.   My sister jumped rope.

   jumped   sister   rope   my

3.   Mother baked a birthday cake.

   birthday   baked   mother   cake

4.   Two friends visited the park.

   friends   park   two   visited

Name _____

Number correct _____% correct _____

1. Mark and Pat are giving a party.

   Mark and Pat is giving a party.

2. The boys jumps the puddle.

   The boys jump the puddle.

3. The children take a test.

   The children takes a test.

4. She isn't at home.

   They isn't at home.

Name _____

Number correct _____% correct _____

1.   senter   center   centr   cinter

2.   middle   midle   middel   midel

3.   fense   fenc   fence   fince

4.   tundr   thundr   tunder   thunder

Name _____

Number correct _____% correct _____

1. <u>growl</u>

   grew
   grumpy
   grand
   grind

2. <u>plot</u>

   please
   plate
   plan
   plum

3. <u>stone</u>

   star
   steal
   stick
   stump

4. <u>through</u>

   these
   those
   thump
   this

Name _____

Number correct _____% correct _____

1. Mom wears a <u>ring</u> on her finger.

    to draw a circle around
    a thin circle of metal
    to give forth a sound
    an enclosed circle of space

2. The bell will <u>ring</u> soon.

    to draw a circle around
    a thin circle of metal
    to give forth a sound
    an enclosed circle of space

3. Draw a <u>ring</u> around the right answer.

    to draw a circle around
    a thin circle of metal
    to give forth a sound
    an enclosed circle of space

4. The elephants performed in the <u>ring</u>.

    to draw a circle around
    a thin circle of metal
    to give forth a sound
    an enclosed circle of space

Name _____

Number correct _____% correct _____

LANGUAGE ARTS COMPETENCY TEST ITEM

COURSE OF STUDY OBJECTIVE #_____   FORM _____ (A or B)

COMPETENCY TEST ITEM #55   GRADE 3

TABLE OF CONTENTS

1. On which page does "Dragon Stew" begin?

   4   16   28   42

2. On which page does "The Magic Pot" begin?

   4   14   16   28

3. Which story begins on page 28?

   "Muffin"

   "Elephant Riddles"

   "Dr. Penny Walters"

   "Lucky Ladybugs"

4. Which story begins on page 42?

   "Dragon Stew"

   "Words of Laughter"

   "The Magic Pot"

   "Muffin"

Name _____

Number correct _____ % correct _____

LANGUAGE ARTS COMPETENCY TEST ITEM

COURSE OF STUDY OBJECTIVE # _____   FORM _____ (A or B)

COMPETENCY TEST ITEM #56A and B   GRADE 3

The Snowman

I like to play in the snow. _____

_____

_____

Word Bank			
five	scarves	coal	mittens
pieces	twigs	three	boots

Name _____

56A Ideas ____% Organization ____% Style ____% Vocabulary/Punctuation ____%

Total Content ____%

56B Sentence Structure ____% Grammar ____% Capitalization ____%

Spelling ____% Total Mechanics ____%

1.

2.

3.

4.

Name _____

Number correct _____% correct _____

COURSE OF STUDY OBJECTIVE #_____   FORM _____ (A or B)

COMPETENCY TEST ITEM #58   GRADE 4

Directions: Mark an X in front of the one word that means the opposite of the underlined word.

1.   <u>bright</u>

A. _____ shiny   B. _____ dull   C. _____ sparkling   D. _____ glowing

2.   <u>wet</u>

A. _____ damp   B. _____ rainy   C. _____ moist   D. _____ dry

3.   <u>happy</u>

A. _____ glad   B. _____ joyful   C. _____ sad   D. _____ cheerful

4.   <u>quick</u>

A. _____ slow   B. _____ fast   C. _____ swift   D. _____ speedy

Name _____

Number correct _____% correct _____

Directions: **Mark an X in front of the one sentence in which the underlined word is used correctly.**

1. A. _____ We <u>eight</u> breakfast after church last Sunday.

    B. _____ My brother found <u>ate</u> pennies.

    C. _____ She <u>ate</u> a late dinner.

    D. _____ There were <u>ate</u> dogs in the show.

2. A. _____ Bicycles are on <u>sail</u>.

    B. _____ That boat has one <u>sale</u>.

    C. _____ Our house is on <u>sail</u>.

    D. _____ The bookstore had a <u>sale</u> on pens.

3. A. _____ Mother bought ten pounds of <u>flower</u>.

    B. _____ Bread, cookies, and cake are made with <u>flour</u>.

    C. _____ We plant several kinds of <u>flour</u> seeds.

    D. _____ The rose is a beautiful <u>flour</u>.

4. A. _____ I wish the <u>son</u> would shine.

    B. _____ Grandpa has one <u>son</u>.

    C. _____ The <u>son</u> is a large star.

    D. _____ He is his father's <u>sun</u>.

Name _____

Number correct _____% correct _____

Directions: Mark an X in front of the base word (root word) of each word given.

1.   unkindly

A. _____ un   B. _____ kind   C. _____ ly

2.   disagreeable

A. _____ dis   B. _____ agree   C. _____ able

3.   incorrectly

A. _____ in   B. _____ correct   C. _____ ly

4.   impolitely

A. _____ im   B. _____ polite   C. _____ ly

Name _____

Number correct _____% correct _____

LANGUAGE ARTS COMPETENCY TEST ITEM

COURSE OF STUDY OBJECTIVE # _____

FORM _____ (A or B)

COMPETENCY TEST ITEM #61

GRADE 4

Directions: Read the article. Use the context to help you determine the meaning of the underlined words.

Over the years, there have been reports of a monster living in a lake in Scotland. Some people who live near the lake say they have seen the monster floating on top of the water. Others who <u>reside</u> near the lake say they can hear the monster roar.

Some people show pictures. They say the pictures are of the monster. Most people believe the <u>photographs</u> are tricks. There have been some tapes made of sounds in the lake. Many people say the sounds are real "monster sounds." Nobody knows if they are <u>authentic</u> "monster sounds" or just sounds made by the water and fish in the lake.

To this day, nobody has given scientific proof that the Loch Ness Monster <u>exists</u>.

Choose the correct meaning for each word as it is used in the article. Mark an X in the blank in front of the correct meaning for each word.

1. reside
   A. _____ live

   B. _____ hear

2. photographs
   A. _____ cards

   B. _____ pictures

3. authentic
   A. _____ real

   B. _____ silly

4. exists
   A. _____ lives

   B. _____ dives

Name _____

Number correct _____% correct _____

Directions: Read the story. Mark an X in front of the best answer for each question after the story.

A hermit crab does not have a hard shell as most crabs do. Its long, soft body makes a nice meal for a hungry fish. It needs a way to protect itself. So it moves into the empty shell of a snail or other sea animal.

The hermit crab lives safely inside its borrowed house. Only its legs and eyes stick out from the shell opening. It can move around with its house on its back and still see where it is going.

The hermit crab has only one problem. The shell cannot grow in size as the crab grows larger. There comes a time when its house is too small.

The hermit crab must keep its old home until it finds another. Finding the right home is not always easy. The crab is like a person shopping for a new coat. It must make sure it gets one that fits properly.

When the hermit crab sees a shell that looks right, it leaves its old one. It backs into the new seashell and tries it on for size. If it is too large, a fish might pull the crab out. If it picks a house that is too snug, it will not be comfortable. The hermit crab searches until it finds a house that is just right.

1. What is the best title for this story?

_____ A Hungry Crab

_____ The Hermit Crab and Its Home

_____ Seashells

2. After the hermit crab outgrows his old home _____.

_____ he dies

_____ he searches for a new home

_____ he cracks the old shell

3. If a hermit crab's home is too large _____.

_____ he can get lost in it

_____ he can break it

_____ another fish can pull him out of the shell

Name _____

Directions: Read the story. Mark an X in front of the best answer for each question after the story.

About 700,000 years ago, the world's weather turned colder. Great sheets of ice moved down and covered the Northern Hemisphere. The earth entered the Ice Age. During the Ice Age, many kinds of animals died out. Yet early humans were able to survive.

To survive, these people needed fire. They needed it to warm and light their caves, to cook their food, and to make their tools. They needed it to hunt. Sometimes hunters even lit fires to drive a herd of animals over a cliff to their death.

It was not easy for early humans to get fire. At first, they had to be very brave. When lightning or a volcano started a forest fire, they picked up a burning stick and carried it back to their caves. To keep the fire alive, they fed it dry sticks and leaves. They took their fire with them when they moved. They held a flaming torch or carried hot coals in an animal horn.

After many thousands of years, early humans learned to make fire. By hitting hard stones together, they could strike a light. Sometimes they could strike a light by rubbing wood against wood.

Humans are the only animals who have ever been able to use fire. For people, fire is nature's wonderful gift.

1. What is the best title for this story?

    _____ Tools

    _____ Homes of Early Man

    _____ Early Man and Fire

2. After early man found fire _____.

    _____ he was able to warm his cave and cook his food

    _____ the weather turned colder

    _____ the Ice Age began

3. Man was able to survive the Ice Age because _____.

    _____ he made tools

    _____ he learned how to build houses

    _____ he discovered fire

Name _____

Directions: Read the story. Mark an X in front of the best answer for each question after the story.

Wilma Rudolph was four years old before she could walk. Then she got sick and nearly died. She pulled through, but she could not move her left leg.

The Rudolph family had very little money, but Wilma's mother took her 45 miles by bus to a doctor. The doctor gave Wilma many tests. He said she might be able to use her leg again, but it would have to be rubbed and worked with every day for years.

Mrs. Rudolph worked at her job all day. When she came home at night, she was tired but she rubbed Wilma's leg until long after the girl had gone to sleep. After a year the leg was a little better. Mrs. Rudolph taught three of her children to help. After that, Wilma's leg was rubbed four times a day.

When she was six, Wilma could hop a little. At eight, she walked with a leg brace. Later that year she was able to go to school for the first time. She wanted to run like other children, and she never gave up trying. With each year her legs became stronger and stronger. Finally, she was able to walk and run like other children.

In high school she joined the girls' track team and at college she became one of the top four girl runners. She loved to run, and she practiced all the time.

Eventually, she won a place on the U.S. Olympic team. Wilma won three gold medals in the Olympics. As a child she had a dream to run and walk like other children; she worked hard and never gave up. She became a champion.

1. What is the best title for this story?

   _____ Wilma Rudolph, Girl of Courage

   _____ A Poor Family

   _____ Olympic Games

2. After the doctor said Wilma might be able to use her leg again _____.

   _____ Wilma nearly died

   _____ Wilma's mother rubbed her leg every day

   _____ Wilma's mother took her 45 miles by bus to a doctor

3. Wilma Rudolph became an Olympic star because _____.

   _____ she went to college

   _____ she had little money

   _____ she worked hard and never gave up

Name _____

Directions: Read the story. Mark an X in front of the best answer for each question after the story.

James Bartley grew up in England. As a boy, he listened to the stories of men who hunted whales. It was because of these stories that he, too, wanted to hunt whales. When he was 20 years old, he signed up on an old whaling ship.

On the deck of the ship, James heard the cry, "There she blows!" This was the cry he had waited so long to hear. He ran to help the men put the longboats in the water.

Everyone was excited and could see the whale across the water. James got into a longboat with some of the other sailors. They went after the whale.

A man with a harpoon stood up in the longboat. The man threw the harpoon. It hit the whale. The whale went down into the water until 500 feet of rope had been pulled away. Then the rope was still. There was no sound but the water hitting against the longboat.

Suddenly the longboat seemed to jump. It was thrown high into the air. The whale had come up right under it! James felt the longboat break into pieces. He was thrown out. He felt the cold water, and then it was dark. It felt like knives tearing at him.

The men watched from other longboats. The whale went down again. The sailors went quickly to the broken longboat. They pulled the wet sailors out of the sea. James was glad to be safe. After this terrible experience, James left the sea and became a shoemaker. He stayed in England the rest of his life.

1. What is the best title for this story?

    _____ The Harpoon

    _____ James Bartley and the Whale Hunt

    _____ The Longboat

2. After the man threw the harpoon _____.

    _____ someone cried, "There she blows!"

    _____ James joined a whaling ship

    _____ the longboat broke in half

3. The longboat broke in half because _____.

    _____ there were too many men in the boat

    _____ it was an old boat

    _____ the whale came up under the boat

Name _____

Question #1 A–D	Question #2 A–D	Question #3 A–D
Main Idea	Sequence	Cause-Effect
Number Correct	Number Correct	Number Correct
_____%_____	_____%_____	_____%_____

LANGUAGE ARTS COMPETENCY TEST ITEM

COURSE OF STUDY OBJECTIVE #_____

FORM _____ (A or B)

COMPETENCY TEST ITEM #63

GRADE 4

**Directions: Read each sentence. There are no capital letters in the sentences.
Read the words below each sentence. Put an X in front of the word
that should begin with a capital in the sentence.**

1. all the students will get their report cards on friday.

   A. _____ students

   B. _____ report

   C. _____ cards

   D. _____ friday

2. this summer our family will vacation in washington.

   A. _____ summer

   B. _____ family

   C. _____ vacation

   D. _____ washington

3. in may, our class will take a field trip to a museum.

   A. _____ may

   B. _____ class

   C. _____ trip

   D. _____ museum

4. our teacher showed a film on life in russia.

   A. _____ teacher

   B. _____ film

   C. _____ life

   D. _____ russia

Name _____

Number correct _____% correct _____

Directions: For each number, put an **X** in front of the one sentence in each group that has the *wrong* punctuation mark at the end.

1. A. _____ Look at the fireworks!

    B. _____ What time is it!

    C. _____ Ouch, I burned my finger!

    D. _____ The team made a touchdown!

2. A. _____ Did you get an invitation to the party!

    B. _____ Get away from the fire!

    C. _____ Sit down, now!

    D. _____ Call the fire department!

3. A. _____ Hurry, there's been an accident!

    B. _____ Look at the falling star!

    C. _____ How much money did you find!

    D. _____ Come here, quickly!

4. A. _____ Watch out for the cliff!

    B. _____ Our family went to the park for a picnic!

    C. _____ Be careful, don't fall!

    D. _____ What a wonderful race!

Name _____

Number correct _____% correct _____

Directions: Read each sentence. Look for the action verb in each sentence. Mark an X in front of the action verb in the list of words below the sentence.

1. He fed the goldfish this morning.

   A. _____ fed

   B. _____ goldfish

   C. _____ this

   D. _____ morning

2. Mother baked a cake for my sister's birthday.

   A. _____ mother

   B. _____ baked

   C. _____ sister's

   D. _____ birthday

3. Our team won the last game of the season.

   A. _____ team

   B. _____ won

   C. _____ game

   D. _____ season

4. My brother drew a beautiful picture.

   A. _____ brother

   B. _____ drew

   C. _____ beautiful

   D. _____ picture

Name _____

Number correct _____% correct _____

Directions: Read each sentence. Look for the noun in each sentence. Mark an X in front of the noun in the list of words below the sentence.

1. She is writing a book.

    A. _____ she

    B. _____ is

    C. _____ writing

    D. _____ book

2. He drew the picture quickly.

    A. _____ drew

    B. _____ the

    C. _____ picture

    D. _____ quickly

3. Mother baked a beautiful cake.

    A. _____ mother

    B. _____ baked

    C. _____ a

    D. _____ beautiful

4. The snow was falling very quietly.

    A. _____ snow

    B. _____ was

    C. _____ very

    D. _____ quietly

Name _____

Number correct _____% correct _____

Directions: Look at the parts of the friendly letter below. On the lines provided, rewrite the parts of the letter putting them in the proper order on the lines. Use margins properly.

Sincerely,

Thank you for the book. I love to read, especially science fiction.

Dear Scott,

Brian

May 5, 1985

Name _____

Number correct _____ % correct _____

Directions: **Read each sentence. Look at the word in the sentence that is incomplete. Look at the list of prefixes below the sentence. Put an X in front of the prefix that will complete the incomplete word in the sentence so that the sentence makes sense.**

1. Tomorrow I will ___pay the money I borrowed.

   A. _____ un

   B. _____ dis

   C. _____ re

   D. _____ mis

2. You must ___cook the noodles before adding them to the soup.

   A. _____ dis

   B. _____ pre

   C. _____ un

   D. _____ mis

3. Stealing the candy was ___honest.

   A. _____ un

   B. _____ mis

   C. _____ pre

   D. _____ dis

4. Icy spots made the road look ___safe.

   A. _____ un

   B. _____ mis

   C. _____ dis

   D. _____ re

Name _____

Number correct _____ % correct _____

Directions: Read each sentence. Look at the word in the sentence that is incomplete. Look at the list of suffixes below the sentence. Put an X in front of the suffix that will complete the incomplete word in the sentence so that the sentence makes sense.

1. She is one of the most honest and truth____ people I know.

    A. _____ er

    B. _____ en

    C. _____ ful

    D. _____ less

2. The lion is a fear___ animal.

    A. _____ en

    B. _____ less

    C. _____ ment

    D. _____ able

3. The farm___ plowed the fields.

    A. _____ ment

    B. _____ able

    C. _____ en

    D. _____ er

4. Stir the cake mix with the wood___ spoon.

    A. _____ er

    B. _____ en

    C. _____ ful

    D. _____ less

Name _____

Number correct _____ % correct _____

COURSE OF STUDY OBJECTIVE #_____   FORM _____ (A or B)

COMPETENCY TEST ITEM #70A   GRADE 5

Directions: Read the story. Mark an X in front of the best answer for each question after the story.

Two American brothers, Orville and Wilbur Wright, were the first to put an engine on wings. The Wright brothers were bicycle makers. In their free time, they made wings, propellers, and a small gasoline engine. The brothers put everything together in one machine. Their machine had two wings. The machine was made of wood and cloth. It had a light gasoline engine. There were two propellers in the back. The propellers were hooked to the engine with bicycle chains.

One day in 1903, the brothers tried out their machine. They started the engine. They let the machine go down a track. Slowly, it went into the air and stayed up for 12 seconds. That same day the brothers made three more short flights.

Orville and Wilbur Wright had made the first airplane. Most people didn't know about the Wrights' flying machine and those who heard didn't believe it.

The Wright brothers worked on making better and better airplanes. Two years later, they made a plane that flew for 38 minutes. This plane could be guided up and down and left and right. Before long, most of the world was to realize that flying had come to stay.

1.   What is the best title for this story?

_____ The Wright Brothers' Bicycle Shop

_____ The First Gasoline Engine

_____ The Wright Brothers Invent the Airplane

2.   After the 12-second flight _____.

_____ the brothers returned to their bicycle shop

_____ the brothers made three more flights

_____ the brothers made a small gasoline engine

3.   After the first flight, the brothers continued to work on making a better plane because _____.

_____ they wanted to become famous

_____ they wanted to quit the bicycle business

_____ they wanted to make a plane that would fly longer and better

Name _____

LANGUAGE ARTS COMPETENCY TEST ITEM

COURSE OF STUDY OBJECTIVE #_____

FORM _____ (A or B)

COMPETENCY TEST ITEM #70B

GRADE 5

Directions: **Read the story. Mark an X in front of the best answer for each question after the story.**

In 1967, Dian Fossey went to the mountains of Africa. She went to study the wild gorilla. Deep in the jungle, Dian built a two-room house. This house was to be her home for more than ten years. All this time, she would study the gorilla.

There may be as few as 500 wild gorillas left in the world today. All of them live in Africa. Little by little, people are moving into the lands where the gorillas live. Since gorillas are afraid of people they move. The places where they can move are becoming scarce. With fewer places to live there is less food to eat. It is possible that the gorillas will starve and die.

Dian Fossey wanted to help the gorillas survive. To help them, she knew that she would have to learn about them. She had to know how they lived, what they ate, and how they acted together. She spent a great deal of time watching the wild gorillas. She recorded the information she gathered about them. Eventually, she would be able to tell people what could be done to save the wild gorillas. She could tell people how to protect the land on which they lived. Dian Fossey loved nature and animals. She devoted her life to saving the wild gorillas.

1. What is the best title for this story?

    _____ A Two-Room House

    _____ Dian Fossey and the Gorillas

    _____ African Jungle

2. After Dian built her house _____.

    _____ she began studying the gorillas

    _____ she went to the jungles of Africa

    _____ she bought a jeep

3. Dian wanted to study the wild gorillas because _____.

    _____ she thought they were funny

    _____ she liked the jungle

    _____ she wanted the wild gorillas to survive

Name _____

LANGUAGE ARTS COMPETENCY TEST ITEM

Directions: Read the story. Mark an X in front of the best answer for each question after the story.

Saving forest lands has become a problem. Scientists warn that within the next hundred years we may face a serious tree shortage. Forest rangers fight hundreds of fires each year. These fires lay bare large sections of forests.

Many fires are caused by careless campers. Campers must be more careful. Those using the forest must make sure campfires are put out. Most people do try to be careful. First, they build fires in areas permitted. They watch the fire carefully. When finished, they pour water on the fire. Then, they spread out the coals. They leave the fire only after making sure it is out.

There is a ray of hope that might prove to be the answer to areas that have suffered forest fires. Scientists are studying the kinds of plants that will live in areas that have been burned. In this way, replanting after forest fires can be done with plants that will flourish in that soil. However, the most important way to save trees is for man to be careful with campfires in the forest.

1. What is the best title for this story?

    _____ A Camping Vacation

    _____ Forest Rangers

    _____ Saving Our Trees From Forest Fires

2. After pouring water on a campfire _____.

    _____ spread out the coals

    _____ light the fire

    _____ gather firewood

3. Forest fires are often caused by _____.

    _____ careless campers

    _____ scientists

    _____ forest rangers

Name _____

LANGUAGE ARTS COMPETENCY TEST ITEM

COURSE OF STUDY OBJECTIVE #_____

COMPETENCY TEST ITEM #70D

FORM _____ (A or B)

GRADE 5

Directions: Read the story. Mark an X in front of the best answer for each question after the story.

One of the earliest homes in our country was the earth lodge of the Mandan Indians. Building an earth lodge was a big task so all the people who were to live in it took part.

The first thing they did was choose an appropriate spot on which to build. When all agreed on the site of the house, one person would drive a strong peg into the soil. This would be the center of the new lodge.

The Mandans then took a strong buffalo-hide rope and tied it to the peg. They tied another peg to the free end of the rope. The peg was dragged to make a circle which would be the circumference of the lodge floor. In this way, they would get an almost perfectly round house. The circumference was usually about six meters.

Within the circle, the people dug out the dirt to a depth of about one and one-half meters. They poured water over the floor and added a layer of grass. They burned the grass and repeated the procedure two or three times until the floor was baked as hard as clay.

Next they placed poles around the circle, about three meters apart. Then they set up four or five poles around the fireplace in the center of the floor. To make the roof, they placed several layers of willow branches on top of the supporting poles. The walls and roof were filled in with sod and loose soil. When the seeds in the sod grew, the grass provided a waterproof cover for the entire lodge.

1. What is the best title for this story?

   _____ Mandan Indians

   _____ Indian Homes

   _____ Building a Mandan Earth Lodge

2. Before the Mandan Indians drew the circumference for their lodge _____.

   _____ they set four or five poles around the fireplace

   _____ they chose a spot for their lodge

   _____ they placed willow branches on top of the poles

3. Grass grew out of the sod in the roof because _____.

   _____ the sod was loose soil

   _____ the soil was full of grass seed

   _____ the sod was stuffed between the willow poles

Name _____

Question #1 A-D	Question #2 A-D	Question #3 A-D
Main Idea	Sequence	Cause-Effect
Number Correct __%__	Number Correct __%__	Number Correct __%__

Directions: Read the article. The main idea has been underlined.

1. <u>Forests have several enemies.</u> Insects rank among the chief enemies of forests. They can destroy trees by eating the leaves and young sprouts or by digging into the bark and trunk. Disease is another enemy that destroys trees, especially the older ones in the western United States. The third major enemy of forests is fire. Fires destroy three million acres of trees each year in the United States. Animals are also destructive to forests. Cattle, hogs, and other kinds of livestock can eat or trample young trees. Animals can also pack down the earth with their hoofs, preventing seedling growth. Because forests are an important natural resource, we must work to control the enemies of our forests.

_____

Mark an X in front of two of the sentences below that support the main idea in the article above.

A. _____ Forests are important.

B. _____ Disease and fire are enemies of the forests.

C. _____ Cattle and hogs are livestock.

D. _____ Insects can destroy trees.

Name _____

LANGUAGE ARTS COMPETENCY TEST ITEM

COURSE OF STUDY OBJECTIVE # _____

FORM _____ (A or B)

COMPETENCY TEST ITEM #71B

GRADE 5

Directions: Read the article. The main idea has been underlined.

2. <u>Animals such as wolves, dogs, and cats use body language to communicate feelings</u>. A cat, for instance, will lay back its ears if it is angry. A dog will do the same thing. Sometimes a dog will put its tail between its legs and let its ears droop if it is sad or ashamed. Wolves sometimes communicate with each other by bites under the chin. The bites are like pats on the shoulders that people give to each other. Wolves use body language as well as sounds to say, "You're my friend."

Mark an X in front of two of the sentences below that support the main idea in the article above.

A. _____ To show anger, a dog will lay back its ears.

B. _____ Wolves are often vicious.

C. _____ Wolves show friendship to other wolves by nipping each other's chins.

D. _____ Cats and dogs make good household pets.

Name _____

Number correct _____ % correct _____

Directions: Read the article. Read the questions below the article and follow the directions.

The following announcement was given on television:

> Join the thousands of people who are purchasing the new Miracle Blender. This amazing machine chops onions, grinds meats, and grates carrots and cheeses. The Miracle Blender operates faster than a conventional mixer. It can whip up a topping in seconds. The twenty different speeds can blend any mixture. Also, the durable plastic container means easy care and convenience. The only blender for the modern kitchen is the Miracle Blender.

1. Read the statements below. Mark an X in front of the *two* statements that express an *opinion* about the Miracle Blender.

    A. _____ The Miracle Blender has a plastic container.

    B. _____ The Miracle Blender is an amazing machine.

    C. _____ The Miracle Blender grates carrots and cheeses.

    D. _____ The Miracle Blender is the best blender on the market.

2. Read the statements below. Mark an X in front of the *two* statements that express a *statement of fact* about the Miracle Blender.

    A. _____ The Miracle Blender has a plastic container.

    B. _____ The Miracle Blender is an amazing machine.

    C. _____ The Miracle Blender grates carrots and cheeses.

    D. _____ The Miracle Blender is the best blender on the market.

Name _____

Number correct _____ % correct _____

COURSE OF STUDY OBJECTIVE #_____   FORM _____ (A or B)

COMPETENCY TEST ITEM #73   GRADE 5

Directions: Read the story. Mark an X in front of the best answer for the question following the story.

1. George was nervous as he stepped up to the plate in the first game of the season. This was the first time George had ever played on a school team, and he wanted to do well. When the pitcher threw the ball, George hit a home run. The team was really excited. They cheered George as he crossed home plate. George looked up in the stands where he saw his family cheering too. George felt proud. The coach congratulated George. He had given his team a good start in the game.

Who is the main character in this story?

A. _____ George's family

B. _____ George's coach

C. _____ George's team

D. _____ George

2. Jan was playing catch in the front yard with her brother and one of his throws went over her head. She turned and watched the ball roll under the car in the driveway. Jan searched under the car, but she could not find the ball anywhere. Her brother blamed her for losing the ball and said she would have to replace it. Then Mom and Dad came out of the house and got into the car. As they began to drive away, the mysterious ball bounced out from under the car. Jan recovered the ball and returned it to her brother.

Who is the main character in this story?

A. _____ Mom

B. _____ Jan's brother

C. _____ Jan

D. _____ Dad

Name _____

3. Thirteen-year-old Ted had to choose either to stay home during the summer to earn money from his paper route and lawn-mowing jobs or to go to his grandparents' ranch for the summer to help with the work. His father said the decision was his. He wanted to go to the ranch, but his grandparents couldn't afford to pay him. He wanted to earn money so he could buy a motor bike like the one his friend Bill rode. Finally, he decided to help out on the ranch and wait another year for the bike.

Who is the main character in this story?

A. _____ Bill

B. _____ Ted's father

C. _____ Ted's grandparents

D. _____ Ted

4. When Sam Houston was fifteen, his mother made him go to work in a store to help support his nine brothers and sisters. He didn't like the work and wanted to be a soldier. Sam ran away and went to live with some Cherokee Indians. He later became a soldier and frontier hero and was president of Texas from 1836–1838.

Who is the main character in this story?

A. _____ Sam Houston's mother

B. _____ Sam Houston

C. _____ Sam Houston's brothers and sisters

D. _____ the Cherokee Indians

Name _____

Number correct _____ % correct _____

Directions: Read each group of words. Mark an X in front of the words that are a complete sentence.

1. A. _____ quickly moved away
   B. _____ the hot water bottle
   C. _____ haven't had breakfast
   D. _____ the clever frog hopped away

2. A. _____ his snowy white beard
   B. _____ hardly understood his grandmother
   C. _____ surely you can whisper more quietly
   D. _____ carelessly drove near the cliff

3. A. _____ my friend is very tired today
   B. _____ useful to know
   C. _____ finally saw his home
   D. _____ the hungry wolf in the woods

4. A. _____ the snake in the sun
   B. _____ you should look for a book at the library
   C. _____ when I was much younger
   D. _____ on the beach by myself

Name _____

Number correct _____% correct _____

Directions: Use the index to answer the questions. Put an X in front of the correct answer to each question.

```
┌─────────────────────────────────────────────────────────────┐
│                          INDEX                                │
│   Coconut, 120–130                 Coffee, 140–148            │
│      How grown, 120–121               How grown, 141–143      │
│      Sale of, 128–130                 Kinds of, 144           │
│      Uses of meat, 123–124            Sale of, 145           │
│      Uses of milk, 124–125            Uses of, 146–148        │
│      Uses of oil, 125–127             Where grown, 142        │
│      Where grown, 122–123                                     │
└─────────────────────────────────────────────────────────────┘
```

1. On which pages could you find out how coconut is grown?
   A. _____ 120–121
   B. _____ 122–123
   C. _____ 128–130
   D. _____ 141–143

2. Which of the following can be found on page 144?
   A. _____ The uses of coffee
   B. _____ How coffee is grown
   C. _____ Where coffee is grown
   D. _____ Kinds of coffee

3. On which pages could you find the uses of coconut milk?
   A. _____ 123–124
   B. _____ 124–125
   C. _____ 145
   D. _____ 146–148

4. On which page could you find where coffee is grown?
   A. _____ 140
   B. _____ 142
   C. _____ 145
   D. _____ 146

Name _____

Number correct _____ % correct _____

LANGUAGE ARTS COMPETENCY TEST ITEM

COURSE OF STUDY OBJECTIVE #_____   FORM _____ (A or B)

COMPETENCY TEST ITEM #76   GRADE 6

Directions: **Read the questions but do not attempt to answer them. Listen carefully to the story the teacher will read aloud to you. Do not attempt to answer questions while you are listening. When the teacher has finished the story, mark an X in front of the best answer to each question that follows.**

1. At the beginning of the story, Dirk told Jan to hold on to _____.

    A. _____ a burner

    B. _____ the basket

    C. _____ a ground rope

    D. _____ the opening of the balloon

2. Why did Dirk turn on the burner jets?

    A. _____ to test the jets

    B. _____ to warm his hands

    C. _____ to use up extra gas

    D. _____ to heat the air in the balloon

3. What did Jan do with the rope when Dirk told her to get in the basket?

    A. _____ handed it to Dirk

    B. _____ kept it

    C. _____ handed it to one of the crew

    D. _____ cut it loose

4. What happened to Jan and Dirk at the end of the story?

    A. _____ they rode the balloon into the sky

    B. _____ they packed the balloon into the truck

    C. _____ they patched the hole in the balloon

    D. _____ they went to get more gas for the balloon

Name _____

Number correct _____ % correct _____

LANGUAGE ARTS COMPETENCY TEST ITEM

Directions: Read the story. Mark an X in front of the best answer for each question after the story.

Frogmen served in our Navy as early as 1776. They destroyed English battleships that were in American harbors. It was during World War II that these underwater experts first served in large numbers. They landed near invasion beaches. They learned as much as possible about the enemy. They cleared the beaches of mines and other obstacles. After the beaches were secured, supplies had to be landed. Frogmen destroyed the remains of any ships that were blocking the landing areas.

Today, frogmen are important in such work as the inspection of ships. They help map the flow of waters under the surface of the sea. In the years ahead, many new and interesting projects will be found for frogmen. They will help us find out more about the unknown world beneath the oceans.

1. What is the best title for this story?

_____ World War II Battles

_____ Frogmen

_____ Jobs of the Sea

2. After securing the invasion beaches during World War II, frogmen _____.

_____ cleared the beaches of mines

_____ landed on the beaches

_____ destroyed the remains of ships blocking the landing areas

3. Frogmen are so called because _____.

_____ they look like frogs

_____ they are as at home in water as on land

_____ they have webbed feet

Name _____

Directions: Read the story. Mark an X in front of the best answer for each question after the story.

When cranberries are ripe, they are ready to be picked and eaten. The ripe berries have a dark red color. The berries usually ripen for harvesting toward the end of September.

Cranberries can be prepared several ways. They are used for sauce. They are also used for making cranberry juice, bread, or cake.

Most cranberries are grown in the United States and come from Massachusetts, Wisconsin, New Jersey, and Washington. They are also grown in Asia and Europe.

When cranberry plants are planted, they are less than ten inches long. They grow quickly. They are planted in a field of sandy soil, called a bog. The bogs are flooded with water to help protect the cranberries from frost.

1. What is the best title for this story?

_____ Cranberry Sauce

_____ Cranberry Bogs

_____ Cranberries

2. Toward the end of September, _____.

_____ it is time to weed the cranberries

_____ it is time to harvest the cranberries

_____ it is time to plant the cranberries

3. Cranberry bogs are flooded with water because _____.

_____ they need the water to grow

_____ they need the water to protect them from the frost

_____ they need the water to protect them from insects

Name _____

Directions: Read the story. Mark an X in front of the best answer for each question after the story.

Will Rogers grew up on his father's ranch. A family friend named Uncle Dan taught him rope tricks. Uncle Dan thought that Will needed a hobby. He hoped the hobby would keep Will out of trouble. Will enjoyed the hobby. He spent hours every day learning to do the tricks.

One day, Will walked through the house practicing roping furniture. Usually his mother did not mind, but that day she had company. She told Will that if he did not stop, she would punish him. He paid no attention to her.

Will's mother stood up to punish him. Quick as a flash, the rope was up in the air and around her before she knew what had happened. At first, she did not know what to do. Then she burst into laughter. Will said that he would let her go if she would not punish him.

1. What is the best title for this story?

    _____ Will Rogers's Rope Trick

    _____ Will Rogers's Life

    _____ Will Rogers's Ranch

2. After Will's mother burst into laughter _____.

    _____ Will roped furniture

    _____ Will paid no attention to his mother

    _____ Will said that he would let his mother go

3. Will's mother did not want him to rope furniture because _____.

    _____ she didn't want her furniture ruined

    _____ she had company

    _____ she didn't like Will doing his tricks in the house

Name _____

LANGUAGE ARTS COMPETENCY TEST ITEM

COURSE OF STUDY OBJECTIVE #_____   FORM _____ (A or B)

COMPETENCY TEST ITEM #77D   GRADE 6

Directions: Read the story. Mark an X in front of the best answer for each question after the story.

The emperor penguin lives near the South Pole. It is one of the largest birds in the world. It can reach a height of four feet and weigh ninety pounds.

Because of the way its black and white feathers are arranged, the emperor penguin looks as though it is dressed in fancy evening clothes.

Penguins spend much of their time in the water. Emperors can dive hundreds of feet beneath the surface. They can stay underwater for as long as eighteen minutes. This is longer than any other bird and most other animals.

A mother emperor penguin lays a single egg. Once the egg has been laid, it is placed between the feet of the father penguin. The egg is covered by folds of skin and feathers from the father's body. When the baby penguin is hatched, the mother returns and cares for the chick.

1. What is the best title for this story?

    _____ Life at the South Pole

    _____ The Emperor Penguin

    _____ Underwater Birds

2. Before the egg is placed between the feet of the father penguin _____.

    _____ the egg is covered by folds of skin and feathers

    _____ the baby penguin begins to hatch

    _____ the mother penguin lays the egg

3. Emperor penguins look as though they are dressed in fancy evening clothes because _____.

    _____ of the way their black and white feathers are arranged

    _____ of the clothes they wear

    _____ of their height and weight

Name _____

Question #1 A-D	Question #2 A-D	Question #3 A-D
Main Idea	Sequence	Cause-Effect
Number Correct __%__	Number Correct __%__	Number Correct __%__

COURSE OF STUDY OBJECTIVE #_____   FORM _____ (A or B)

COMPETENCY TEST ITEM #78   GRADE 6

Directions: **Read each paragraph that follows. For each paragraph mark an X in front of the sentence below the paragraph that was used as the *topic sentence* in the paragraph.**

1. Monarch butterflies migrate south during the winter. While migrating south some monarchs travel as much as two thousand miles. Monarchs begin their migration in the fall just as birds do. They head south for areas like California, Mexico, and Central America. They seem to hibernate in the south in order to store fat in their small bodies for the long trip back north in the spring.

   A. _____ They head south for areas like California, Mexico, and Central America.

   B. _____ Monarch butterflies migrate south during the winter.

   C. _____ While migrating south some monarchs travel as much as two thousand miles.

2. The lake trout that lives in the Great Lakes is easily identified. Like most deep-water trout, it is not brightly colored. Small pale yellow spots cover its body. Its tail is deeply forked. The lake trout usually weighs 15 to 20 pounds. Its flesh is slightly oilier than that of most other trout, but it has a fine flavor and is considered a good food fish.

   A. _____ Small pale yellow spots cover its body.

   B. _____ The lake trout usually weighs 15 to 20 pounds.

   C. _____ The lake trout that lives in the Great Lakes is easily identified.

Name _____

3. The bodies of reptiles are covered with scales. Turtles and some other reptiles have hard shells which are partly made of some very big scales. Reptiles have very short legs or no legs at all. All reptiles are cold-blooded animals. That is, the temperature of their bodies changes with the temperature of their surroundings. Reptiles have very interesting characteristics.

    A. _____ Reptiles have very short legs or no legs at all.

    B. _____ Reptiles have very interesting characteristics.

    C. _____ All reptiles are cold-blooded animals.

4. Some of the most frightening occurrences in history were the outbreaks of the disease called the Black Death. This fatal disease killed thousands of people. During one outbreak in Europe it left one-fourth of the population dead. Not knowing its cause people panicked and fled from the cities only to die on the roads. Scientists learned the disease was caused by a germ carried by fleas. Strict methods for the prevention of the disease are now in use.

    A. _____ This fatal disease killed thousands of people.

    B. _____ Strict methods for the prevention of the disease are now in use.

    C. _____ Some of the most frightening occurrences in history were the outbreaks of the disease called the Black Death.

Name _____

Number correct _____ % correct _____

LANGUAGE ARTS COMPETENCY TEST ITEM

COURSE OF STUDY OBJECTIVE #_____

COMPETENCY TEST ITEM #79

FORM _____ (A or B)

GRADE 6

Directions: Mark an X in front of the simple subject of each sentence.

1. He listened for the sound of footsteps outside the door.

   A. _____ He

   B. _____ sound

   C. _____ footsteps

   D. _____ door

2. Her best friend is planning a surprise party.

   A. _____ best

   B. _____ friend

   C. _____ surprise

   D. _____ party

3. The clowns juggled balls at the circus.

   A. _____ clowns

   B. _____ juggled

   C. _____ balls

   D. _____ circus

4. The excited basketball team celebrated their victory.

   A. _____ basketball

   B. _____ team

   C. _____ their

   D. _____ victory

Name_____

Number correct _____ % correct _____

LANGUAGE ARTS COMPETENCY TEST ITEM

COURSE OF STUDY OBJECTIVE #_____

FORM _____ (A or B)

COMPETENCY TEST ITEM #80

GRADE 6

Directions: Mark an X in front of the verb of each sentence.

1. Tom planned to spend the summer at camp.

   A. _____ Tom
   B. _____ planned
   C. _____ summer
   D. _____ camp

2. The delivery boy brought the pizza to our house.

   A. _____ delivery
   B. _____ brought
   C. _____ pizza
   D. _____ house

3. Our family purchased a new car last week.

   A. _____ our
   B. _____ family
   C. _____ purchased
   D. _____ week

4. My uncle arrived by plane yesterday.

   A. _____ uncle
   B. _____ arrived
   C. _____ plane
   D. _____ yesterday

Name _____

Number correct _____ % correct _____

COURSE OF STUDY OBJECTIVE #_____   FORM _____ (A or B)

COMPETENCY TEST ITEM #<u>81</u>   GRADE 6

Directions: Mark an X in front of the sentence in which the part that is underlined is the complete subject.

1. A. _____ The tallest trees <u>were covered with snow</u> and ice.

    B. _____ The tallest trees were covered <u>with snow and ice.</u>

    C. _____ <u>The tallest trees</u> were covered with snow and ice.

    D. _____ The tallest trees <u>were covered</u> with snow and ice.

2. A. _____ <u>The clever elf</u> danced a jig around the fire.

    B. _____ The clever elf danced a jig <u>around the fire.</u>

    C. _____ The clever elf <u>danced a jig around the fire.</u>

    D. _____ The clever elf <u>danced a jig</u> around the fire.

3. A. _____ The exhausted boys were relieved <u>to find the path home.</u>

    B. _____ <u>The exhausted boys</u> were relieved to find the path home.

    C. _____ The exhausted boys <u>were relieved to find the path</u> home.

    D. _____ The exhausted boys <u>were relieved</u> to find the path home.

4. A. _____ Four brave children hunted for the lost kitten <u>in the dark.</u>

    B. _____ Four brave children <u>hunted for the lost kitten in the dark.</u>

    C. _____ Four brave children <u>hunted for the lost kitten</u> in the dark.

    D. _____ <u>Four brave children</u> hunted for the lost kitten in the dark.

Name _____

Number correct _____ % correct _____

LANGUAGE ARTS COMPETENCY TEST ITEM

COURSE OF STUDY OBJECTIVE #_____

FORM _____ (A or B)

COMPETENCY TEST ITEM #82

GRADE 6

Directions: Mark an X in front of the sentence in which the part that is underlined is the complete predicate.

1. A. _____ <u>Mother</u> decorated the birthday cake with pink and white icing.
    B. _____ Mother <u>decorated the birthday cake with pink and white icing.</u>
    C. _____ Mother decorated the birthday cake <u>with pink and white icing.</u>
    D. _____ Mother <u>decorated the birthday cake</u> with pink and white icing.

2. A. _____ The funny clown <u>made the children giggle and laugh.</u>
    B. _____ <u>The funny clown</u> made the children giggle and laugh.
    C. _____ The funny clown made the <u>children giggle and laugh.</u>
    D. _____ <u>The funny clown made</u> the children giggle and laugh.

3. A. _____ The batter hit the ball <u>over the pitcher's head.</u>
    B. _____ The batter <u>hit the ball over the pitcher's head.</u>
    C. _____ <u>The batter</u> hit the ball over the pitcher's head.
    D. _____ <u>The batter hit</u> the ball over the pitcher's head.

4. A. _____ <u>His little sister</u> learned the names of the colors and letters of the alphabet.
    B. _____ His little sister <u>learned the names</u> of the colors and letters of the alphabet.
    C. _____ His little sister <u>learned the names of the colors and letters of the alphabet.</u>
    D. _____ His little <u>sister learned</u> the names of the colors and letters of the alphabet.

Name _____

Number correct _____% correct _____

LANGUAGE ARTS COMPETENCY TEST ITEM

COURSE OF STUDY OBJECTIVE #_____   FORM _____ (A or B)

COMPETENCY TEST ITEM #83   GRADE 6

Directions: Read each sentence. Mark an X in front of the word below the sentence that is used as an adjective in the sentence.

1. The beautiful rainbow spread across the sky.

    A. _____ beautiful

    B. _____ rainbow

    C. _____ spread

    D. _____ sky

2. The little puppy wagged his tail.

    A. _____ little

    B. _____ puppy

    C. _____ wagged

    D. _____ tail

3. Mother baked a delicious pie.

    A. _____ Mother

    B. _____ baked

    C. _____ delicious

    D. _____ pie

4. The carpenter built a sturdy birdhouse.

    A. _____ carpenter

    B. _____ built

    C. _____ sturdy

    D. _____ birdhouse

Name _____

Number correct _____ % correct _____

LANGUAGE ARTS COMPETENCY TEST ITEM

COURSE OF STUDY OBJECTIVE #_____   FORM _____ (A or B)

COMPETENCY TEST ITEM #84   GRADE 6

Directions: Mark an X in front of the word or words that correctly complete the sentence.

1. That basketball player is really _____.

   A. _____ tall

   B. _____ tallest

   C. _____ more tall

   D. _____ most tall

2. Which of the two boys is _____?

   A. _____ most handsome

   B. _____ more handsome

   C. _____ handsomer

   D. _____ handsomest

3. Dad bought the _____ car he could find.

   A. _____ cheap

   B. _____ cheaper

   C. _____ cheapest

   D. _____ more cheap

4. Tim is _____ to win than John.

   A. _____ more eager

   B. _____ most eager

   C. _____ eagerer

   D. _____ eagerest

Name _____

Number correct _____ % correct _____

Directions: Mark an X in front of the misspelled word in each item.

1. A. _____ hopped
   B. _____ skipped
   C. _____ grined
   D. _____ ripped

2. A. _____ cried
   B. _____ buried
   C. _____ replied
   D. _____ carryed

3. A. _____ bike
   B. _____ time
   C. _____ lif
   D. _____ kite

4. A. _____ takeing
   B. _____ riding
   C. _____ waving
   D. _____ biting

5. A. _____ women
   B. _____ rabbits
   C. _____ foxs
   D. _____ wishes

Name _____

Number correct _____ % correct _____

Directions: For each item look at the underlined word. Put an X in front of the word below the underlined word that would come after it in alphabetical order.

1. <u>grant</u>

   A. _____ grasp

   B. _____ grammar

   C. _____ grain

2. <u>tragic</u>

   A. _____ trade

   B. _____ transfer

   C. _____ track

3. <u>flame</u>

   A. _____ flair

   B. _____ flash

   C. _____ flake

4. <u>drink</u>

   A. _____ drill

   B. _____ drift

   C. _____ drive

Name _____

Number correct _____ % correct _____

Directions: Use the dictionary entry to decide which meaning of a given word fits the use of the word in the sentence. Write the number of the correct meaning of the underlined word in front of the sentence in which the word is used.

> **hand** (hănd) *n.* **1.** The end part of the arm. **2.** A share in doing something. **3.** Applause. **4.** A hired laborer; a worker.

_____ We gave the performers a big <u>hand.</u>

_____ Jan broke her wrist, and the cast covered her entire <u>hand.</u>

> **line** (līn) *n.* **1.** A rope. **2.** The boundary of a place. **3.** A row of words across a page. **4.** Any long, thin mark. **5.** A group of persons in a row.

_____ There was already a <u>line</u> waiting to enter the theater.

_____ The teacher drew a <u>line</u> under the title of the book.

Name _____

Number correct _____ % correct _____

LANGUAGE ARTS COMPETENCY TEST ITEM

COURSE OF STUDY OBJECTIVE #_____   FORM _____ (A or B)

COMPETENCY TEST ITEM #88A   GRADE 7

Directions: Read the story. Mark an X in front of the best answer for each question after the story.

If you like gingerbread, you might be interested to know that people may have been eating it 5,000 years ago! The history of spices is a long one. For thousands of years people have used spices. Nearly 3,000 years ago Arabs from Egypt and nearby countries were making their living by selling spices to people from other parts of the world. Shortly after 700 A.D., Italian sailors began bringing spices back from Egypt. Later, people began to travel further for spices. In 1271, Marco Polo, an Italian, made his first voyage to China with his father to bring back spices and other Chinese goods.

India also became an important source of spices. By 1600 A.D., English sailors were bringing many spices back from India each year. Later, U.S. sailors made similar voyages to India for spices.

When people began to settle in the United States, they brought along the spices they had used in their homelands. This resulted in the variety of spices found in America today.

1. What is the best title for this story?

   _____ Marco Polo

   _____ Making Gingerbread

   _____ History of Spices

2. After Marco Polo journeyed to China for spices, _____.

   _____ Arabs began using spices

   _____ U.S. sailors made voyages to India for spices

   _____ Italians began using spices

3. We have a great variety of spices in America today because _____.

   _____ Marco Polo brought us spices from China

   _____ settlers coming to the U.S. brought spices from their homelands

   _____ Marco Polo was an Italian

Name _____

Directions: Read the story. Mark an X in front of the best answer for each question after the story.

California has been the site of many important historical events. One of the most famous is the beginning of the Gold Rush in 1849. Gold was discovered at Sutter's Mill by James Marshall, a miner, on January 24, 1848.

But long before the discovery of gold, other historical events took place in what is now known as California. First, Spanish and Portuguese sailors landed there. Shortly after that, in 1769, a Spanish missionary founded the first mission. The land, called California, became a territory of the United States in 1846. Later, in 1850, it became a state.

The Central and Pacific Railway, which ran east from Sacramento, California, made its first run in 1863. When refrigeration cars were developed, the first trainload of California oranges left Los Angeles for the east in 1886.

The history of California contains many facts both interesting and tragic. The state has been the movie capital of the United States since 1907 when the first movie was made there. Just a year earlier, in 1906, an earthquake destroyed parts of San Francisco.

1. What is the best title for this story?

    _____ Gold Rush

    _____ California History

    _____ Movie Capital

2. Before California became a state, _____.

    _____ the first movie was made there

    _____ James Marshall discovered gold at Sutter's Mill

    _____ an earthquake destroyed parts of San Francisco

3. It was possible to send oranges from California to the east because_____.

    _____ refrigeration cars kept them from spoiling

    _____ growers had lots of gold

    _____ the earthquake did not destroy the orange groves

Name _____

Directions: Read the story. Mark an X in front of the best answer for each question after the story.

For years people have wondered how they might predict the weather. One old way of telling temperatures was to count the number of times a cricket chirped in 14 seconds. To this was added the number 40. Sometimes that worked. Sometimes it did not.

Today's scientists use computers to record temperature and air movement. They use the computer to chart and predict the weather's progress. The result is fairly accurate for a three-day prediction. It is still almost impossible to forecast weather beyond that time limit.

During the 1940s weather scientists began to try to change the weather. Cloud seeding (dropping dry ice into clouds) was frequently tried to speed up the rain. Scientists believe that at least one hurricane was controlled by such a method; its fast winds and moisture slowed down when seeded.

1. What is the best title for this story?

    _____ Predicting the Weather

    _____ Cloud Seeding

    _____ Preventing Hurricanes

2. After scientists began using computers to chart and predict the weather's progress, _____.

    _____ they used crickets to help determine their results

    _____ they learned to seed clouds

    _____ they were able to make fairly accurate three-day weather predictions

3. When dry ice is dropped into clouds, _____.

    _____ the clouds freeze and do not change form

    _____ hurricanes develop

    _____ moisture in the clouds becomes cooler and it rains

Name _____

Directions: Read the story. Mark an X in front of the best answer for each question after the story.

Robert Goddard was born in 1882. He became interested in math problems and scientific experiments. His boyhood experiments were not always successful. More than once, he nearly destroyed his relatives' house with his attempts to build a rocket. He kept trying. Robert filled many green notebooks with the dream of building a giant rocket.

When he was 38, he used these notebooks to produce a plan for the "Goddard Rocket." He wrote a book called *A Method of Reaching Extreme Altitudes.* The book told how a rocket might be made to go to the moon.

In 1926, his first liquid-fueled rocket took off. It made a short but successful flight. At first, people laughed at the idea. Many years and many rockets later, the world realized the importance of Robert Goddard's dreams and work. At the time of his death in 1945, he was already known as "the father of rocketry and space travel."

1. What is the best title for this story?

    _____ Rocket to the Moon

    _____ Robert Goddard—Father of Rocketry and Space Travel

    _____ Scientific Experiments

2. After his first liquid-fueled rocket took off, _____.

    _____ people continued to laugh at the idea of rockets

    _____ Robert became interested in math problems

    _____ Robert's boyhood experiments were often disastrous

3. Successful space flights have been made because _____.

    _____ of the groundwork and study of Robert Goddard

    _____ men like Robert Goddard gave up when laughed at by others

    _____ Goddard was discouraged by failures

Name _____

Question #1 A-D	Question #2 A-D	Question #3 A-D
Main Idea	Sequence	Cause-Effect
Number Correct ___%___	Number Correct ___%___	Number Correct ___%___

Directions: Read the story. Mark an X in front of the best answer for each question after the story.

Marty had to go all the way across the bubble that covered this section of the moon every morning. School and his parents' apartment were both on the perimeter but almost exactly opposite. This did not present much of a problem. Marty had to walk only a hundred yards to pick up an autocabin. After that he punched his destination on the dial and the robots took over, swinging the cabin out onto the overhead moving cable and plotting the course which would take him most directly to the school depot. He had timed it once at twenty-and-a-half minutes, and knew it would never vary by more than seconds. It could have been a bore, but he usually had enough homework held over to pass the time. The dial panel served as a desk.

1. This story takes place_____.

    A. _____ on a school bus

    B. _____ in an autocabin

2. This story takes place_____.

    A. _____ in the present

    B. _____ in the future

Name _____

Directions: Read the story. Mark an X in front of the best answer for each question after the story.

Storms came early with rain, and between the rains fierce winds struck our island and filled the air with sand. Most of the days I spent fashioning a spear to catch a giant devilfish. I had seen a spear made, as I had seen my father make bows and arrows. I remembered how it looked and how it was used. From my memories I made a spear after many errors and many hours of work. I worked a sea-elephant tooth down to a head with a barbed point. I then made a ring and fastened it to the end of the shaft.

On the first day of spring, I went down to Coral Cove with my new spear. I pushed my canoe into the water and drifted toward the reef where the devilfish lived. Far down, the sea ferns moved as though a breeze were blowing there, and among them swam the devilfish trailing their long arms.

It was good to be on the sea with the new spear in my hand. When the sun was high I speared a giant devilfish and returned to our cave to prepare our dinner over the fire.

3. This story takes place_____.

   A. _____ on an island and on the sea

   B. _____ on an island and on a pond

4. This story takes place_____.

   A. _____ in the present

   B. _____ in the past

Name _____

Number correct_____% correct_____

Directions: Mark an X in front of the correct form of the possessive.

1. _____ dog ran after the rabbit.

   A. _____ Ted

   B. _____ Teds

   C. _____ Ted's

   D. _____ Teds'

2. The _____ jacket is on the hook.

   A. _____ boy

   B. _____ boy's

   C. _____ boys

   D. _____ boys'

3. The _____ books are on the shelf.

   A. _____ children

   B. _____ childrens

   C. _____ children's

   D. _____ childrens'

4. Both _____ dresses are red.

   A. _____ girl

   B. _____ girls

   C. _____ girl's

   D. _____ girls'

Name _____

Number correct_____% correct_____

LANGUAGE ARTS COMPETENCY TEST ITEM

Directions: Mark an X in front of the possessive pronoun that correctly completes the sentence.

1. The pilot landed the aircraft just as _____ wing caught fire.

   A. _____ its

   B. _____ his

2. Diane could not graduate unless she found _____cap and gown.

   A. _____ her

   B. _____ hers

3. Pat and her partner presented _____ report to the class.

   A. _____ theirs

   B. _____ their

4. Dad reminded me not to forget _____ goggles.

   A. _____ mine

   B. _____ my

Name _____

Number correct _____% correct _____

LANGUAGE ARTS COMPETENCY TEST ITEM

COURSE OF STUDY OBJECTIVE #_____

FORM _____ (A or B)

COMPETENCY TEST ITEM #92

GRADE 7

Directions: Mark an X in front of the word or words that correctly complete the sentence.

1. Tom _____ newspapers for his brother when he is busy.

    A. _____ deliver

    B. _____ delivers

    C. _____ delivered

    D. _____ am delivering

2. I put the wall hanging that mother _____ on my wall.

    A. _____ wove

    B. _____ weave

    C. _____ weaves

    D. _____ will weave

3. We _____ the horse if you brush it.

    A. _____ saddles

    B. _____ saddled

    C. _____ will saddle

    D. _____ are saddling

4. David _____ television while he eats lunch.

    A. _____ watch

    B. _____ watched

    C. _____ is watching

    D. _____ was watching

Name _____

Number correct _____ % correct _____

Directions: Mark an X in front of the adverb that completes the sentence.

1. The children play _____.

    A. _____ games

    B. _____ often

2. With more help, Dad will finish the job _____.

    A. _____ easy

    B. _____ easily

3. Mom bakes _____.

    A. _____ daily

    B. _____ cookies

4. Our basketball team will practice _____.

    A. _____ regular

    B. _____ regularly

Name _____

Number correct _____ % correct _____

LANGUAGE ARTS COMPETENCY TEST ITEM

COURSE OF STUDY OBJECTIVE #_____

FORM _____ (A or B)

COMPETENCY TEST ITEM #94

GRADE 7

Directions: **Number the sentences in each group from 1 to 4 in the order in which they would have happened.**

1. _____ The two stared at each other for a moment.

   _____ He looked in and found himself eye-to-eye with a fish.

   _____ My cat slowly approached the aquarium.

   _____ Then the fish winked at the cat and swam away.

2. _____ The magician ran off the stage screaming.

   _____ Then waving her wand over the hat, she said some magic words.

   _____ The magician calmly took her hat from her head.

   _____ Suddenly a fiery dragon appeared.

3. _____ The big dog looked at her as Patty jumped out of bed.

   _____ She called to her German shepherd, who was asleep beside her bed.

   _____ Then Patty sat with her arm around the dog and thought of the prize they might win.

   _____ When Patty woke up, she remembered the dog show was to take place today.

4. _____ The English settlers who came to this country filled pie shells with meat.

   _____ Thus, a new American dish, called pumpkin pie, was invented.

   _____ Later, the American Indians introduced the English to cooked pumpkin.

   _____ Then the English tried putting the pumpkin into pie shells.

Name _____

Number correct _____ % correct _____

LANGUAGE ARTS COMPETENCY TEST ITEM

COURSE OF STUDY OBJECTIVE #_____   FORM _____ (A or B)

COMPETENCY TEST ITEM #95   GRADE 7

Directions: Use the two underlined words in each test item as guide words on a
dictionary page. Mark an X in front of the word below the guide words
that would be found on that page in the dictionary.

1. helmet   hike

    A. _____ hire

    B. _____ hitch

    C. _____ hearth

    D. _____ hesitate

2. sparrow   sprawl

    A. _____ spur

    B. _____ sprain

    C. _____ souvenir

    D. _____ spaghetti

3. parade   peddler

    A. _____ peer

    B. _____ papoose

    C. _____ peculiar

    D. _____ parachute

4. exhibit   export

    A. _____ extend

    B. _____ exhaust

    C. _____ excellent

    D. _____ explosion

Name _____

Number correct _____% correct _____

LANGUAGE ARTS COMPETENCY TEST ITEM

COURSE OF STUDY OBJECTIVE #_____   FORM _____ (A or B)

COMPETENCY TEST ITEM #96 A and B   GRADE 7

Directions: You are a reporter on the school newspaper. Use the facts given below to write a single paragraph news article for the paper about the football game between Plainville and Tealtown. Use the top part of the paper to compose a rough draft. Correct your rough draft for main idea and supporting details, organization, style, choice of words, complete sentences, correct grammar, correct punctuation and capitalization, and correct spelling. Use the bottom part of the paper to rewrite your rough draft in final form. Be sure to title your article. If you run out of space, use the back of the page.

FACTS: Plainville Panthers versus Tealtown Tigers
            Football game, Tuesday, September 9, 4:00 P.M.
            Played on Plainville Junior High School football field
            Score: 14 Panthers   Touchdowns by John Baker and Steve Fields
                     7 Tigers   Touchdown by Brad Smith

_____

_____

_____

_____

_____

_____

_____

_____

_____

_____

_____

_____

_____

_____

_____

_____

_____

_____

_____

_____

_____

_____

Name _____

#96A Ideas____% Organization____% Style____% Vocabulary____% Total Content____%

#96B Sentence Structure____% Grammar____% Punctuation/Capitalization____% Spelling____%

Total Mechanics____%

Bibliography

The following bibliography represents the sources that were used to gain the knowledge base necessary to write this guide to competency-based education.

ASCD Committee on Research and Theory, *Measuring and Attaining the Goals of Education.* Alexandria, VA: ASCD, 1980.

Baker, Eva and Edys Quellmaly, *Educational Testing and Evaluation.* Beverly Hills, CA: Sage Publications, 1980.

Brandt, Ron, "On Standards and Public Policy: A Conversation With Arthur Wise," *Educational Leadership,* October 1983, pp. 41–44.

Freeman, D. J., et al, "A Closer Look at Standardized Tests," *Arithmetic Teacher,* 1982, 29, pp. 50–54.

Gronlund, Norman E., *Constructing Achievement Tests.* Englewood Cliffs, NJ: Prentice-Hall, 1968.

———, *Measurement and Evaluation in Teaching.* New York: Macmillan, 1976.

Ingram, Craig, *Fundamentals of Educational Assessment.* New York: Van Nostrand Reinhold, 1980.

Jaeger, Richard M., and Carol Tittle, eds., *Minimum Competency Achievement Testing: Motives, Models, Measures, and Consequences.* Berkeley, CA: McCutchan, 1980.

Lacey, Colin and Denis Lawton, *Issues in Evaluation and Accountability.* New York: Methuen and Co., 1981.

"List of Skills," *Critical Academic Skills: A Program in Minimum Competencies.* Planning and Development Branch, Cincinnati (Ohio) Public Schools, 1980.

Madaus, George F., "NIE Clarification Hearing: The Negative Team's Case," *Phi Delta Kappan,* October 1981, pp. 92–94.

Mager, Robert F., and Peter Pipe, *Analyzing Performance Problems or "You Really Oughta Wanna."* Belmont, CA: Fearon, 1970.

"Management Options for Competency Testing in Ohio: A Guide for Implementing the Measurement Component," a booklet published by The Riverside Publishing Company, 1984.

Popham, W. James, "The Case for Minimum Competency Testing," *Phi Delta Kappan,* October 1981, pp. 89–91.

Popham, W. James, and S. C. Rankin, "Minimum Competency Tests Spur Instructional Improvement," *Phi Delta Kappan,* May 1981, 62, pp. 637–639.

Probst, Robert E., "Competency Testing in English," *English Journal,* October 25, 1983, pp. 22–25.

Sullivan, Howard, and Norman Higgins, *Teaching for Competency.* New York: Teachers College Press, Columbia University, 1983.

Trent, E. R., and E. Golden, "Impact Evaluation of Locally Developed MCPs in Four Ohio Districts," *North Central Quarterly,* 1981, 56, pp. 14–26.

Wise, Arthur E., *Legislated Learning: The Bureaucratization of the American Classroom.* Berkeley, CA: University of California Press, 1979.

Index

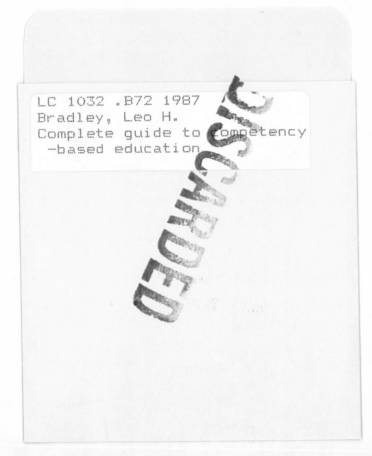